The Golden Retriever Puppy Handbook

About the Author

R. Ann Johnson became a Golden Retriever person in the 1960s when she acquired her first Golden as a companion for her aging German Shepherd. She has been intimately involved in Goldens ever since. She is the founder of Gold-Rush Kennels, located in Wrightstown, New Jersey. Her Goldens (owned, bred, or sired) have produced more than 300 American champions and numerous Canadian champions. Her national record holders include Am. Can. Bda. Ch. Cummings' Gold-Rush Charlie OS SDHF (Top Sporting Dog in the country and #1 Golden in 1974 and 1975, sire of 59 champions), Ch. Stone's Gold-Rush Shilo SDHF (#1 Golden in 1980), and Ch. Lizzie's Gold-Rush Echo OS SDHF (#1 Golden in 1985, sire of 18 champions). Other prominent dogs in the history of the breed, all descendants of Charlie, were Ch. Gold-Rush's Great Teddy Bear OS, sire of 50 champions and Ch. Gold-Rush Copper Lee Apollo OS, sire of 42 champions. Two outstanding dogs, Ch. Russo's Gold-Rush Sensation and Ch. Gold-Rush Wild Trout OS, earned the dual title CH.-OTCH. Many progeny of dogs of her breeding have excelled in obedience, as working dogs, and even as Junior, Master, and Senior hunters. Gold-Rush dogs have also been utilized as guide dogs for the blind, as narcotics- and explosive-detection dogs, and as therapy dogs.

Ann holds an A.B. in Biology from Douglass College and an M.S. in Zoology from Rutgers University, where she completed her Ph.D. research in Developmental Biology. While at Rutgers she received a National Science Foundation traineeship grant and taught courses in Comparative Anatomy, Embryology, and Genetics. In the 1970s she taught at Georgian Court College and was Coadjutant Professor of Biology at The College of New Jersey, where she taught courses in Anatomy and Physiology, Developmental Biology, Embryology, and Principles of Biology. At the high-school level, she also taught Advanced Placement Biology, Chemistry, Earth Science, and Genetics.

In the 1980s, Ann turned her attention full time to maintaining and improving her Golden Retriever breeding program and was listed frequently by *Golden Retriever World* as one of the top breeders (in terms of number of champions bred each year). She maintains a special interest in educating those newly involved in and devoted to Golden

Retrievers. She has helped in Animal Rescue, has judged at her Club's Specialty Show, and has been corresponding secretary for her Club, where she has been a Board member and participated on the Committee that developed "Principles, Responsibilities and Guidelines" for Club members. For clients and friends, she publishes an occasional newsletter that addresses current issues and concerns pertaining to the breed.

Ann is a member of the American Association for the Advancement of Science and keeps current in matters of science and scientific research through journals such as *Bioscience, Nature, Science,* and *Scientific American*. She is listed in *Who's Who in Dogs* (Howell, 1998) as one of "a small number [of people in the sport of purebred dogs] who has made a lasting and significant contribution."

A member of the Golden Retriever Club of America (GRCA) for 29 years, Ann has made it her goal in recent years to bring a group of talented individuals who can work together to maintain the tradition and type set forth by Gold-Rush Charlie and to improve the breed.

The Publisher

THE GOLDEN RETRIEVER PUPPY HANDBOOK

The Care and Training of a
Golden Retriever Puppy from
Seven Weeks through Twelve Months

by

R. Ann Johnson

Including
"Your Puppy's First Visit to the Vet," An Interview
with Jean H. Cunningham-Smith, VMD

Illustrations by Karin Walter

The Darwin Press, Inc.
Princeton, New Jersey

Library of Congress Control Number: 2004103872

ISBN 0-87850-163-0 (hardbound)
ISBN 0-87850-164-9 (softbound)

Darwin® Books are printed on acid-free paper and meet the guidelines for permanence and durability of the Committee on production guidelines for Book Longevity of the Council on Library Resources.♾

Published by:
The Darwin Press, Inc.
Box 2202, Princeton, NJ 08543-2202 USA
Tel: (609) 737-1349 Fax: (609) 737-0929
E-Mail: books@darwinpress.com
Web: www.darwinpress.com

Printed in the United States of America

Dedicated to all the folks at Gold-Rush
Who have contributed so much
to the Breed and to

Charlie

Who was the true founder of Gold-Rush

Contents

Part I:
Before Selecting a Puppy

Part II:
From Seven Weeks through Four Months

Part III:
From Five Months through Eight Months

Part IV:
From Nine Months through Twelve Months

Part V:
Health Concerns

**Part VI:
Additional Training for Specific Purposes**

Part VII:
Special Topics for New Owners

III: The Focus of Modern Research
  Genetics vs. the Role of the Environment

Preface

There was once a physicist who never took part in discussions with his colleagues and also didn't want to publish anything. His colleagues believed he was quite intelligent and very knowledgeable, but they were not sure and, to remove all doubt, they kept urging him to publish. One day, he yielded to their requests and finally published an article, and everyone in his department read it. And when afterward they talked about it, everyone agreed . . . they still didn't quite know for sure.

Well, I've been asked by numerous people to write on the topic of the care and training of puppies, but I'm feeling like the inscrutable physicist who was urged on by his colleagues to publish in order to remove all doubt about his competence. Why inscrutable? Because this is a subject about which, I believe, there are no easy answers. And I know you want answers.

There are many breeders who have opinions, but I submit there are almost as many variations on the "truth" as there are breeders. If you have an opinion on any of the subjects presented here, and you differ in your opinion, all I can say is, "you may be right." For those of you who are confused about, or unacquainted with, any or all of these subjects, perhaps I can help you by offering a way of looking at the subject as I do and by suggesting guidelines about what to do and what to look for.

It's really not possible for me to predict the outcome of all the factors that combine to go into the development of your Golden, who must cope with you and your unique world. I will try to explain the Golden's innate nature so that you may better meet his needs and mold him into the companion that you desire. As a breeder, my responsibility toward the Golden Retriever and toward the breed and to you—as owner, guardian, and caretaker—is truly one that I regard as a privilege.

A scientific approach to responsible breeding remains a top priority for me. By this I mean that "science" implies a dimension of change; we are learning and changing our perceptions and perspectives almost on a daily basis. Truth in understanding also is not immutable. Hypotheses explain the data, but as more is learned, the hypotheses (the interpretation of reality) need to be changed or revised to fit new observations. For instance, I believe not everything is known about so-called genetic defects. For breeders and owners to focus exclusively on the genetic component and not take into consideration environmental influences ignores a major component of what goes into producing healthy Goldens. Breeders have an added responsibility to know how certain bloodlines mix; they also need to have the freedom to make the best decisions on their own in the interest of breed purpose, type, and soundness.

* * * * * * *

For more than thirty years I have been raising my Gold-Rush Golden Retrievers and have enjoyed seeing these puppies go off to become happy members of many families. The relationship between the Golden and his family is very special because nothing pleases the Golden more than to be with his family.

My purpose in writing this book is to help members of the human family recognize and meet the needs of the Golden Retriever they are fortunate to own. These pages are designed to acquaint you with an overall picture of the breed as well as the many specifics you will need in order to manage a puppy properly and to allow him to develop into the best dog possible.

Further, I hope this book will be of value both to new puppy owners as well as responsible breeders of Golden Retrievers who address questions posed by owners of their new puppies. These observations and ideas of course are based on my own experience, reading, personal research, and interactions with responsible breeders past and present, and I trust they may be of some benefit to those who believe, as I do, that a thorough knowledge of the breed will enable us to enjoy better the unique qualities of our beloved Goldens.

I do not regard this book as a definitive work on puppy management and training, or a reference book on canine pediatrics. It is basically a compilation of responses to questions people have asked me during the course of more than three decades of working with new puppy owners and their families. In addition I refer to matters that I have found interesting as a biologist and to situations and "laws of nature" that have helped me understand those Goldens that have been such a great part of my life.

This book is not intended to supplant the contribution of the veterinarian responsible for the health of our puppies, but it does contain material, including my interview with Jean H. Cunningham-Smith, VMD, that, I hope, will be helpful in understanding the valuable contribution of your veterinarian to the lifetime care of your puppy.

Acknowledgments

Many people have helped me understand the breed by sharing their knowledge, by giving me feedback, and by asking questions, sometimes difficult questions, where the answers are not readily apparent. To all, I can only express my grateful appreciation, for it is quite impossible to thank properly all of the people who helped with the process of writing this book from conception to completion. For that reason, the following list is woefully incomplete.

Since I'm at heart a people person, I always rely on friends and relatives to help with any project; I have seldom been let down. In response to my pleas for input, once again, many close friends and associates readily responded with their personal expertise and suggestions. At the beginning I must mention Jean H. Cunningham-Smith, VMD and Larry Smith, VMD, whose advice through the years has been exceptional and unconditional. Kim Johnson and Robin Meirs have stood by me and have shared so much of their lives in dogs, almost on a daily basis. I have been able to count on other special friends through the years, who, without fail, have always gone the extra mile for me: Craig Westergaard, Judy Breuer, and my fabulous illustrator, Karin Walter, and her husband Dick Walter—all of whom have been special friends for many years and a part of Gold-Rush from its beginning.

Ed Briggs, who co-owns two champions with me and is the author of our website, was one of the first people to suggest that I write a handbook on puppy care and training; his constant encouragement kept me hard at work completing the task of finally writing this book.

My thanks to Nancy Talbott and Cathie Turner, who graciously agreed to read the manuscript and made helpful comments.

Larry C. Johnson deserves a special word of recognition: His contribution to Gold-Rush during its initial decade in the 1970s was paramount to its very existence.

There are those whose contributions to Gold-Rush Charlie's career and to the modern history of the Golden Retriever breed are incalculable: Janet Bunce, Joan Tudor, Mrs. Robert V. Clark, Jr., Betty Trainor and Bill Trainor, and Gerry B. Schnelle, VMD.

So many others, including friends who have passed on, have contributed each in their own way over the years, and have offered support at strategic times. From the bottom of my heart I shall be eternally grateful to them as well as to the many associates and helpers who through the years have been so important to our success. And to all my dear personal friends and family, who gave me unconditional love, encouragement, affection, and much needed support during the difficult times of my life, I give you my undying love in return.

I'm particularly grateful to the members of the Garden State Golden Retriever Club and Golden Retriever Club of Western New York for their courage in standing up in the best interests of the breed.

A special thanks to Jim Plastine who has worked for Gold-Rush since the age of fourteen and more recently as a college student, who attended to the technical details of composition and format.

I shall be forever in debt to my editor and publisher, Ed Breisacher, of the Darwin Press, who launched this project, believed in its importance, encouraged me, saw every draft through its rough spots to the final phases, and designed the final production. Thank you.

My life with Golden Retrievers, I feel certain, would probably never have happened had it not been for Janet Bunce. In 1972, I was interested in purchasing a female puppy and visited many breeders. My research led me to Janet, who suggested that my husband and I come to the Long Island Golden Retriever Club Match to meet her. We took Charlie and knowing nothing about showing or having any intention of doing so, went to the match to meet her. With her help and urging, she found us a show lead and my husband, Larry, took Charlie into the ring. Charlie won, and that was the beginning of his career and of my relationship with Janet. In the days and years that followed, she not only bred her champion bitches to Charlie and finished many of the offspring, but she was in fact my mentor and source of inspiration and was also Charlie's true mentor. This is an example of Janet's contribution to the breed, for she has always put the good dogs she has met ahead of her own personal goals.

Last but not least, I thank Charlie, the true founder of Gold-Rush who changed my world, who guards me even today and gives me a purpose that keeps me sane, and whose constant presence is still felt everyday in my life.

Notes on Style and Content

A few words on style and content are in order to help the reader recognize what I consider some of the more important elements discussed.

My use of boldface type in the text is intended to point out useful concepts or sentences that deserve attention and re-reading as matters of the highest importance.

You will find KEY WORDS capitalized. These words relate to attitudes that may help you relate to your Golden throughout his life.

In some cases, underlining of dates (for example, in the chapter on "Feeding and Nutrition") make the time periods clearer or provide other useful items to remember.

Extensive endnotes serve as references to sources or additional information that will help with an understanding of the topic, often incorporating bibliographical references to noteworthy books for further reading. I have tried to list literature that is easily accessible to non-specialists.

In the Glossary, keywords relating specifically to the breed and to science are explained.

In the Index, I have not listed commercial products or trade names.

PART I:

Before Selecting a Puppy

Chapter 1:
Choosing the Breed

A Brief Description of the Golden Retriever

To describe a Golden Retriever, I would always begin with temperament. The Golden is foremost a companion devoted to his owner-guardian, family, and indeed other animals that the Golden recognizes as part of the family. His family actually includes most of his world: the postman, the neighbors, the children at the park—all are immediately assumed by the Golden to be old friends he can't wait to see again. It is this open, playful and loving temperament that is the embodiment of the Golden Retriever personality.

Those who own a Golden puppy are showered with love and kisses. Quickly the Golden's energy raises the spirits of each member of the family, bringing joy and inner contentment in being loved. No one can be lonely; no one can remain depressed. Each person is inspired to become a better person and the family is thereby strengthened. The Golden's joy for life uplifts people, making so many feel good about themselves.

The antithesis of the guard dog, Goldens have no concept of guarding. They can perceive danger when unknown sounds are heard, and they may bark and sound an alarm, but when that sound is perceived to be coming from a human being, all the signs of fear and protection immediately fade away, to be replaced by a wagging tail and a friendly greeting. There is an old joke among Golden owners that, when left to guard the house, the Golden will happily show the burglar where the silver is located.

The Golden has a high pain threshold, and is very forgiving if by chance an accident occurs and the puppy is unintentionally injured, which may sometimes happen in an active family. Though at first confused, the puppy will not understand this event as something hostile, nor become aggressive and counterattack. On the contrary, he will demonstrate that he is the family companion, will resume his playful ways, and will be as ever giving and trusting. Whatever you want to do, your Golden will be on board.

If there was ever a canine that wants to please, it is the Golden Retriever. The round face and large eyes (as with the human infant) engender in us feelings of happiness, love, and concern. With such qualities, the Golden has much to offer: They are playful companions when we are in the mood for fun. When we are lonely or sad, they are loving companions, which heightens our sense of well-being. When we become agitated, apprehensive, or tense, they are calming companions. And they still carry out their age-old duties of alerting us to intruders approaching our homes.

There are those who do not share this love of dogs, and they are missing a great deal. They are missing an amazingly rewarding relationship between man and animal. The people who are caring guardians of a Golden Retriever can look forward to having the benefit of this special relationship. It is certainly a medical fact that the calming influence of the company of a friendly Golden Retriever reduces blood pressure and may therefore lower the risk of stroke or heart attack. The act of petting a dog has a "de-stressing" influence that is valued in today's stressful urban life. It is my goal to increase one's appreciation of the extraordinary end product of canine evolution that rushes up to greet you every time you open the front door.

Bred first of all to function as a working retriever, the Golden today remains one of the most trainable and eager to please of all canines, and one of the most popular breeds to share their lives with Mankind.

What to Consider before Choosing Your Puppy

Before choosing a puppy, you want to be sure that this new member of your family is suited to your lifestyle and meets your expectations and those of your family. Only then will you want to begin to investigate the puppy's bloodlines and genetic endowment.

As a lover of Golden Retrievers, I cannot sing their praises loud enough, but that does not mean that the Golden is the perfect dog for everyone. For instance, their success as a companion means that they need companionship. Isolation is apparently as painful for them as solitary confinement is for prison inmates. Therefore, unless you have the time for a Golden, or are going to provide for these needs some other way, you should not have a Golden, at least not a young one. Older Goldens are still fun loving and wonderful, but they are more content spending hours a day sleeping until their master returns. Also, other family pets provide a degree of companionship for the Golden.

We humans tend to think that, because our Golden loves us so much, we are the only one who can fill our Golden's need for companionship. This is not true, but the fact remains that, as our Golden's guardian, we have a responsibility not to ignore this basic requirement.

In addition to companionship, he needs to be trained. The Golden strives to please, and nothing focuses him more than learning basic obedience and good manners. Nothing makes him happier than the praise he receives for a job well done. Untrained, his exuberance can be annoying, and any expression of anger from his trusted master is confusing and unpleasant. Therefore, the untrained dog is a two-time loser: He misses the opportunity to receive praise from his master, and his untrained behavior creates negative emotions in his owner, which in turn distresses him. Clearly, if you are to acquire a Golden, you must understand what undertaking this commitment means—to you and your Golden.

Another responsibility that comes along with a Golden is that of his care, feeding, combing, bathing, trimming, nail clipping, tending to ears and teeth, as well as frequent expensive trips to the veterinarian—all part of the package. That's in addition to cleaning up after a Golden, because these dogs have lots of hair, and the daily contribution to the disarray of the house is considerable.

Furthermore, the sheer size of a mature Golden must be considered. The wagging tail can play havoc to any coffee table arrangement. Windows and doors will never be the same again due to the footprints and nose prints galore.

On the other hand, once a Golden steals your heart, you will never be the same again. Hair and footprints are minor annoyances. To have a friend who loves you above all else . . . who will go with you anywhere, anytime, with pure enjoyment in his heart, will make your life more worthwhile. You'll find you are planning your vacation not only to include him but choosing places he will enjoy. Even your choice of the car and house you buy will be made with your beloved Golden in mind. And when he dies your grief will be immense. Only to be placated by the acquisition of your next Golden.

Although the breed is considered to be dual purpose (that is, field/companion), there are variations in the way a Golden looks as well as variations in personality and in traits such as intelligence, birdiness, energy level, and retrieving ability. Because the Golden Retriever is a very versatile and intelligent creature, the breed serves well in rescue work, as a guide dog to the blind, as a narcotics-detection dog, as a therapy dog, in rescue work, and as a noble companion; he is also well suited for agility, obedience, field work, and the show ring—to name some of his most important endeavors.

Male vs. Female

Many people ask me whether they should buy a male or a female. The answer really lies within one's expectations. There are, of course, gender differences. Most of these differences center around the presence of the hormone testosterone. In general the male is larger and generally weighs about 15 pounds more than the female. Because of his testosterone levels, he develops secondary sex characteristics after adolescence: His head becomes broader primarily due to the growth of the frontal, temporal, and masseter muscles on either side of the skull; he has a more pronounced "stop"; he develops a longer coat and a greater ruff (the coat on the chest); and he has a greater amount of musculature in general and is taller than the female.

There are a number of personality characteristics that are also peculiar to the male. The male seems to worship the pack leader; he is concerned with his master's moods and feelings. This behavior may be derived from the position of males within the ancestral pack, where the

Male

Female

Female

Male

Male

Female

pack leader is of utmost importance in the hierarchy of the males and the survival of the group. On the other hand, if the male is neutered, the physical and behavioral differences between male and female are minimized. (More about "Neutering the Male" in Chapter 17, pp. 178–79.)

The female is smaller, of course, than the male. The female is devoted, affectionate, even needy, and may come across as more submissive. Somewhat less worshipful of her master, she may be seen to have greater drives to meet her own needs for food and shelter, perhaps historically from the need to provide for her offspring.

The fact that the female will come into heat twice a year is an annoying problem. The estrus cycle lasts 21 days, during which time she must be kept under lock and key due to her attractiveness to male dogs in the neighborhood and her own natural desire to escape and roam in order to attract even more males. In addition there is a bloody discharge, which also produces an unpleasant odor. (More about "Spaying the Female" in Chapter 17, pp. 179–80.) I feel that the female is harder to housebreak probably because submissive urination is part of, and quite normal to, the young female personality. Also, the immature female is more prone to cystitis because of her short urethra and the low levels of the estrogen hormone, which are present until maturity. (More about "Cystitis" in Chapter 15, pp. 140–42.)

Some people prefer males because they are larger and more magnificent, but their weight and size makes them harder to handle. Other people prefer females just because they are smaller. Until he is neutered, the male may hump children or dogs as a show of his dominance, and even challenge strange males, although many males do not demonstrate these traits.

Both males and females can be aggressive with strange dogs if they are not correctly socialized early on with other dogs. **It is the responsibility of the human caretaker to supervise and control a Golden's behavior when he is interacting with other dogs.** The Golden has the ability to identify fully with his human family to the point of thinking of other dogs as foreign creatures. Good management can minimize many of the negatives of both sexes mentioned above. Owners need to recognize the physical and behavioral differences in making their choices.

Goldens, Children, and the Family

Golden Retrievers have an innate love for children. I remember well my Ch. Cummings' Gold-Rush Charlie who held all the breed records for twenty years. In the early seventies, he was the number one Sporting Dog (and still the only Golden so ranked) and was known for his sparkling personality in the show ring. The reason for his marvelous showmanship was that Charlie especially loved children. He would study the gallery until he saw a child; then he would focus entirely on the child and spontaneously wag his tail. The gallery loved it.

The Macha family with their two Goldens

The Golden Retriever is one of the most popular dogs for families. The adult's patient and gentle nature, intelligence, willingness to please, and playfulness have justly given the breed the reputation as an ideal companion for children. Goldens are social animals, and can bond to all members of the family, including other pets. Goldens, especially puppies, will view young children as playmates. A puppy has sharp teeth and nails and cannot resist treating children to its own "play" behavior, which includes nipping, jumping, barking, chasing, and even growling. This behavior can frighten a toddler, who will often react by screaming and running away. Thus, a bad cycle can develop because a puppy will see the child's behavior as an invitation to play. To avoid this, **parents must monitor the play of children with the puppy and not allow rough-housing, chasing, wrestling, and the like.** Young children should be protected, as the puppy also must be protected. Older children should be coached in short periods of calm play with the puppy, while adult members of the family can train the puppy and take on the feeding and grooming duties.

Because the adult dog is a large, strong, enthusiastic creature, training must be initiated while the Golden is young and manageable. Care and training are activities that will develop a close bond between the Golden and family members and foster the desired behavior.

Chapter 2:
The Role of the Breeder

Ethics and Responsibilities

Responsible breeders have goals and reasons why they acquire certain dogs and plan certain breedings. They are trying to improve the breed and to keep what they value at the same time. Taking time to discuss these issues with the breeder will give you a better idea whether the breeder is breeding for the type you are looking for.

It is important to choose a breeder who senses the responsibilities that breeding involves. Breeding for such reasons as to allow the dogs to have sex, to have puppies to entertain children, or to make money—and having even an accidental mating—are unacceptable today in view of the numbers of unwanted dogs and the high cost of veterinary expenses. Dogs today are valued members of the family and much care and concern should be devoted to their breeding, just as there is planning and forethought in choosing to have children.

Choose a breeder who is an ethical person. Golden Retriever clubs have written guidelines and responsibilities to which breeders should comply. But do not have too high expectations of perfection, for it is the total dog that you experience. Dogs are no more perfect than other living beings. It would be a mistake to look for excellent ratings in one area—hips, for example—and disregard the overall quality of the dog and its temperament and trainability.

It is important that there be full disclosure of all pertinent facts with regard to the pedigree, parents, and the status of certain key areas where problems are likely to occur. In the Golden Retriever it is generally agreed that the main area of concern is that of hip dysplasia. (For a full discussion, see Chapter 22, "Perspectives on Hip Dysplasia.") There are certification programs, such as the OFA (Orthopedic Foundation for Animals), where radiographs of the parents are evaluated and rated by board certified radiologists. There are also certification programs for the Golden's heart and eyes. Other areas of concern

13

are the status of elbows, thyroid function, and a propensity toward allergies. In each of these areas there is a large environmental influence as well as the genetic endowment the puppy receives from each parent. It is important to have an open, honest relationship with the breeder so that there can be a discussion of problems that inevitably arise. In this way solutions can be better obtained and information shared.

Like Usually Begets Like

Although a puppy will not be exactly like his parents or siblings, he will be more like his own family members than like other Goldens. Each puppy receives half of his genes from his sire and half from his dam. In selecting a puppy, the goal will be to choose the puppy that has the traits of parents that you value, which have come together in the puppy. If you like the parents and other relatives of the puppy you select, you will have a greater chance of obtaining a dog that you admire, given that you provide the correct environment. For this reason it is important that you feel you are in agreement with the value system the breeder employs.

Often puppies will resemble closely a grandfather or grandmother or other ancestor (sometimes called a "throwback.") This is because there are certain combinations of genes that were present in that ancestor, which produced his particular characteristics, but were lost in the recombination of genes that produced the next generation; yet, by chance, they can come together in one of the puppies of the current generation.

The Role of Good Early Care On Development

Although the Golden Retriever is probably one of the best of the canine breeds to serve as a human companion, the Golden's pleasant nature is more than just a product of inborn genetic endowment. Correct socialization and nurturing begin essentially from the moment of birth.

Nurturing

The Environment

Important events have already occurred in a puppy's life before you meet him—such as the amount of mother's milk available, the presence of pathogens, and the odors and sounds that play a role in imprinting. The task of the breeder is to assure the highest quality of initial care during the first weeks of a puppy's life, which is important in order to create a robust, beautiful, outgoing, healthy puppy.

Cleanliness is paramount. Puppies cannot thrive if they are not clean, and they may die because of an overabundance of bacteria. Parasites and pathogens must be kept to a minimum. Puppies raised under unhealthy conditions will have an "unthrifty" appearance; that is, they will be characteristically smaller and thinner, and have a refined (thin and narrow) face and less coat, and what coat they do have is dry and dull. The whelping area must be kept clean and the bedding changed frequently.

Proper temperature of the whelping room needs to be maintained, monitored continuously, and regulated accordingly—a matter that cannot be underestimated, because the puppy has little ability to regulate his own body temperature during the early days. Puppies must receive a great deal of nutrition from their mother, and if they are not warm enough, they cannot digest and assimilate the nutrients they need, and will not thrive. In general, healthy, well-fed, warm puppies are either suckling or sleeping for the first three weeks. Crying, agitated young puppies are usually cold and are not having their need for warmth met for maximum growth.

Social interactions and external stimuli have a profound impact on the early development of the puppy. In the process of tending to the needs of the mother and her litter, the breeder is also handling the puppies, which ensures imprinting on human odors and sounds as well as on those of their canine mother and siblings.[1] Because early imprinting is important, puppies must spend their early weeks carefully nurtured by their mother, surrounded by littermates, and gently attended by human caregivers. (More on "imprinting" in Chapter 5, pp. 43–44.)

Social interactions

Besides imprinting on human as well as canine smells and sounds, the puppy's nervous system is stimulated by being gently handled on a daily basis. As puppies are moved and talked to, these stimuli are recorded in their early brain as normal, familiar stimuli and will help make the puppy a confident dog in the human world.

Nutrition

The value of nutrients that a puppy receives during his early development cannot be underestimated. Here the role of the mother assumes importance. Even before the mother gives birth, there is variation in her blood supply to a particular fetus. After the puppies are born, the size of the litter, the health and care and feeding of the mother, and the nurturing characteristic of the mother all determine how much food each puppy receives. The human attendee must be astute in observing the development of each puppy in order to intervene if necessary. The dedication of the breeder to overseeing every hour of the new puppy's ability to feed is the only way to ensure that each and every puppy grows sufficiently every day.

Starting at approximately four weeks, the breeder will probably augment feeding of every litter with solid food. If a puppy has not made normal gains in the initial four weeks—for any number of reasons, such as not receiving enough nourishment from the mother, or being smaller in size and not having access to the mother because of sibling competition—these "missed gains" in the initial four weeks cannot be made up quickly.

The size and appearance of the six- to seven-week-old puppy is not only a matter of what genes he received from its parents but also of the care he received from the mother and breeder during the initial few weeks of life. In addition, his personality and intellect are also influenced by both these environmental and genetic factors.

* * * * * * *

Thirty some years ago I, too, obtained my first Golden Retriever puppy. He was to be sure a thing of beauty and a joy to behold, but he was far more than that. There was a mystical quality about him and a presence that changed the course of my life forever.

Goldens cannot be simply described as the best canine companion. It has been said that the Golden has a Great Heart. They have that, but even more: As they greet the world with their pure, open, and positive attitude they bring out the best in those they meet and open doors for those that follow their lead. It is into this world that I welcome you. But know that your life, too, will be changed forever.

Charlie at fifteen months of age

Chapter 3:
Understanding Your Golden
Retriever's Evolutionary Origins

Introduction

In order to determine the suitability of the Golden Retriever for your lifestyle and what responsibilities you will be assuming as you welcome this new member into your family, you should learn as much as you can about the breed and dogs in general. After all, this is a commitment that may last a lifetime, and a breed that, to my mind, you will want to identify with and to cherish.

The purpose of this chapter is to help you understand the origin and evolution of the canine so that you can more fully understand its behavior. An appreciation of the evolution of the dog increases our understanding of what we can expect and what we may encounter with a puppy—what things are important and what are not. I shall try to share with you my experiences and understanding so that we may better relate to our Goldens to bring out their potential.

Where, for instance, did your puppy's ancestors originally come from? What was he before he was a member of the modern domestic species known as *Canis familiaris*? What are the characteristics we share, and how do we differ? And how has the Golden Retriever itself evolved since its own origins as a specific breed in the late nineteenth century?

A Brief Look at the Evolution of the Dog

Around 12,000 years ago, the great ice formations that covered most of the Northern Hemisphere of our world for millennia had in large part melted and receded, although large remnants remained. At that time, in a remote area of the Middle East near the Mediterranean Sea, a man died and was laid to rest and alongside him was a puppy—a relative of an ancestor of our present-day dog.[2] What is significant about this burial is that it shows that the relationship between Man and Dog had already become more than one of mere association and domestication. The man chose the dog to accompany him into eternity.

Canines belong to the same taxonomic grouping as we humans—Class Mammalia (Mammals)—and they, like us, came from parents that did not die in infancy. They passed on their genes unchanged for many generations, except for random, albeit important, mutations.[3] With the union of the parents, however, new combinations of those genes occurred, some being more successful than others in that the successful individuals grew and survived to reproduce so that their genes were the ones that were passed on to the next generation. Another reason for the success of certain individuals in passing on their genes to the next generation was that they survived through the benefit of behaviors that, in canines, we call pack behavior; they also began to evidence adaptations that enabled them to cohabit with humans.

Social Behavior

The canine achieved its present form even before *Homo sapiens* came into existence as an upright, bipedal creature. When one thinks about why the canine is successful, one is struck by its main survival skills: such as teeth, strength, and speed. Its key survival trait, however, is his pack behavior, and **the canine's success is due to its social evolution in the pack**. In its role as a hunter of game, a dog would be more likely to survive in the wild because it belonged to a pack rather than living alone. We, too, have been more successful because of our roles in a society. The early ability of the dog to bond to the pack, and us to our family is something that we share. Early imprinting and learning is seen in many species where the formation of a society offers a selective advantage.

Furthermore, the relationship between Dog and Man has come about because of the advantage both of them have by their living together, joining forces so to speak.[4] This symbiotic relationship proba-

Co-evolution

bly began more than 20,000 years ago, when humans were still in a Stone Age hunting society, and the dog was useful to chase or fetch prey. When the hunting ethos of humans became more hunter-gatherer and then developed into an agricultural society (probably around 15,000 to 12,000 years ago), this relationship probably received an added impetus. Mutual security also became important, and canines served as watchdogs and guardians. They also helped humans in other, rather direct ways—by destroying vermin, pulling sleds or carts, and of course offering companionship. As companions, they were given permission to freely roam the abode. In turn, our part of the bargain was that we fed them and provided care and shelter. In the Middle Ages, there were probably no more than a dozen different types of dogs in Europe, mostly as working dogs. With the Industrial Revolution there was a great explosion of the different dog breeds, and the working dog was soon outnumbered by the new companion dog, a development closely linked to the growth of urban and suburban Man.[5]

With fewer tasks being expected of them, and with dogs assuming their main role as a companion, canine traits were selected according to what made them appealing to us, and these traits still prevail. Our canines offer us what few other species do. We have an affectionate affinity for them; basically we like them, and they like us. Why is this so? Perhaps we recognize some of our own characteristics in them. I mean, they exhibit a consciousness not entirely unlike ours. They recognize who we are by our movements and voice, although not necessarily by our individual features. They dream like us (and like us may even make noises in their sleep), and display emotions such as sadness or happiness, and sometimes, if they are unhappy or jealous, they may sulk or express displeasure through their body movements.

In the ancestral dog, as in the wild dog of today, both dominant and submissive behaviors probably played an important role in the survival of the pack. Dominant individuals prevent the reproduction of other less dominant dogs, thus giving a selective advantage to the more robust individuals that can maintain their position. The dominant dog's genes will contribute (be passed on) to the next generation. A dominant male will drive other males away from breeding females. The dominant female will fight and overwhelm more submissive females to maintain her position in the pack hierarchy. Only the dominant female will successfully mate and raise a litter of puppies. Either the less dominant females will not ovulate, or if they do conceive a litter, the more dominant female will destroy the litter. Because too many puppies can be unhealthy, and could deplete the amount of food and space available for each individual in the pack, the continuance of this behavior serves to control population size, for the greater good of the pack. Non-breeding, submissive individuals, however, do contribute to the success of the pack; for instance, their presence has the advantage of increasing the pack's numbers, thus allowing the pack to be more effective when hunting. In addition, submissive females who do not raise litters of their own will join in caring for and feeding the dominant female's litter, thereby contributing to the puppies' well-being.

Herein lies the advantage of submissiveness and hierarchy to the pack. The value of both dominant and submissive individuals can be seen to enhance the survival of the pack. It is, therefore, also important to preserve the genes of submissive individuals. How is that done? As the submissive female matures, and the dominant female ages, the more submissive female will eventually "be allowed to" successfully raise a litter, and thereby contribute her genes to the next generation.

Submissiveness is one of the basic traits that endeared dogs to us as companions in the first place; indeed, it was probably one of the most important traits when it came to deciding whether a dog was acceptable in human society. If a dog that joined forces with humans was too dominant and would challenge or attack its benefactor, the relationship would end. But dogs that had the submissive trait were already in the ancestral-dog gene pool to be selected. So it is even today. In addition, if the dog provided feelings of play and warmth to its human "pack" leader, and could perform useful duties besides, it was accepted into the human pack environment. Over the millennia, through man's selection, the dog was seen to adapt to its new role in relationship to man.

And what do we do for them? Two things: First, just as we value consistency, **our companions demand consistency from us.** Nothing can be so confusing or upsetting to a puppy or dog than the uncertainty of inconsistency. Second, we also feed them; thus, they are doubly dependent on us for their survival.

Although there are many mongrels in the world today, the breeders of purebred dogs (that is to say, dogs bred according to the standards of each specific breed) have maintained that only with expensive, purebred dogs is there sufficient caretaking of the animals to meet their needs. Purebred dogs such as the Golden Retriever are more valuable to human society, because the mongrel dog, on average, may have been raised under conditions of neglect or as a feral dog, and is, therefore, more likely to be a burden to society. Such dogs can give all dogs a bad name.

With their new role as companion dog, breeds have been refined and dog shows have been organized so that the competitive showing of dogs has become a big business. The numbers of purebred dogs in the United States are quite staggering. It is estimated that there are 40 million such dogs with us today. Given an estimate of 50,000 to 52,000 Golden Retrievers registered each year, with an average lifetime of, say, a little more than ten years, that means that in the United States alone there are probably more than 500,000 Golden Retrievers alive today.[6]

Since Golden Retrievers are being raised as high-quality companions for people, it behooves the responsible breeder to minimize the problems that can occur and to breed out traits that are not satisfactory, thus enhancing the value of these dogs as companions and as part of our social structure.

The Dog's Bark

The dog's bark evolved as a complicated means of communication among dogs.[7] Dogs are virtuosos at barking when compared to their distant relative, the wolf. And each dog's bark is distinctive; that is, you can tell who is barking by the sound and tone of his bark.

In general, the Golden Retriever is a dog that does not bark as much as other breeds. I believe there has been selection, and continues to be selection, for those individuals who are not barkers, because incessant barking is considered to be annoying, and the breed is not one that is chosen to be a guard dog. A barking dog is of no value in the field, and only of small value, as an alarm, in the home.

The most common dog bark is usually associated with defense of the home territory. It is a protest against a perceived threat. This bark is a canine alarm and is meant for other members of the pack. The message conveyed by the bark is that there is potential danger out there. The bark has two effects on other dogs and puppies: First, adult dogs may immediately join in when one dog sounds the alarm. The dogs do not know whether the arriving person is a friend or foe. Once the new arrival has been identified, the Golden Retriever's barking will be replaced by a friendly greeting. Second, an adult dog sounding an alarm bark will raise fear in the minds of puppies, with the result that puppies will often run and hide. This can be observed especially when puppies are being raised in a situation where there are other adult dogs around, as may happen in the new home of the puppy. A puppy may panic if he hears dogs barking; he needs reassurance from his guardians to remain calm and secure.

There are, of course, barks that express other emotions, including loneliness, distress, and pleasure as well as the kind of bark to alert other dogs or people to changes in the surroundings.

The loudest and deepest barks are related to defensive and offensive threats, social insecurity, and physical distress. Higher, more harmonic barks are used as a signal for social play and active and passive submission to other dogs or person, and when making social contact. Play barking is often associated with other behaviors such as wrinkling of the brow, raising hackles, pinning back ears, lifting a tail, or other postures.

Other reasons why dogs bark are: to gain information; to know what is happening; and to be fed. When a dog knows food is being prepared, his anticipation is portrayed by a particular bark. Owners learn to differentiate barking for food, barking for going out, barking when the dog feels abandoned, and barking when sensing an intruder approaching.

Howling

Although dogs bark more than wolves, they howl less. On occasion, though, a Golden Retriever will howl. The Golden leads a life of perpetual puppydom and needs to reinforce his attachment to the pack; howling seems to have that function. In the wild, the effect of howling is to attract the other members of the pack to come together or just to hear oneself "sing." The Group Chorus of howling reinforces the pack cohesiveness.

Because his world is his family, the Golden Retriever is not generally away from his "pack." But sometimes it is necessary to forcefully shut him away by himself. It is then that one can hear the howl of loneliness. I remember a time when I had a small brick cottage and built a fence around it to make it a comfortable home for Champion Gold-Rush Alltheway. However comfortable the cottage was for him, as long as he was by himself, he began to howl—a clear sign of loneliness. When given another companion dog to live with him, the howling ceased and "Tank," as we called him, became happy with his new living arrangement. As long as the Golden Retriever lives in the home of a caring human or another canine companion, he will not normally howl.

Nevertheless, there are Goldens that will howl in response to a siren wailing, to singing, or to the playing of a musical instrument. Many years ago I had a young Golden that would howl when my son practiced the piano. We needed to remove the Golden and have him wait outside during such times until my son finished his practicing. Perhaps this is a vestige of the more primitive wolf-pack instinct.

Some male dogs that never howl under normal circumstances are known to howl when they are shut away from a female in season. Again the message here is: "Join me."

Tail Wagging

Tail wagging is primarily a greeting. A puppy not only wags his tail when he first sees you, but also when he wants you to pay attention to him. The tail wagging greeting is only used by the dog when in the presence of friends, whether it be other dogs or its master. Dogs that do not know each other do not wag their tails in greeting; rather, they display themselves as tall and menacing by stiffening themselves. Once they perceive the newcomer as friendly, the tails will start wagging.

Newborn puppies can slowly wag their tails, and it can be observed that when they are nursing and the milk begins to flow in the milk let-down, there is a rapid twitching and stiffening of the tail, which can be interpreted as the forerunner of tail wagging in response to the pleasure of feeding at this early age. True tail wagging is present when the puppies reach four weeks of age, and by six weeks they will wag their tails in greeting each other or their mother or their human family.

Play Behavior

Play behavior is commonly found in mammals and birds. Play behavior appears to be exaggerated normal behavior with no specific reason or goal compared to mature behavior, but using the same skills that are seen in the adult. Play behavior does, however, have several important functions, such as aiding in the development of motor skills, furthering the development of learning processes, and gaining understanding of the environment. It is also important in learning social skills (including the development of dominance relationships). In each case, play behavior allows the puppy to develop and perfect necessary skills before they are needed in real life situations.[8]

Of all canine breeds, I believe the Golden Retriever excels in juvenile characteristics. He is known for his lifetime of playfulness. During the course of evolution, we ourselves became juvenile apes, retaining our childhood curiosity and playfulness through our adult lives. It was this change that gave us our remarkable inventiveness and is at the heart of our success story. The Golden Retriever shares with us this extended playfulness. Just as we are, in a sense, juvenile apes, so the Golden Retriever is the juvenile wolf. This phenomena has been called "neoteny"; that is, the preservation of the juvenile stage into adulthood. However, a more recent way of looking at this process is that the organism has further evolved to have traits that are like the more immature stage of development of its ancestors. This process is called paedomorphosis.[9] It is not a process of immature development but is a change in the rate of growth. In paedomorphosis there is a slowing of the growth rate, which results in a less complex structure in the descendant form. These changes can occur through the selection of a few genes, for example the hox (homeotic or homeobox) genes, which control growth rates, rather than involve selection for the many genes for each and every trait. It is quite probable that, when early man took young pups from their mother, the puppies that possessed more juvenile characteristics made successful human companions and were therefore kept and bred, which led to the evolution of the modern dog resembling the youthful stage of its ancestral roots.

Canines are programmed to explore everything in their environment. Dogs are opportunists in the wild and must develop a broad knowledge of everything in their world in order to survive, which also led to their successful evolution; and the modern dog has retained this ancestral behavior. As an adult the Golden Retriever remains unusually curious and playful, even after it has reached an advanced age.

In order to indicate to other dogs or to people that they are in a playful mood, they exhibit certain behaviors that are related to submissive behavior. Since play often involves mock fighting and mock fleeing, it is necessary to indicate to others that a particular action is only in fun and not to be taken seriously. This is done by exhibiting play invitation displays. The most important of these play signals is the "play-bow," where the Golden dramatically lowers the front half of its body while keeping its rear end raised. It may be said that a dog doing a play-bow is a dog mimicking stretching and is, therefore, interpreted as being non-aggressive. In this position the playful dog stares intently at his companion and makes small forward movements designed to entice his companion into play. If the other dog responds, there follows play-chasing or play-fighting that never leads to a real fight, or the fleeing and capture that never results in a serious bite. In the chase game the dogs repeatedly switch roles. The fact that they switch indicates that they are not experiencing moods of real aggression or fear.

There are several other typical, canine play-invitation signals such as the so-called play-face, where the lips are pulled back horizontally, the jaws slightly open, but where there is no baring of the front teeth. (If they were, this would be interpreted as aggressive.) Play-face is completely non-aggressive. Other inducements to play are: nudging, pawing, or offering a prized object to another dog. In offering an object to another dog, the first dog lays down an object, but the moment his companion attempts to pick it up, the dog snatches it and runs off, hoping the companion dog will follow. If he does not, then the object is presented once again.

It is important to understand the behavior of the dog or puppy in order to correctly interpret his behavior when he tries to play with you. Novice owners are sometimes afraid of play-fighting behavior, for example, because the puppy can inadvertently inflict pain. In general, it is better not to indulge a puppy in canine play behavior, and it is far better to remain in the leadership role, limiting interaction to stroking and quiet praise. Nevertheless, active interactions are best when they utilize throw toys (such as a "cotton bone") that give the puppy a chance to respond to the fetch command, for which he can be praised and thus learn that his owner is indeed his leader. If one understands that play behavior is natural and necessary and even desirable to the development of the young dog, one can be more patient with its annoying aspects. (For an additional discussion of the importance of "play" in training your puppy, see "The Role of Play" in Chapter 7, pp. 70–72.)

Canine Senses

Like us, and like so many other species, canine survival was predicated on acute senses, which enabled the species to escape predation as well as to allow them to function as a pack predator. Some canine senses are more refined and indeed far superior to ours. The main areas of superiority are in certain aspects of vision, smell, and hearing.

Vision. For many years it was believed that canines had no color vision and lived in a totally black-and-white world. It is now known that they see color but that color is not as intense for them as it is for us. Eye cones are sensitive to color, but a dog's eyes do not contain as many cones as human eyes—which explains their diminished response to color. On the other hand, canines have a higher ratio of rods to cones than the human eye, and since rods are responsible for black-and-white vision in dim light, their nighttime vision is sharper than ours. The greater number of rods in the eyes of dogs, moreover, allows them to see better early in the day or in twilight, when light is dim.

Another related adaptation in dogs is a light-reflecting, pigmented layer called the *tapetum lucida* located at the back of their eyes. This layer intensifies light, thus enabling the eyes to make more use of what little illumination there may be. This is what makes dogs' eyes shine in the dark.

A dog's eye, I believe, is also exquisitely sensitive to movement, but probably less so to the detail of the object in question when compared to our perception. For instance, if a dog comes upon a new object or even a familiar human, it may not immediately recognize them without additional sensory data such as movement, scent, or voice. If the human stands still, even when close to a dog, the person may remain unrecognized. On the other hand, a moving object will easily gain his attention. Hence, the Golden's value in retrieving falling game. A non-moving object may be easily missed. This is the reason why so many prey animals "freeze" and stand motionless when they become alarmed—in order not to be spotted by the predator. Even though a dog may not detect its owner at close range, a dog can see a waving hand signal at a great distance. The ability of a dog to detect the slightest unusual movement, or to observe something unusual in the physical or verbal behavior of its owner, may be the basis for the so-called sixth sense often attributed to canines.[10]

Smell. During evolution, the advantage of an acute sense of smell in order to locate and track prey at a distance meant the difference between life and death for the ancestral dog. Those individuals who possessed greater olfactory abilities thus had a better chance for survival and would thereby pass on their genetic endowment to their descendants. It is this refined ability that our Goldens have inherited.

The olfactory (smell) sense in dogs has been said to be from fifty to one hundred times better than ours to as high as even a thousand times better. For comparison, there are estimated to be approximately 220 million smell-sensitive cells (olfactory receptors) in a dog's nose compared to only five million to ten million in a human being.[11]

A dog experiences a great variety of odors with a subtlety and sensitivity that is as far from our comprehension as higher mathematics is to the dog. However, the comparison can only be made with regard to a particular chemical substance. With some odors dogs perform little better than we do because these odors have little significance for them—such as the fragrance of flowers. But with other substances such as the butyric acid found in sweat, it has been shown that some dogs have a sensitivity that is at least one thousand times sharper than ours. For instance, the tracking dog will follow individual human scent for miles through areas where many others have walked.

Canine assistance has been sought in many spheres of scent detection. With training, Golden Retrievers have been successful in such areas as drug-detection, bomb-searching, and the rescue of victims of earthquakes and fallen buildings, as happened after the collapse of the twin towers of the World Trade Center. When it comes to distinguishing smell, the dog's nose is far more efficient than any machine.

There is also a phenomenon that helps me realize how strong scent is to a dog. When you open a door or gate for a puppy to come in, the puppy in the beginning cannot seem to go around the barrier to locate where the opening is. This is because the puppy is following scent, and cannot logically figure out how to get around obstacles— they are programmed to go straight ahead through the door. In contrast, primates have more ability to solve puzzles based on perceptions. (Squirrels also are better at getting around open gates, because they are programmed to run back and forth in their searching behavior.)[12]

Hearing. With regard to auditory perception, the dog's hearing ranges higher and lower and over more frequencies than the range of human hearing. At the higher pitch the dog is far superior to us. When we are young, our upper range is about 30,000 Hz (a Hertz, or Hz, is one cycle per second). This sinks to 20,000 Hz by the time we are young adults and to only 12,000 Hz by the time we reach retirement age. Dogs have an upper limit of 35,000 to 40,000 Hz or higher.

This gives the dog the ability to hear sounds that are to us ultrasonic. The evolution of such sensitive hearing is clearly related to the ancestral dogs' hunting needs, allowing them to detect the presence (squeaks and movements) of rodents and other small prey.[13] An interesting result of this perception is that dogs can react to tiny clues that make their behavior seem almost telepathic.

Less well-known is how well developed their perception is on the low end of the scale, where I suspect there is a kind of communication that goes on, related in some way to an instinctual perception of danger, as in distant thunder or a barely audible rumble. A low rumble, on one hand, can sometimes induce alarm growls or barking in an older puppy; on the other hand, talking with a puppy in a high or squeaky voice is generally perceived as non-threatening if not pleasurable, and it can also be exciting and play-inducing.

Applying an Evolutionary Point of View

There is probably no branch of veterinary medicine or behavioral psychology that cannot benefit from an evolutionary approach. Indeed, in today's scientific world the study of evolution has found many practical applications. One may even gain insight into many of the problems that involve the puppy if one thinks of the modern dog's relationship to the ancestral dog, for often the problems that occur with our puppy/dog result from a mismatch between formerly evolved adaptations and the dog's current lifestyle as part of the human pack. These problems arise from the constraints of history that a dog brings to the present. Certainly a dog's behavior can be seen as containing many remnants of his wolf-like ancestor.

There are genes that are associated with hereditary diseases that may be viewed differently in the light of the dog's evolutionary origin. Many of the conditions and diseases that plague the dog today come from new factors in our environment. It is unlikely that the more common disease-causing genes represent mutations that have not yet been weeded out; rather, many are probably genes that in other genetic combinations or in the other sex, or in another stage of development, are advantageous. Disease-causing genes may be deleterious only in the modern environment. There are evolutionary explanations for the vulnerabilities that lead to disease. Infection, tradeoffs at the level of genes and traits, compromises, and historical constraints can all be understood better if seen in their evolutionary context.

There are also compromises among the benefits that certain genes give to the dog, which cause difficulty in other instances. An example of this is the genes that cause aging, which, although necessary to the early development of the dog, lead in the end to his aging and demise.[14]

The needs of Goldens can best be understood, too, in an evolutionary sense, and their recent development has occurred in combination with our own needs, in the sense that they are in large measure dependent entirely on us. They flourish in the company of their human companions, who are their guardians. Is it any wonder that we want to provide the best living conditions for them, that we want to protect them from all ills? In any case, **it is the goal of the responsible breeder to perfect the Goldens' structure and to improve their overall health by means of selective breeding, recognizing that environmental conditions also play a dominant role in their development and survival in "human" surroundings.**

The breeder's role, then, is one of artificial selection rather than natural selection. In addition to selection with regard to improving the known health concerns of the breed, the breeder also wishes to retain and perfect the instincts, temperament, and purpose for which the Golden Retriever was originally intended.

Goldens were originally bred to be hunting dogs, to fetch game for hunters. The evolution of these instincts began originally when they were members of a pack. It is easy to see how bringing home the game enhanced their survival. These hunting abilities led to their survival during the course of their evolution, and their non-aggressive behavior, as followers if you will, contributed to their usefulness to the human hunter. In today's world these same traits are cherished by families who love their Goldens as members of the family, always willing to be playful and to enter into retrieving behavior. Could this be what we perceive as a "giving personality"? It is the hallmark of the Golden Retriever.

* * * * * * *

Starting from this premise as caregiver, we owe our charges an understanding based on the most current knowledge we have available, and an environment that speaks to their needs. We have a responsibility to offer them consistency, kindness, protection, patience, and reward—and a perception of themselves in a hierarchy that mimics or represents their original one—as a beloved and accepted member of the pack.

The Golden Retriever: Origins and Purpose

Historically, the forbearers of the present Golden Retriever breed were first bred in 1868 by Lord Tweedmouth (formerly Sir Dudley Coutts Marjoribanks) at Guisachen, Scotland, to be a hunting dog, and to sit quietly in a boat or a duck blind and wait for the bird to be shot and then, with enthusiasm, to retrieve the downed bird—whether on land or in the water—back to the hand of the owner. Selectively bred to get along with other people and dogs, and not to be distracted or aggressive toward other dogs, they were most respected among the hunting canines in the early years.[15]

Goldens were first imported into the United States, probably in the early 1930s or even earlier, from England and from Canada for the hunting pleasures of well-to-do landowners, the sport of the leisure fancier who had open space and time to enjoy the woods and fields, lakes, ponds, and marshes that characterized so much of North America in those days. The owners were accustomed to the ambience of the fireplace at night, with the Golden at their feet, weary and tired and fulfilled after a day working and roaming in the outdoors.

Nowadays, still retaining the traits developed in those early years, they are just as much appreciated, even though no longer so much as a duck hunter. The soft mouth of a Golden is a desirable trait to ensure that the duck is not destroyed, and, similarly today, if the Golden takes hold of your hand or your arm in his joy that you have returned home, he would do so gently, and his teeth would not hurt you. His energy, those quick bursts of speed, and his persistence and eagerness to find the game, accompanied by his keen sight and sense of smell, are traits that endear him to so many even today.

Goldens belong to the world. When the Golden Retriever Club of America (GRCA) was incorporated on May 6, 1938, in Colorado, the Articles of Incorporation stated as follows: "Realizing that the Golden Retriever is a gun dog, the purpose of the Club shall be to encourage the members to perfect, by selective breeding, the type most suitable for such work. The Club shall do all in its power to protect and advance the interests of Golden Retrievers in the field and on the Bench by holding Field Trials and Bench shows under the rules and regulations of the American Kennel Club." Goldens attained their preeminence in sporting dog circles in the United States as a result of the enthusiasm and efforts of Colonel S. S. Magoffin and other early proponents of the breed. One of the additional goals of the original members was to improve the type and to make readily available outstanding Goldens, not to hoard the breed. These Goldens distinguished themselves in field and obedience trials by exemplifying the best working qualities of the breed: "eagerness for work, desire to please, and stamina of character coupled with a most friendly disposition" (Henry W. Norton, GRCA President, 1946).[16] Outstanding Goldens of today are still molded in this great tradition.

PART II:

From Seven Weeks through Four Months

Chapter 4:
Selecting Your New Puppy
and Preparing the Home

Getting Started

Let us assume you have already investigated and selected the parentage of the puppy you wish to have. You have investigated his pedigree, invested time deciding upon type (appearance and temperament), and personality traits you would like in your soon-to-be puppy, and are aware of the requirements of raising the puppy. You are sure this is the breed you wish to live with and are committed to giving the puppy the care, attention, time, a social life, and devotion for a truly meaningful existence for the remainder of the puppy's life. Now you are ready to choose your new family member. Where do you begin?

Having decided on either a male or female, you would first separate the puppies according to sex. Then, taking an overall look at your group of puppies, remove, if possible, any that you are sure you do not want: If you are looking for a smaller-sized adult, you will remove the largest puppy; then you remove the darker ones if you are sure you want a lighter one, or the lighter ones if you want a darker one. The color of the ear of the young puppy is indicative of the future color of the adult dog. Now you are ready to find your puppy.

Evaluating the Puppies

Having reduced the number you are evaluating, consider taking them to a place, usually outside, where there are no other dogs to distract them and you. There you can appraise their overall look as you watch them freely move around. If you are having trouble telling them apart, mark each one in a different place with a magic marker. As you spend time with the puppies, you will begin to realize their differences.

Each puppy should be checked, usually with the help of the breeder, for anything deviating from the norm, such as the bite, undescended testicle(s), length of back, the angulation of the front leg or upper arm with the shoulder and the rear angulation between the bones of the hind leg with each other as they connect to the pelvis. If the breeder "stacks" the puppy (that is to say, places the puppy in a perfect standing position) for you, it will be easier for you to see this. However, it is probably more important for you to evaluate the appearance of the puppy moving freely. The puppy should look balanced— that is, the head should be proportionate to the body, and the front should appear suitable to the rear.

If the breeder holds two puppies together at a time, with their heads side by side, you can evaluate the head. Look for an expression that basically appeals to you. Taste is often based on one's previous experience, on the dogs you have owned and admired in the past; therefore, two people may not exactly prefer the same "head piece" (as the look of the head and face is often called).

For example, a Gold-Rush head has several defining characteristics: a broad, smooth forehead without many furrows; variable shading above and to the side of large dark eyes set well apart; fairly small, close-fitting ears. The planes of the top of the head and the bridge of the nose are roughly parallel with a relatively steep stop (forehead). The muzzle is broad and deep and there is a squared-off lip line; that is to say, not having a pointed or "snippy" muzzle. Below the eyes, to each side of the muzzle, there is a visible "cheek," which, together with the overall shape of the head, gives it a look of breadth and depth. The expression is kindly. Bruce Weber, the well-known Vogue photographer, has called the Gold-Rush face a "Story Book" face. Other lines of Goldens are known for slightly different "head pieces." The differences are subtle and each can be considered correct.

Temperament Testing and Personality

Temperament testing has been in vogue in recent years. For example, one rolls a puppy on its back to see if he struggles, which is supposed to be a definitive predictor of whether he will be dominant or submissive in years to come—or more importantly, whether he will be a pleasant, cooperative member of the household. However, I feel the temperament of the parents is a far better predictor of the temperament of the puppy. The temperament of the parents, taking into consideration their own early training, is the most important clue about the innate nature of the puppy. The puppy is more like his own parents than other Goldens.

Much of the personality of the puppy is inherited. If you have owned dogs over several generations, you can clearly see the similarities being passed down. True, these dogs are being raised in similar environments, but a breeder also often witnesses the impact of improper handling on puppies by new owners. Indeed, poor handling or insufficient positive handling of the developing puppy can have disastrous effects on the behavior of the grown-up dog.

Regarding my own personal belief on the matter of temperament testing, I would say that much depends on the environment in which the puppy is raised, and the impact of the environment on the puppy plays a major role in his development. Proper socialization involving exposure to many different positive experiences will greatly affect how your puppy reacts to various situations. Therefore, all of these things influence his personality. Indeed, what you do with your puppy during the first year of his life is as important if not more important than which puppy you select from a well-bred and cared-for litter. According to Warren Eckstein, an animal behaviorist and TV personality, your impact on the puppy is probably responsible for 80 percent of the adult dog's behavior.[17]

Dr. Katherine A. Houpt, VMD, Diplomate, American College of Veterinary Behaviorists, who has studied the subject in depth, says, "'Dogs change a whole lot between 7 weeks and 2 years of age." Further, she believes that the "psychological underpinning is determined by physical and mental attributes, both inborn and acquired . . . and that temperament tests are not useful on puppies." She believes that "temperament testing is best done on mature dogs, two years of age and older."[18]

The Final Decision

As you study the puppies you may see differences that are meaningful to you, and you should follow your instincts. Each person has different ideals in mind. My feeling is: If you have come this far, you will not go wrong at this point in your selection, and it is a very personal decision the breeder can no longer help you with.

* * * * * * *

A word of caution: puppies tire quickly. You have entered into this puppy's life abruptly—from his point of view. If he is a young puppy, you may be taking him outside for the first time. Give him a few minutes to adjust to the new environment before you evaluate him. **Please be understanding. At seven to ten weeks of age, a young puppy cannot do this for more than thirty minutes without becoming exhausted.** Being a Golden, he will be delighted to play with you and will mobilize his energy reserves to do so. With each passing week a puppy becomes stronger and can handle more activity.

Preparing the Home for the New Puppy

It is important to have a place to put the puppy when you arrive home. A very young puppy under 12 weeks of age should not have free run of your house. Because he needs to urinate frequently, you will probably not want to confine him to a crate. I suggest a puppy playpen that is available through a mail-order dog-supply catalogue. Although such a playpen is an expensive investment, it is ideal for caring for a puppy too young for confinement to a crate, and it can house an adult dog quite nicely if the grid-floor is located on the floor. Alternatively, one can set aside a portion of a large room with an exercise pen or pieces of plywood, which will be the puppy's area. An empty small room with a gate across it is often used.

In the puppy's living area there should be nothing that the puppy can destroy. The floor should be bare and impervious to damage. You can place a dog crate in this area but, in the beginning, leave the door open. Newspapers can be placed in one area if the puppy is so young that it is unlikely that you will be able to get him outside to relieve himself often enough. I would suggest that this place be close enough to the family so that he can be heard in order for you to respond to his whines when he wants to go out, but it should not be the kitchen unless there are no other options, because the puppy will be under foot when one is working or eating there. In his place he should have a stainless steel bowl or bucket or crock bowl for water and another bowl for food. You should have gates to confine the puppy to various rooms where he is spending time with human supervision. Outside, one should also have a convenient secure area such as a fenced yard or kennel to leave the puppy. If a doghouse is provided, you can leave the puppy there for longer periods. Good equipment takes the stress out of raising and caring for dogs.

Equipment

A Shopping List for Your New Puppy

A list of essentials you will need to get started:

Puppy Food (any high-quality, commercial puppy food, small-sized kibble to start, often labeled Small Breed).

Stainless steel pans—at least one-quart size.

Water pails:

> inside crate, two quart size.
>
> outside pen, four-quart size.

Double-ended snaps to attach water pails.

Leash: light-weight, six-foot length.

Collar to wear: light-weight, adjustable buckle or clasp.

Collar for walking: light-weight nylon choke collar about 14 inches to start.

Crate—large size or extra large if you have the space to accommodate.

Comb—greyhound, seven inches long, chrome plated, with coarse and fine teeth 1¼ inches long.

Nail clippers; Quick stop (stops bleeding from a nail cut too short).

Child gates for doorways.

Safe toys: rag, fleece, hard rubber, rope bone, booda, and the like—*not* plastic or breakable toys.

Essentials

Chapter 5:
A Short Course on Bonding

A Positive Attitude at All Times

The puppy wants to please, but he also wants to know where he fits into the new hierarchy. The puppy is eager to learn and eager to test the limits of his new environment. Your first approach to addressing this situation begins with an attitude—a POSITIVE attitude. Along with this attitude is your CONFIDENCE, which presumes that you know what you are doing or believe that what you are doing is the correct or optimal approach. This attitude and this confidence are grounded, I believe, in an appreciation of the warm, cuddly creature who is now in your charge.

Imprinting

Imprinting is an irreversible form of learning that takes place in many animals during critical times in their lives.[19] Through imprinting, animals attach themselves to other individuals of their own kind or even other species. If puppies are not bonded—that is, if they do not "imprint"—on humans during the early critical period, they can never be fully at home in the human world. I have met older puppies or adults from other breeders that have not had this early imprinting or bonding. Such dogs appear insecure and nervous in the human setting, but can be relaxed and content when returned to their canine companions. It is very difficult to reverse what is established in this early critical period, which, from my experience ends in the fourth month. As I raise and work with my own puppies, I use the appearance of the second set of teeth, which emerge around four months, as a marker of whether I am on course with the early bonding process. Dogs can learn by trial and error all of their life; however, the ability to form specific attachments, which are based on key stimuli such as the look, smell, and sound of humans, only occurs when contact occurs in this early period.

Importance of Bonding

Your puppy has been handled from birth by humans. Although the earliest bonding associations are derived from the mother and litter-mates, along with the stimuli from the human caregiver, it is still important that the puppy bond to his human master without the presence of other dogs or puppies. The bonding process is a time when you will be working out a personal relationship that you will have with your puppy for the rest of his life. You build on the early associations. The bonding process is ongoing. It is therefore important that a Golden puppy form a close bond with his human "Alpha" (leader) before four months, which falls within the critical imprinting period.

Relating to Your Puppy: Specific Steps

Bonding begins as soon as you walk out the door with your new puppy. Your first interactions set the stage for the remainder of your relationship and begins the bond of TRUST.

The very specific steps would begin around seven weeks of age, and are known as initial bonding, play bonding, and leash bonding. We repeat these often during the first 12 weeks of the puppy's life, and beyond. It is a method that has not failed us and the results are immediate and dramatic. Whether this method can be transferred to other breeds or all lines of Goldens, we cannot say. We can only speak from our experience, and we can vouch for it. Remember the steps: Initial Bonding, Play Bonding, and Leash Bonding.

Initial Bonding

I believe it is important to begin the bonding process immediately. The puppy needs to be close to you. You speak to the puppy while positioned at his own level—sitting, kneeling, squatting—but never stooping over or standing.

Sit with the puppy in a quiet place. No distractions, no other people or children or dogs or loud noises around. Your puppy is sitting beside you, or you are holding the puppy in your arms. You may also want to stroke your puppy on his breastbone. Talk to him, praising him with soft words, or even in whispers, so that the puppy is focused on you. (Whispering to a puppy will usually get his attention. It is also a useful bonding technique.) Whisper to him what life will be like, how he can trust you, as you praise his beautiful ears, eyes, nose,

Dominance position

tongue. While this may sound a bit strange to some people, I can tell you it works for me. The puppy wants to hear the gentle tone of your voice. There is time for play later, a lot of time.

Then place the puppy in a position that demonstrates your dominance—that is, holding him or cradling him from the rear, his back against your chest or arm, in a comfortable position. Stroke his chest gently. You are holding him at "eye level" and are periodically gazing fleetingly into his eyes. ("Eye contact" is another important concept to remember. You may not realize that this demonstrates dominance but, in fact, it does.) The puppy is concerned that you are a member of the pack, but you want to establish your position in the pack in a most compassionate way. You are not a being from another planet and your intention is not to frighten the puppy or force him into doing something alien to his way of thinking. For instance, we move slowly, calmly, but deliberately when in the bonding mode. (Fast motion elicits fast reactions. What we want is attention, not a reactive response.)

Canines are more hard-wired in their behavior than humans. That is to say, they act in certain ways that are genetically programmed and therefore think in ways different from us, and that thinking is a basis for their survival. By controlling the puppy in a very pleasurable way and using a strategy that is natural to him, you are building a relationship based on trust.

You have probably seen two dogs approaching each other for the first time; they stand still and stare at each other, often with tails raised and perhaps moving slowly, and sniffing. They are trying to establish, or at least determine, the social hierarchy between them. In a similar way, you are establishing yourself as the pack leader as you engage your puppy with eye contact. But do not hold that eye contact too long because you don't want to frighten the puppy. You are the compassionate leader, not a tyrant, and you do not want to break the bond of trust. Also, you will not want to fail to assume your role as leader; "bad dog" behavior is related to your puppy's perception of you as an equal or a playmate or, worse yet, an underling. This is an example of an area of the canine's innate behavior that you can understand and use to build behavioral patterns in the puppy that are desirable to humans.

As you learn more about your Golden you can mold other behaviors into those you desire. The Golden has much to offer us, and we in turn express our better nature with the relationship we develop with them, and this relationship can, and will, last a lifetime.

Play Bonding

Appropriate for puppies eight weeks and older, play bonding is as important as initial bonding, and can continue for a lifetime. Let us say you have spent five, ten, or fifteen minutes in your initial first stage. (Remember, too, you can return to this first stage at any time, because it is one of the most satisfying moments you can spend with your companion during his lifetime.) Now, you can move on to the "play" stage. Play is what your puppy was born to do. Since your puppy was bred to serve as a Hunting Dog, and that behavior is "in the genes" so to speak, your puppy will look forward eagerly to a game of throw and fetch.

You can start off with a slow, but short, throw. The first throw should be slow so that the puppy can mark the position of the "cloth throw" or "rope bone" and follow it with his eyes through the air. The younger puppies are very limited in their ability to follow the toy and also need time to investigate the nature of the toy once it is on the ground. The puppy will go after the toy and perhaps with some encouragement, or perhaps with none, will bring it to you. You can receive the toy while kneeling or squatting, so that you are more or less at the same eye-level position as the puppy.

You would do well to praise the puppy at each return. The puppy likes to hear the praise, which reinforces the bond of trust and introduces the puppy to the pleasure of approval, which should be fun for you and the puppy.

You may want to give your puppy a small reward—a biscuit—when he returns the cloth rope to you successfully. This will reinforce his desire to fetch and return the bone. A reward given two to three times in a row should be sufficient to imprint the positive idea of retrieving. It is important, however, to limit the use of food rewards so that the puppy doesn't become overly focused on food and develop the bad habit of going after the food too forcefully, as if entitled.

At this stage you can also introduce his name (instead of just

"GOOD PUPPY"). The words are simple: "GOOD FIDO," or "GOOD MISSY." Always say it; never tire of it. The two words, spoken in a tone that shows you really mean it, are the magic words.

A word of caution, however. Never use the words "Good Puppy" before the puppy has completed the behavior correctly. The game can continue for another five to ten minutes, and you can pause in between throws (or to keep the puppy guessing when the next throw will take place), which will also allow the puppy to recover and prevent unnecessary stress to the muscles.

You can also vary the exercise by moving the rope bone in a semi-circle on the ground in front of you. Your puppy will chase after it, trying to grab it with his paws. Allow him to succeed, perhaps not every time. This little game is highly successful in play bonding.

When the puppy becomes tired, he will slow down naturally. **You should never push or overstress a puppy or even a young dog by excessive play or by running any distances.** Sure, you can force a puppy to do this, because the puppy will want to please you

Play Bonding

and will respond to you as the leader. But you are asking for trouble in the puppy's development by doing so, and are setting the stage for symptomatic hip dysplasia. (More on "hip dysplasia" in Chapter 15, pp. 153–58 and Chapter 22, "Perspectives on Hip Dysplasia.") Play can be a fun time. It is a time for bonding, and when it's time to go home, perhaps a little early, the puppy will follow, and you will have successfully opened the door to the third stage of bonding: Leash Bonding.

Leash Bonding

On the way home, you can do a little leash bonding. First, you would take a light nylon leash with a nylon choke collar and place it around the puppy's neck, leaving it to dangle, so that the puppy can become used to it. It is not advisable to begin walking the puppy until the puppy accepts the collar, which he may or may not do. It really doesn't matter at this stage.

If the puppy accepts the lead and wants to walk with you, then just let the puppy follow you. (He may very well want to keep close to you because you have bonded successfully and your games have been both fun and pleasurable.) If the puppy wants to walk with part of the lead in his mouth, allow him. It will hasten his acceptance of the lead, and he won't want to hold the lead all the time. If the puppy seems to balk, allow the puppy to get used to the leash and follow you around. But still try to keep the puppy close to you, to have him want to be with you. (As your attachment to the puppy grows stronger, and you are walking together or the puppy is close to your side, the puppy may occasionally look up to you for reassurance, and that is a good time to reach down and stroke his head gently, to express your companionship and your affection. It's a simple gesture, but important, and cannot be taken for granted.)

If the puppy wants to run away, try to call him back by playing the game mentioned on the previous page with him: Sitting, squatting, or kneeling on the ground, you run your hand in a circle in front of you. The puppy will follow your hand and then grab your hand with his paw to stop it. Of course, you will praise the puppy, too. The purpose of the game is to have the puppy bond with you, to want to stay close by you.

If the puppy balks with the leash on him, then squat down and call the puppy to you. Invariably, he will come to you when you are at his level. The puppy must see you as the play giver, the provider, the companion, and he will soon become accepting of the leash. Do not pull on the leash or in any way choke the puppy. The puppy will get the feel of the collar, and will be sensitive and responsive to any pressure when he goes to the end of the leash.

The puppy must never pull you, and you must develop the habit of not pulling on the leash in a steady fashion, but if necessary, give two or three gentle but quick jerks. It may take more than one jerk to get the puppy's attention but the release of pressure between successive jerks acts as a positive reinforcement to the act of not pulling in response to the jerk.

The initial training must take into account the age of the puppy, his innate personality, and what other experiences he has had. The steps you use to engage your puppy may need to be done over and over, until the puppy and you are "leash bonded."

* * * * * * *

A well-socialized puppy is a wonderful asset for the home and family, for friends and neighbors, and you have a responsibility to do everything you can to know how to raise your puppy properly in the company of other human beings. Don't expect a puppy to do this all by himself, just because he has the innate temperament and the genetic makeup to do so. He cannot do this alone. Neither can human children raised without proper socialization, or without a role model for speech, function in human society. They, too, turn out feral. Only through the closeness of bonding and the affection we bestow in this little puppy will he develop in his devotion to us and become confident in the human world—both qualities we appreciate so much in the Golden Retriever.

Chapter 6:
Caring for Your New Puppy

The Puppy Crate

Why Use a Crate?

A dog crate is a convenient, handy place to put a puppy that cannot be watched. The puppy perceives the crate as its den or lair, which represents the instinctual home of the ancestral dog. A crate therefore provides your puppy with a secure retreat.

When you raise a puppy, you strive to manage him so that there are as few failures as possible. Using a crate gives you more control over the puppy in order to train him. In this regard, there are many benefits from using a crate.

1. The crate is very helpful in housebreaking the puppy. (See "Housebreaking, " pp. 57–58.)

2. A crate is useful in preventing destructive chewing and costly changes to your home.

3. A crate prevents a puppy from roaming freely in the home with the potential that, when unattended, he is at risk for getting into potentially dangerous toxic substances and electrical wires.

4. A crate serves as a safer way to transport your puppy in a car and prepares him for airline travel. Many motels will accept puppies and dogs if they are crated in their rooms.

5. In his crate, he cannot offend visitors with his overly friendly greeting; and he is safe in his crate if children or workmen neglect to close doors behind them.

6. A crate teaches him to be happy by himself. Among other things this enables him to stay away from home, happily, when, for example, he is with a groomer or veterinarian.

51

To sum up, a crate is a tool that helps you manage your puppy successfully so that he is an appreciated member of the household.

What Is a Crate?

A crate is a rigid enclosure that is designed to contain a dog. Crates come in many different styles and sizes. Choose one that will be large enough for an adult Golden of your puppy's sex. It must be large enough for the adult to lie down in comfortably and to stand up and turn around in without difficulty. In general, I recommend getting one as large as will comfortably fit in your available space. There is no advantage, however, in having a crate more than a couple of inches taller than the head height of the standing adult Golden. I recommend the plastic airline crates because the hair does not escape and accidents are easily cleaned up. These crates also provide the dog with a den-like, more enclosed, living space. In addition, they are readily available and tend to be less expensive than the wire crates. Wire crates, however, also work well. They have the advantage of allowing heat to escape, and they can be folded up and are fairly portable.

What to Put in the Crate

Place a towel in the bottom of the crate. Newspaper is not a good idea because the puppy may already associate newspaper with a place to eliminate. Furthermore, newsprint will rub off and change the color of the puppy's coat. The puppy will invariably begin chewing the papers, which makes for a great deal of fun for him, but a lot of clean-up for you. A towel is better suited for the crate because it can be washed frequently and can serve as a soft bed—not unlike the experience the puppy was used to when he curled up with his littermates to sleep.

Handling the Crate and the Very Young Puppy

I would suggest that a very young puppy be cordoned off in an area or room that is large enough to contain the crate and give the puppy space to play; a few sheets of newspaper can be placed off to the side for "paper training" and the food and water dish set down in the area. This may be a laundry room, a powder room, enclosed porch, part of the

Wire Crate

family room, or a space enclosed by an exercise pen. The door of the crate should be left open and fastened in an open position so that it cannot accidentally be closed by the puppy's activities. The puppy will, quite naturally, probably go into the crate to sleep and also naturally use the newspapers you provided to eliminate on. You should still make an effort, whenever possible, to take the puppy outside to eliminate. If the puppy does eliminate on the newspapers, the newspapers should be replaced as soon as possible. Keeping the puppy's environment clean will foster his natural instincts to keep his nest clean and eliminate away from his den. As the puppy matures and as you learn to understand his behavior, you will soon learn how to read the signals and recognize when to take him outside. If he can be left outside to play, his house training goes more easily. If he is brought inside to play, he will need to be monitored, and as he tires, after one more trip outside, you can return him to his confinement area for a nap. If you pay attention and are responsive, you will find he is almost always eliminating outside by 10 weeks of age.

Crating guidelines are as follows:

Crating Guidelines and Time Intervals when Puppy is Awake

Puppy's Age	Average Length of Time in Crate During the Day
7-10 weeks	30-60 minutes
11-14 weeks	1-3 hours
4 months	3-4 hours
6 months	4-6 hours

After you are sure you can meet his need to get outside of the crate to eliminate, you can begin shutting the crate door. When he begins to cry, take him outside to relieve himself. When he has accomplished that, praise him, bring him back inside and allow him free time outside his crate in an area that is puppy-proof. The puppy must be monitored so that he can be taken out frequently.

Any puppy will usually be able to last up to six hours when he is asleep at night.

Where to Put the Crate

I would suggest putting the crate in a convenient place that is not too far from the family's high-traffic areas but removed far enough away so that he will not be in the way. I prefer the crate to be located in a place close enough to a heavily used room so that people often pass by and can check on him. However, it should also be in a place that people can move away from, so that the puppy cannot see them, because what a puppy cannot hear or see is soon forgotten and he will most likely go to sleep more quickly. As stated above, the seven-week-old puppy is better off in a closed-off area in which the crate can be placed, with the crate door left open. As the puppy matures, and he is no longer using the newspapers in his area, the papers should be taken up and the puppy taken outside to meet his needs. At this time you may want to shut the crate door to help extend the periods between taking him outside. The puppy area is still a good play area inside if he has had sufficient time outside to eliminate. If the puppy is spending most of his playtime outside in a fenced-off enclosure, it may not be necessary to have the play area inside. One would still be using the crate, however, at night, when the puppy cannot be watched inside. Once the puppy is using just the crate, the crate can be located so that he is not totally removed from watching the activities of the family. You need to be close enough so that you can hear the puppy's movements or restlessness and respond before the puppy eliminates in his crate. But you need not allow the placement of the crate to override the needs and desires of other members of the family.

Add safe toys to the crate to distract him during the first moments of separation from you. When you first place the puppy in the crate or in the area containing the open crate, talk to him in a reassuring, gentle-pitched tone of voice. You will probably find that the puppy will cry at first. This is a natural way for the puppy to reconnect with his family, and in the wild this behavior would be necessary for his survival. You will probably have to go through a few nights of crying, and it is probably best not to return if he cries at first; it would be better to wait and see if he does not quiet down in a few minutes. If the crying or barking (as with the older puppy who is not introduced to the crate gradually) continues and escalates to a tone that shows he is very upset—or so upset that he will need to defecate—then you will need to take the puppy outside to give him a chance to eliminate. If he does, you have then learned about his behavior or needs; if he does not, you have also learned that you need to be more patient in *not* responding to his demands for your company. Confidently repeat the happy reassuring process of returning him to his crate with yet another dog biscuit or toy, and this time you will be able to leave him with the confidence of knowing that he does not need to eliminate and will not soil the crate. In your absence he will soon go to sleep.

If you are using a crate exclusively, rather than the crate within the puppy play area, urge him to enter the crate using a familiar phrase, such as "Kennel up" or "Get in," while you gently but firmly place the puppy in the crate. Quickly give him a dog biscuit and while he is focused on that quickly close the door. Throwing a dog biscuit into the back of the crate as the puppy approaches the crate will usually cause the puppy to enter the crate on his own. Praise the puppy in a happy tone and leave the room. Later when the puppy awakens and begins to whine softly, you must respond and take the puppy outside before he urinates in the crate. The younger the puppy is, the more often he will need to urinate. Therefore, I do not recommend using the crate with the door shut until the puppy is three-months old, except for a short period when you know you can get back to the puppy to take him outside before he needs to eliminate.

During the day, gradually lengthen the amount of time your puppy is allowed to play free in the most indestructible room of your house. By the time he is three-months old, he should be able to control himself for an hour between trips outside, and by five- to six-months old, up to two hours. That same puppy will, however, be able to sleep through most of the night without soiling.

The crate is also useful as an aid in curbing destructive behavior such as uncontrolled chewing. By the time he is a year old he will be mature enough to be trusted to walk around the house for most of the day once he was been taken outside to relieve himself. But keep the crate set-up with the door open anyway. He will become attached to it as his own private "den" and will continue to use it. It will probably prove useful, too, when visitors come or when he is being left alone for a number of hours.

Safety Tips
You must never leave a dangling collar or leash on a puppy or dog, because it could get tangled around the puppy or hooked on to the wire of the crate. The "S" hook of the rabies tag is notorious for this.

Make sure your puppy is warm enough in winter and cool enough in the summer. Never leave an unsupervised dog inside a car during warm weather, whether in a crate or not, and always leave a window open for fresh air to circulate.

Overuse of the Crate
The crate is the puppy's bed and can be used as such for as long as you want. But it is still just a bed. The puppy cannot be confined to his bed for long periods of time without it impacting negatively on the growth and development of his structure and mental state. The puppy

must have adequate exercise, mental stimulation, social interactions, and training to develop satisfactorily and remain in good health.

Housebreaking

The puppy has an innate desire not to soil his sleeping quarters. His desire not to soil the bed can be observed as early as three weeks. The puppy's ability to respond to that desire is a function of his maturity. Your young puppy will always urinate as soon as placed on the grass outside (and for that matter he could eliminate on a rug in a distant part of the house not perceived as his home). Therefore, it is your task to get the puppy outside often enough so that he does not soil his living quarters, which he may do only because of the small size of his bladder and inability to get outside. As the puppy grows he will quite naturally stop using the papers you have provided on the floor (or the rug if you have not confined him and gotten him outside before his bladder was too full) and urinate as soon as he goes outside. I see housebreaking a Golden as merely an enabling process; its success is almost inevitable. As the puppy matures and you show him the way outside, he will quite naturally wait until he is outside before relieving himself.

The general approach to housebreaking is to bring the puppy to the proper place to eliminate. Consistently taking the puppy to the same place every time will speed up his understanding of where to go, so that soon he will naturally urinate there almost immediately. He will most likely defecate after running around for a few minutes. Because a puppy is easily distracted, leave him alone; or if you must wait, watch quietly. Quite often a puppy will move his bowels twice as he plays, so allow enough time for him to do so. As soon as possible, allow the puppy to walk to the house and through the doors to the inside. This may not always be possible, but remember: When you always carry the puppy in and out you are not allowing him to learn this very necessary part of being housebroken—that is, to know the route to the outside. Ideally, you should have the patience to help the new puppy walk in and out. In the beginning, carrying the puppy out may be necessary in order to inhibit him from urinating along the way as he goes. When the puppy is inside and cannot be watched, he must be confined to a small area that he thinks of as his bed or lair. His natural instinct will be not to soil that area. After the puppy has been outside and is brought in, he can be let loose in the room.

A puppy should be watched for sniffing and circling, which indicates that he is looking for a place to eliminate, and should be taken out immediately. If an accident should happen, the puppy should be picked up and taken outside. A loud "No!" may be helpful if the puppy can be caught in the act. Outside, the puppy will soon urinate again and can be praised. All accidents must be cleaned thoroughly. The puppy responds to the odor of urine and will urinate again on that spot. This is a useful phenomenon outside, but inside it is one of the main sources of failure in housebreaking.

Feeding Your Puppy

Selecting a puppy food, usually a dry kibble, that is of good quality and high in protein is of utmost importance. The amount fed and the frequency of meals, however, depend upon the age of the puppy. The younger the puppy the more frequently he must be fed. The older the puppy the more food he will consume each day. (Please see also the overall guidelines in Chapter 14, "Feeding and Nutrition," pp. 127–29.)

Stress and Its Effect on Your Puppy's Appetite
The first week in his new home can be very difficult for the puppy and often results in a loss of appetite. The puppy has been riding in a car for the first time, changing homes, leaving the companionship of littermates he has felt closely bonded to; and now, newly separated, he is not yet fully at home in his new surroundings. As will be discussed below ("The Problem of Stress in a New Environment," pp. 64–65), all of these new situations contribute to his distress. In addition, puppies are delighted to meet new people and respond to that stimulation by

mobilizing their adrenaline. Adrenaline has the effect of suppressing the puppy's immune system as well as his appetite. If the immune system is already overloaded as a reaction to the first immunization, and the puppy is now coming into contact with bacteria for which he has no maternally obtained antibodies to suppress, a bacterial overgrowth may occur in his digestive tract. This can result in gastro-enteritis, the first sign of which is also loss of appetite. (See also "The Problem of Stress in the Environment," pp. 66–68.)

There is also a change in the desire to eat due to a lack of visual stimulation: Your puppy's eating behavior was stimulated by the littermates' act of eating, and a puppy by nature (pack behavior) is interested in what other puppies are eating and will quickly join them. Without littermates eating, the puppy doesn't have that visual stimuli to eat.

New owners presented with a puppy with a poor appetite may have some success in inducing the puppy to eat by stirring the food in front of him or even pretending to eat the puppy's food. As bizarre as that sounds, it does tend to work. Not that this is my recommendation. It is far better to recognize that a puppy under stress during his first week in his new home needs some special attention. This can take the form of adding small amounts of chopped meat or chicken or canned puppy food, which acts as a flavor enhancer, but more importantly it is a matter of making sure the puppy is given ample opportunity to rest and, in some cases, I even give a few days of mild antibiotics to suppress the bacterial overgrowth. All of these things will help the new puppy during the transition period—that is, after he has been taken from his litter and when he must confront, deal with, and adjust to his new environment. Later, there are many other things that can suppress a puppy's appetite, such as the following:

After the initial transition period, I would expect a loss of appetite to be related to such things as the presence of worms or other parasites, various puppy bacterial or viral illnesses, stress from being left behind, new experiences, too much stimulation, car sickness, and vaccinations as well as extremes in the amount of exercise or even temperature fluctuations. Such are the number of situations that can suppress your puppy's appetite. (See Part V: Health Concerns.)

Feeding Frequency and Amounts

Note: Puppies vary in their appetite and requirements from day to day. (See also Chapter 14, "Feeding and Nutrition," pp. 127–29.) My approach (and the reasons and experience supporting my conclusions) is as follows:

Seven Weeks: At seven weeks of age, and for the following three to four weeks, the puppy can be fed all he wants. Although the puppy may be slightly fat as a result, the extra weight on its skeletal system is not detrimental since the puppy is still relatively small and light. There is a concern that the sheer weight of a dog will contribute to problems of the joints, and this is certainly true as the puppy grows larger, but I maintain that in the very young puppy, with a total weight under 20 pounds, the negative effect of the weight is offset by the positive effect that full nutritional support has on the developing muscle mass and skeletal system. It seems to me that a certain amount of weight provides a desirable reserve to the puppy in case an acute digestive disorder occurs. This is the most immediate risk to the puppy because he is in the process of exploring the environment with his mouth and developing resistance to new bacteria and other pathogens. The chance of the puppy having diarrhea is always high until the puppy's immune system has had time to respond—that is, to develop antibodies to all the foreign microorganisms the puppy is encountering. Hence, if a puppy has a bout of diarrhea or vomiting owing to an enteritis caused by a bacterial overgrowth (see pp. 65–67, below), I am always happy to know that the puppy has some reserves to draw upon. In spite of immunizations, keep in mind that serious diseases such as parvo, are not out of the question.

Because the seven-week-old puppy has a small stomach, he must be fed frequently. For this reason "Ad lib" feeding (see p. 128–29) is well suited to the young puppy. This means that dry food is left in a bowl or container that cannot be easily overturned. From this bowl the puppy will nibble from time to time throughout the day. Many times the puppy seems to eat more when fed "free choice" with dry kibble than when fed wet or moist meals four times a day, even when the meals contain flavorful additions. However, it is also beneficial for the puppy to have some additives—such as milk (preferably goat's milk), meat and chicken, or even boneless fish—for their nutritional value. These are only guidelines. Use your common sense and firsthand knowledge of your puppy to determine the appropriate amounts to feed.

Ten Weeks to Twelve Weeks: At ten to twelve weeks of age it is probably time to give up the self feeding and to feed two or three meals a day. At this point, the puppy will usually start to become excessively fat and the amount fed will need to be limited. The rule of thumb on numbers of feedings is to drop one feeding when the puppy loses interest in his food before completing the meal.

Sixteen Weeks through Twenty Weeks: Between four and five months of age, the food may be divided between two meals. As the puppy grows, his total daily food requirement continues to increase. It is only after much of the puppy's growth is completed and his stomach sufficiently large (beyond six months) that I feed just one meal a day. The maximum amount of food is consumed at about nine months and that would be about six cups a day. Thereafter most adults require just three or four cups a day, sometimes less. The amount of exercise, the size of the dog, time of year (temperature) as well as other factors all influence the amount of food required.

Veterinary Care

The new owner will take a newly purchased puppy to visit a veterinarian soon after purchase. Take along his health records. (See Chapter 19 for an in-depth discussion of what a veterinarian looks for during the first visit of the Golden Retriever client.)

The veterinarian will examine the puppy and determine the status of his health and will check for parasites that might have survived the initial de-wormings. The veterinarian will also prescribe heartworm preventative.

The puppy will need a series of vaccinations given every three to four weeks until about fourteen weeks. The vaccinations contain material to develop immunity to the more serious diseases that affect dogs. (See Chapter 13, "Vaccinations," p. 121–25.)

Bathing Your Puppy

In general, the cleaner the Golden Retriever, the fewer problems there are with the skin, coat, and ears. The young puppy is prone to dermatitis (superficial skin infection) until he has developed sufficient immunity to the germs of the environment (see pp. 142–43). Lowering the germ level on the puppy's skin will help prevent such skin infections.

It is probably not advisable for the newly acquired puppy to be bathed immediately upon reaching his new home. The puppy has already had a big day and there is danger in doing too much to your puppy at once. A seven-week old puppy can be bathed, but he will be chilled unless the weather is very warm. Every precaution must be taken to keep the puppy warm until he is completely dry. A puppy will usually sleep after he is bathed.

I use a large, deep basin or bucket, which I fill with warm water. To this I add a small amount of a good liquid dish detergent, or a strong shampoo. The puppy can be immersed in the warm soapy water up to his neck. As one bathes the puppy, every inch should be scrubbed using a cloth. The soapy cloth should be rubbed over the head, face (not the eyes), and ear leathers (inside and out), and then the soapy water can be flushed into the ears until any wax and dirt is removed.

The proper bathing of a puppy is a repetitive and painstaking process, not to be done superficially. Yet, it must be done deliberately and quickly in order not to overtire the puppy's patience. Every inch of the puppy should be scrubbed with a washcloth several times.

It is important to reassure your puppy with a happy tone of voice. If the puppy becomes too unhappy, you may go immediately to rinsing the puppy and save the more thorough bath for the next time. It is always important to have every experience be a happy one for the puppy. With experience, you can gauge how far to go, and can be flexible and "feel" yourself through each new experience. You will be repaid dividends by always ending on a positive note.

Washing the Ears: There are no "halfway" measures when it

comes to washing ears. If the ears are left dirty, or worse, wet and dirty, bacteria and yeast will flourish and inflammation will set in. The ear canal is delicate, and I would advise not to probe into the canal with the washcloth or even cotton or Q-tips, because you may abrade the wall of the ear canal. The outside of the ear, however, can be moved back and forth to help dislodge any material inside and then flushed with volumes of soapy water. The inside of the ear canal should then be thoroughly rinsed with clean water.

Rinsing: The puppy is rinsed with volumes of clean warm water. When working in a laundry tub, the puppy can be rinsed underneath the faucet or with a spray attachment. The water must be warm and the puppy must be thoroughly rinsed. The puppy's face should be rinsed, but you need to avoid splashing soapy water in his eyes. Water must also be kept out of the nose so that the puppy does not breathe water into the lungs or become frightened. It is very important to rinse every part of the puppy. A "conditioner" rinse is often used to reestablish the slightly acidic pH of the skin.

Similarly, after the ear, too, is rinsed with clean, warm water, an otic solution should be used and allowed to remain in the ear, to re-

Washing the Ears

establish the acidic pH of the ear canal. (See also "Ear Infections," in Chapter 15, pp. 144–45.)

When you are rinsing the puppy, you can look carefully for any fleas and ticks. As the water passes through and parts the hair, these parasites can be identified. If you see any, pull them off or scratch them free of the coat and flush them down the drain. Once the puppy is thoroughly rinsed, the puppy is ready to be towel dried and then put in a warm place to finish drying.

Drying: I need to stress that a young puppy will be in danger of chilling; thus, a warm towel in a warm room will help prevent that. The puppy can be placed in a crate with several dry towels and will probably go to sleep after shaking the water out of his coat and rubbing himself on the towels. Keep the puppy warm until fully dry. Later, the puppy can be combed. The hair tends to stick together when wet, but will separate with combing, and the puppy will look fluffy when dry.

The Problem of Stress in a New Environment

The effect on the puppy of changing to a new home is far more stressful than one imagines.

What "Change" Means to Your New Puppy

As you watch your new puppy playing, delightfully greeting every new person, and joyfully investigating everything in his new home and yard, you may overlook how all this activity can have a negative impact on the puppy. You may be so used to thinking of puppies as enjoying this stimulation, enjoying going places and doing things, that you may fail to consider the stress that "change" means for a puppy who is away from home for the first time and may be missing his littermates and their games. You need to remember that this stress can be dangerous. Let us look at some of the reasons why this is so.

The word stress is a commonly used term today, but it was not always so. The term was coined a generation ago by a researcher named

Hans Selye, who first identified the "fight-or-flight" mechanism, whereby an animal prepares itself to meet a stressful situation. That response was defined by showing that the adrenal glands of mammals, including those of puppies, when stimulated by stressful events, produce adrenaline (or noradrenaline) or epinephrine, which are hormones released into the blood stream. (The term applied to these hormones is collectively called catacholamines). These hormones have the effect on the body of preparing the animal for the fight-or-flight response. The sudden release of the epinephrine in response to this stimulation will raise the blood pressure, will increase the blood supply to the liver and muscles, will increase the blood sugar concentration, will stimulate respiration, and will increase the cardiac output and enlarge the air passages. All of these events enable the body to cope better with what is going on—in other words, to prepare the animal for fight-or-flight. There is survival value in this for an animal to have all its resources mobilized for a quick response.

The problem, however, is this: Under stress, the body shuts down certain bodily functions that are not involved in the fight-or-flight response, such as the immune system. Another effect caused by the release of adrenaline is the reduction in the number of lymphocytes that produce antibodies. (For this reason, hormones from the adrenal glands are often used as immunosuppressive agents to inhibit graft rejection.)

When these hormones suppress the puppy's immune system, the body is vulnerable to an overgrowth of bacteria. In addition, immunizations themselves have been observed to repress the production of lymphocytes peaking at five days after the vaccine is given.[20] We know that a puppy is born with circulating antibodies that have come from the mother's immune system, and these protect the young puppy for a number of weeks, after which they are lost. Thereafter, the puppy must make his own antibodies. In addition, if a puppy goes into a new environment for which he has received no maternally obtained antibodies he has no protection. It will take a few days for his immune system to respond to these new bacteria and for antibodies to be made to defend the puppy against these new bacteria. In the absence of any antibodies, these bacteria will immediately begin to multiply in the intestine, and a few days later there will be a bacterial overgrowth, resulting in an enteritis (an infection of the intestine), which results in diarrhea. Couple this with the fact that a puppy has few reserves (little food storage capacity) at this age and will exhaust himself very quickly, and you can begin to understand how difficult it can be for a puppy going to a new home. If at this time you have a puppy that has played at length, has traveled in a car, has mobilized his adrenaline to adjust to the smells and sounds of a new environment, has been given a bath, immunized, de-wormed, and so on, you can see why a puppy may be totally overwhelmed. From the puppy's point of view there are just too many changes that he must adjust to. It is traumatic enough for the puppy to go to a new home after having left his birthplace and the security of a familiar environment.

I have repeatedly observed that approximately five days after a puppy is in his new home, he may suddenly develop diarrhea. As stated above, the bacteria have grown unchecked because the puppy has no antibodies to suppress them and because not enough time has elapsed for the puppy's own immune system to stimulate the lymphocytes to produce antibodies necessary to suppress the bacteria present in his new environment. The puppy enters his new home armed only with the resistance that is due to the presence of antibodies in his blood stream that came from his mother before he was born. As these maternally obtained antibodies fade away, and as he is exposed to new bacteria that are essentially foreign to him, time is required for his own immune system to respond. Until that happens, there will be unchecked growth of these bacteria in his intestine. The first sign of this is usually the diarrhea. (See also the section on "Diarrhea" in Chapter 15, pp. 137–39.) This is dangerous because diarrhea dehydrates the puppy. Subsequently the puppy becomes nauseous, loses his appetite, and often starts to vomit. The situation may become more serious as the state of dehydration increases; within a few hours the puppy becomes lethargic and needs immediate attention.

If you were studying the intestine of these puppies, you would probably find coccidia, which is a protozoan commonly found in the intestine of puppies. Coccidia is an opportunistic organism, meaning that it flourishes and starts to reproduce dramatically when the intestine is compromised by the bacterial overgrowth. This organism is found in the lining of the intestine under normal conditions, but it causes irritation when it starts to multiply and proliferate. The new colonies of coccidia develop in the wall of the intestine and break out through the intestinal lining and so pass out of the body. This process contributes to the enteritis. Often one will see a little drop of blood in the stool, which is a result of the epithelium (the lining) of the intestine becoming fragile. This is a signal most commonly associated with a puppy suffering from a coccidial overgrowth. The puppy will become quite ill, and the situation calls for intervention. It is important that the puppy be treated properly.

Through the years my experience has been that the veterinarians' approach has changed as medication available has changed. Currently the procedure directed by my veterinarian is to give the puppy mild antibiotics that will suppress the bacterial overgrowth. Clavamox (augmented amoxicillin) is quite effective. Sulfadimethoxine and Metronidazole, which are called Albon and Flagyl, respectively, will be very effective if used in concert to suppress the coccidia and the bacterial overgrowth. The puppy that has very quickly become ill will, with treatment, also very quickly become well. Usually one 125mg tablet of Clavamox followed by possibly a second one in 24 hours, followed by a 5-day regime on the Albon and Flagyl, is usually sufficient to get the puppy back to normal. I have found that the safest way to prepare young puppies for the transition is to give them Albon and Flagyl every day for the first five days in their new home and so prevent the whole bacterial overgrowth episode. It is also important to realize that all the factors first mentioned, which lumped together add up to the term "stress," will help the puppy avoid becoming sick—if they are kept to a minimum. Your veterinarian can assist you in this regimen.

I have also seen a similar, but more immediate response, in an older puppy or dog taken on a long trip, when he has never before experienced traveling. If there are several factors coming together—

such as the fear of traveling, motion sickness, and recent shots—these may then work together to result in diarrhea. If a puppy has a low-level of parasites in its intestine, these stressors may even precipitate blood in the diarrhea. Although this can be alarming, a day's rest will usually rectify the situation.

Motion Sickness

Many puppies are prone to motion sickness. Most puppies (but not all) will grow out of the condition. The most likely cause of motion sickness is attributed to stimulation of the inner ear. However, fear of the vehicle can possibly be a contributing factor, as it may be observed even in a dog in a non-moving vehicle.[21] In most cases it is *probably not due to* visual stimulation. Therefore, placing a towel over the crate will probably not be an effective preventative. However, I have observed puppies that will become motion sick in one vehicle but not in another.

Once you learn that your puppy is one that can become car-sick, you will find that it is better not to feed the puppy before the trip. One should be prepared to travel with towels and trash bags. Frequent short trips help the puppy overcome his car-sickness. Traveling in a crate makes it much easier to clean up after the sick puppy.

Traveling to places the puppy enjoys, such as a park or a lake, helps to make positive associations with traveling, which seem to diminish the tendency to motion sickness by overcoming his fear of the car. Another strategy to help your puppy overcome his resistance to the unpleasant association of riding in the car is to feed the puppy in his crate in the car, but not go anywhere. After several days of this, the puppy will eagerly get into the car.

Sometimes, you can give a rawhide to a car-sick prone puppy in his crate, which will distract him enough to prevent him from becoming car sick.

Chapter 7:
Early Socializing and Training: Understanding your Puppy's Behavior

Training Begins with Your First Interactions with Your Puppy

Proper puppy training is one of the most important aspects of your interaction with your new puppy. It begins as soon as you arrive in your home with your new puppy in your arms or on his lead.

If you are a novice, you can begin to correct some of the mistakes you may already be making—mistakes that are often evident to the breeder as early as the selection process. And you may have received some instruction from the breeder about them. If you have already had a close relationship with a dog, the following paragraphs may still contain a few things that may enhance your awareness. For instance, not all dogs are the same, even dogs from the same kennel. The more knowledge and skill you have, the better you will be able to bring out the best behavior in your dog. Now your puppy is ready to show you what he is all about.

The puppy is not exactly a *tabula rasa* (a blank slate) because, as mentioned in Chapter 3, he has already learned some things and has certain instinctual behaviors that have come to him through generations of evolution as a carnivore/pack animal. The ancestral dog's survival was based upon the relationships that the pack members establish with the puppy. These relationships were based on trust, respect, affection, and communication.

69

These same factors will be a part of your relationship with your dog. As your young puppy stumbled around and across his littermates, your puppy began the process of learning. Initially the puppy learned that his littermates offered warmth, and his mother offered food and warmth. If he became separated from them, he became cold and uncomfortable. At this point and because of instinctual as well as learned behaviors, the mother represented largely a source of food *and* warmth. As the puppies grew older, they were handled and fed by humans; transferred from one pen to another, or carried outside, they learned more about the world. They also learned to relate to humans and to look to them for food and support, developing trust along the way. Human companionship, however, was not organized in any teaching mode to establish bonding—that will come later, with the new owner(s). Still, bonding of a sort has taken place—the necessity to become confident with humans. To this point the puppy has had a comfortable and pleasant experience. It is important that this world-view continue in order to retain his happy, giving, and forgiving attitude. The learning experience should be a continually positive one.

With regard to the initial human-puppy interaction, nothing is injected that is negative during this early period: there is no "bad puppy," no "noes"—at first. This early period reinforces the pleasure-seeking in the puppy's genetic makeup. Accidents that inflict pain are to be avoided for they will break the bond of trust, and though puppies are very forgiving, they need reassurance should a mishap occurs. Through your kind, loving overtures of trust and respect, affection and communication are being established in your relationship with the puppy. Nevertheless, "bad behavior" also needs to be addressed and corrected early on. Our initial approach is this: We give a puppy lots of "rope," but then we also install firm boundaries.

The Role of Play

Early on in the puppy's development, the process of "play" has begun. Play has several functions in the developing puppy. Cognitive and motor skills increase. Recognition of the world around him is being calculated so that he can better adapt to living in a world of expectations and surprises. Also, the puppy is building social skills. Play can take the form of dominance-contest behavior, stalking and prey capture, chasing, jumping, play fights, and the like. While learning to enjoy the social interactions of other puppies, the puppy is also acquiring a sense of his position in the pack. As part of the socializing process within the litter, puppy play may be rough at times, but this is part of the social setting, establishing a hierarchy, learning where each fits into the scheme of things—all this is dictated by the evolutionary process whereby selection occurred to produce the innate pack behavior. Much of the play had to do with the predator-prey contest, perfecting skills that were necessary to the ancestral pack. Some of the puppy's innate behavior and early learning experiences are useful to his relatively new Pack, the Human Family; others are not.

In your first interaction with your puppy, play is an essential bonding experience. Play can be viewed as practice for adult behavior, such as hunting, rank ordering, fighting, and mating. In addition, play behavior helps dissipate a young animal's extra energy.

"Play bow"

In his 1998 book, *Animal Play*, Marc Bekoff, of the University of Colorado, proposes that "experiences with play promote learning about the intentions of others."[22] And in an article in the *Quarterly Review of Biology* (June 2001), Bekoff proposes another theory—that "play is training." Bekoff says that play helps animals to be prepared for the unexpected, that unexpected challenges can be rewarding, and that play may be "emotionally exciting and rewarding while at the same time being relaxed." So, in addition to preparing an animal to "cope," play also means "having fun."

In our desire to keep the puppy safe from harm and disease, and to protect our possessions, we necessarily limit, at times, the puppy's play behavior. Although this in itself is a discord, we must seek to find a way around it. Since we are removing a very important part of a puppy's development, we must substitute other activities and problems for the puppy to solve in order to give him proper stimulation—such as toys, walks, meeting people at playgrounds, and gentle retrieves.

It is important to organize the puppy's daily schedule in much the same way as one does for a young child. Your goal is to bring out the most desirable behavioral patterns, to maximize his development, and to mold him into the best possible companion.

Discouraging Development of
Less Desirable Canine Attributes

There are, unfortunately, puppy behaviors that are less valuable, even detrimental to the puppy's success as a human companion. As an animal caregiver, your task at hand is to limit the development of undesirable behaviors so that upon maturity, when the dog's thinking ability has been stabilized, certain behaviors are no longer part of his repertoire—such as biting, growling, and jumping.

Let's take human development as one example: We are familiar with the ability of children to learn languages or music quickly at an early age and know that this ability to learn rapidly is missing or often lost later in life. So, too, the puppy can learn easily early in life; later, it is far more difficult, if not impossible. Couple this with a dog's instinctual behaviors coming from his past generations as a wild-dog carnivore, and one can see how important it is to handle your young puppy properly in order to accentuate the positive and diminish, or suppress, the development of less desirable canine traits within the human culture.

Some of these behaviors can be seen as ways in which the puppy tests his position in the family hierarchy. This is somewhat innate in his nature. Your response will vary. It may be that you will allow the puppy to be a little undirected in this testing period, to see if the puppy's behavior will change, as it often does. If it doesn't, then the important part of the puppy's education will be up to you—to set *boundaries*. This will probably occur sooner rather than later, so be prepared.

One of the most important aspects of teaching puppies is to make corrections only at the time they misbehave. This is always the case in the ancestral pack. A puppy will not make the association or connections if you bring him back to the mess hours later "to rub his nose in it" in order to punish him. This action will only serve to break his bond of trust with you and reduce his respect for you. He will not connect your discipline with his misbehavior unless you make your correction as he is in the act.

Communication with your puppy involves body language and short sounds, not unlike the canine barks. You cannot reason with a puppy. You cannot use grammatical language. On the contrary, develop a few sounds to be used to inhibit the puppy's behavior. A sharp "no," a loud sound like "aehh," a "stoppit" or a painful "ow" can all be communicated to a puppy to inhibit his behavior along with your physically stopping him. The pitch of the sound is very important. The ancestral growl is low and gutteral. When you are inhibiting a puppy you should use a low, sharp tone. On the other hand, when a mother greets her puppies, she whines in a high pitch. Praise and greet your puppy with a high-pitched tone of voice. As your puppy grows he will recognize more and more words, and the learning process will continue for years. In the beginning, follow these rules and keep it simple.

Dogs associate words with certain actions. When you use a word, you must follow through with an action that brings the response you desire, then follow through with praise. In general, you teach the puppy by doing, not by talking to him. Some of these "natural" but annoying behaviors will be discussed below:

Nipping (Play Biting, Holding On)

Nipping is an important matter to address and understand early on. First, the young puppy explores the world with his mouth, testing the environment with his teeth, exploring the environment by chewing—whatever he needs for examination. Second, the teeth and jaws are necessary tools for survival and puppies must learn how to use them, not only to communicate with their playmates in the hierarchy (such as getting their attention by pulling), but also to defend themselves against predators in the wild by using their equipment effectively. Third, and most importantly, the puppy needs to know how to obtain the food he enjoys eating.

You, as the puppy's "pack mate," are part of this inborn method of discovery; you are part of what he must learn about. You are setting limits that the puppy must learn about, too. Young children also play with each other physically—wrestling, pushing, and pulling each other in play—but rarely hurting each other. When things get too rough, you may step in with words of advice to set limits. So it is with puppies. After all, underneath they are probably not far removed in time from their original wild state (just as some modern humans also display evidence of not having evolved much farther than the Upper Neolithic Stone Age in relating to "others" of our species). However, if your first interaction with the puppy becomes a negative experience for the puppy—that is, the puppy greets you happily by taking hold of your hand, only to be met with a "NO" or a scream or, even worse, with physical pain—you are interfering with *the bond of trust* that you want to establish.

You need to teach the puppy what has been called "proper bite inhibition." (Fortunately, aggressive biting has not been a problem with Goldens when contrasted with other dog breeds; their temperament is justly regarded as one of the best in the world of canines.) Nevertheless, puppies must learn not to nip or play-bite their human guardians. Unfortunately, children may not be able to cope with the "play-biting" phase that puppies go through. One breeder suggests that the parent use an aerosol breath spray on the child's hand to discourage the puppy when he tries to nip or hold on. Another breeder recommends gloves and long pants to help a child avoid the puppy's sharp teeth and nails.

The following is suggested as a way to gradually wean your friendly little puppy away from nipping or chewing on you, without compromising his bond of trust:

From the beginning, express your discomfort to the puppy with an "ow" or "ouch." Then hide your hands from the puppy's mouth. Play with the puppy with toys at first. Later, play gentle games of fetch. This serves two purposes: It keeps the puppy from biting you, and it gives the puppy a way of doing your bidding, for which the puppy can be praised. This is an important lesson and is part of the initial bonding process. At the same time you are showing understanding that play-biting is a necessary part of the puppy's behavior; however, play biting is not to be a rewarded activity for the puppy. (As I have said, it is also not a good idea for you to inflict any kind of pain on any Golden because it can break the bond of trust. On the other hand, if you accidentally hurt a puppy, remember that Goldens are very forgiving and will always assume you didn't mean to hurt them. Puppies are ever alert to your attitude and want to please.)

If the puppy's behavior shows no sign of diminishing, you will always use a firm "NO" in a voice that allows for no negotiation. There is no bargaining when behavior needs to be corrected. **Undesirable behavior must be corrected.** For example, when a puppy clamps down on something of yours, that is unacceptable. You can place your hand over his muzzle, firmly saying the magic words, "NO NIP" or "NO BITE." When the puppy lets go, you say, "GOOD PUPPY," or "GOOD [Puppy's Name].

Correcting undesirable behavior

In other breeds, one method is to pop your hand upward under the puppy's chin, along with the strong sounding command: "NO." And, as a last resort, when the behavior is unrelenting, you pick up the puppy and hold him by the scruff at the back of the neck, and say, "NO." A puppy's dam may also sometimes move a puppy around in this fashion. When you wish to stop a particular behavior, this is a natural spot to hold on to, where the least pain is inflicted on the puppy. Both of these methods of correction, however, are not what I would consider desirable approaches.

When you have a behavior that does not respond to your first corrections, it is probably better to remove the puppy from your presence. Return him to his place and give him a toy and leave him alone for a while. A little social deprivation will bring out the behavior you want. He will be glad to be with you and will have forgotten about the game he was playing with you. Alternatively, one could take the puppy for a walk because, once outside your house, the puppy always looks to you as the leader and not as a playmate. In each case, when the bad behavior stops, you lavish the puppy with praise using the words "GOOD PUPPY." After a puppy has learned to be a "good puppy," you now have a useful tool in training your puppy whenever you find annoying behaviors you want to correct. (See also a shorter discussion of this problem as part of the teething process in "Teeth," pp. 149–51.)

Chewing

Dogs enjoy chewing. It is similar to many of our human activities such as knitting to pass the time of day or chewing gum—possibly just to occupy oneself to reduce tension. Also, chewing is often related to the teething period. Teething is one of the most difficult times because the puppy's gums are swollen and uncomfortable. This usually occurs at about the 16th week of its life. For some puppies it's no problem. Others experience a difficult time, and you may be faced with excessive nipping, mouthing, and chewing. A tasty rawhide or other bone may be the answer—to give the puppy chewing satisfaction—as long as the bones won't be swallowed (when they become smaller bites through attrition).

With regard to chewing on objects, use a similar approach: If the puppy happily begins to chew on you, or your favorite rug, do not let the puppy continue, but say "No" and then pick him up and thereby distract him, and then praise the puppy with strokes when setting the puppy down, and distract him further with a toy. This is a more positive approach. **You must remember *always* to follow your correction, once the puppy has stopped the bad behavior, with "GOOD PUPPY" in order to reinforce acceptable behavior;** in other words, when he ceases to engage in undesirable behavior, he is rewarded. Never send a puppy away with "NO" still ringing in his ears.

Should you become proficient in these exercises, you may even be able to guide your puppy/dog by "remote control," from across the room—just by using these simple word "No" followed by "Good Puppy." **There must always be praise when the puppy ceases the undesirable behavior.** This is the uplifting part, and it is very important. The puppy will appreciate knowing what his boundaries are, and you will feel better, too.

Undesirable Play Activities

Play is fun and training can be play. The puppy will eagerly look forward to the next session. There are forms of playing, such as fetch, that are natural to a puppy/dog, and there are others that are natural to a dog but unacceptable in human society:

For instance, the "Tug of War" is not a desirable game. On the savanna, wild dogs and jackals still play this game while eating their prey, but it is more than a game; it is a matter of survival (the way they tear up game to smaller pieces), and it is also very competitive, a matter of life and death. Now that dogs have processed food that comes in small bites and have tasted the pleasures of domestication, we need not participate in a game that can lead to competitive, aggressive behavior even though it served them well in the wild, and is still played out amongst litter mates. Children should be taught not to play with puppies in this manner because it is pack behavior and leads to competitive, even aggressive, behavior. This can be very dangerous if it unleashes this aggressive survival instinct. Children are *not* to be construed as equals in the pack—never.

"Chase-Me" is another type of play behavior to be avoided. Children, especially, like to play in this fashion. But again this is a

"Tug of War": Undesirable Behavior with Children

firm no-no, since it teaches a puppy/dog always to run away. Again, a puppy's instinct is to run away from the bigger animal—a matter of survival. The behavior to be encouraged is for the puppy/dog to *come to you—always!*

Jumping Up

This behavior is more difficult than nipping or holding on, because it does not naturally go away with time, at least not for many years. To help you through this difficult time, when your puppy is so glad to see you that he cannot contain himself, I can suggest several approaches:

a. By far the best approach always is to greet your puppy by bending over before he has time to jump on you. The puppy derives a great deal of pleasure by touching you; if you bend over to his level fast enough, he will not receive what to him is the pleasure of touching you by jumping up.

b. Another approach is to teach your puppy to sit, so you can give him the "sit" command when you first come to him. Then you can bend over and touch and praise him without being jumped upon. You can also give him a reward when he obeys your command, which is an effective reinforcement. Be sure not to pet or praise the puppy unless all four feet are on the ground.

c. You can offer him a toy or have an old towel available to hand the puppy when you first come home.

d. For more show-minded folks, you can give the puppy a skill that helps distract him from you when you first approach him—such as teaching him to Stand-Stay for a treat. In the show world, similar behavior is called "baiting." (See Chapter 18, "Beginning Show Training," p. 185.) If you put a dog in the standing position, and then say "STAY," and then reward him when he stays there for longer and longer intervals, you will develop a skill that you can employ when you first come home. Similarly, your puppy will be much less likely to jump on you if you go through a Sit-Stay and reward when you arrive home. As the puppy matures into adulthood, you can do a Stand-Stay or a Sit-Stay when guests arrive. What you don't want are failures. The puppy enjoys leaping on you, so the sensible way to approach the problem is to work on it from the start. Remember, what is tolerable in a puppy will not be so tolerable when he reaches 75 to 80 lbs.

e. Sure, as the puppy grows into a mature dog, he will still have his moments on a frosty morning where he would love to show you his exuberance by jumping up on you. Correct him as you did when he came to you as a puppy. Be sure that all four feet are on the ground before you praise him. You need to plan ahead on your interaction. If you are athletic enough, you may want to raise a knee to protect yourself from an older puppy, and while that may knock him off balance, it should not hurt him and will not destroy his trust in you. If possible, quickly placing a leash on him will give you more control. If he continues to leap, pull the leash up (rather than down, because he will dislike this more when feeling that he is losing his footing) and this will discourage him. Always praise him when he has his feet on the ground.

f. One more thing that may be helpful: Moving away from a leaping dog will not give him the reward he is looking for. If you can walk away from a puppy jumping up on you, this will help extinguish the behavior. As is always the case, if you respond to a dog doing something you don't like, he will be getting the social contact he wants, and this reinforces the bad behavior. Walking away quietly may be the best strategy. When the puppy is standing quietly, you can bend down to his level and touch him and praise him, "GOOD PUPPY."

Possessiveness

Possessiveness is not too common in a Golden and it can be easily extinguished. However, any tendency toward possessiveness should be attended to immediately. As a matter of course, toss your puppy a toy and then take it back. Watch the puppy's behavior: He will usually look puzzled, but as you quickly praise him, he will wiggle all over and realize he did the right thing by giving it up, and indeed got it back again. Using the word "GIVE" will be helpful, so that later in life he will quite readily give you whatever it is you do not want him to have. Start this exercise at a very early age and repeat it often, especially if there is any sign of possessiveness. This is one exercise children should be immediately taught to understand, and they should be part of the training. If you have concern that the puppy may growl at you over your taking a prized possession from him, pick the puppy up first and talk to him in a high pitched, happy tone, before you take the possession from him. Follow with praise and repeat the action of "giving and taking" the possession. With the puppy in your arms, you decrease his sense of security, and he is much less likely to growl at you.

Family Matters

In addition to the above undesirable canine behaviors you may encounter, there are still a few more that must be mentioned, such as: begging at the table; stealing food from the table; getting into trash; jumping up on the bed or furniture; tearing up bathroom tissue; chasing cars, cats or rabbits, or other moving objects. During the first four months of a puppy's life, especially, you should not allow these "bad" behaviors to develop by having the young puppy experience them in the first place. Put the puppy away before meals are served, store the trash where the puppy cannot see it, have him on a leash when there is a high likelihood of cars or other animals coming by. If the puppy has not had the opportunity to experience the situations that bring on these bad behaviors, it is less likely that these bad habits will develop.

Exercising Dominance

It is always useful to exercise "dominance" after playing with a puppy so that you are not viewed as a playmate in the pack. The best way to do this is to talk quietly with your puppy, and then, having established a relationship of relaxed closeness, carefully and gently move the puppy on to his back on your chest, so that you can softly stroke his chest. The puppy will usually go along with this because you are doing it in a quiet manner. After a short (or longer) period of time, you release the puppy on your own terms. You determine when. The puppy does not make the decision; you do.

Encouraging Good Behavior
When Meeting New People

To develop good manners in your puppy, you should meet people off your property—at parks or along the sidewalk or at the mall. The puppy will be naturally more cautious away from home, and having the puppy automatically on a leash will give you the control you need. It is also a good idea to hold the puppy securely in front of you and have him sit against your legs so that you are in no danger of losing control. Every time your puppy successfully greets people without mouthing or jumping, you are closer to your goal of a well-mannered dog.

Do's and Don'ts

DO:

    1. Be careful when using a leash, and be gentle when handling a puppy.

    2. Be kind to your puppy or dog at all times. This may be the best companion you will ever have. Besides, it's illegal, uncivil, and inhumane to be cruel or abusive in any way to Mankind's best friend. If possible, consider your puppy/dog to be your nicest, closest relative, in whom you are well pleased.

    3. Try to speak to your puppy/dog in a quiet, relaxed tone, which aides in bonding and is soothing to your companion's ear. Low tones demand attention; high tones mean play and positive reinforcement.

    4. Exercise your puppy every day, to build muscle tone and togetherness. Short periods of fetch are desirable. For example, a puppy may be overtired if forced to keep up with you when running long distances (i.e., over a quarter mile). Being overtired can also result in damage to joints and lead to stress. On the other hand, a puppy/dog cannot be deprived of exercise. He must have a proper amount of exercise for his mental and physical well-being.

    5. Use commands always with actions to get the desired result.

6. Use rewards during and immediately after those behaviors that you want your puppy to learn.

DON'T:

1. Handle a puppy/dog roughly. Inflicting pain confuses a puppy.

2. Pull a puppy or dog so that you are choking him.

3. Let children rough-house or chase a puppy/dog.

4. Be angry for very long with a puppy/dog, and don't raise your voice unnecessarily, except as a corrective. Always follow with praise.

5. Run with a puppy/dog for long distances, neither fast nor slow. It would be better for puppies to set their own pace over short distances in order to find their own level of exercise tolerance.

Early Training Sessions

In Chapters 2 and 5, I pointed out the importance of early imprinting of puppies on humans. Formation of the bond of trust is another important early development task. The establishment of human caregivers as pack leaders is also important. Finally, a working relationship that comes about through training makes the dog a pleasure to have.

Training sessions with your puppy will not only instill the desired trained behavior but also reinforce your position in his pack as leader. *You* control the puppy, not the other way around. Our recommendation is that you work with your puppy a little every day or so. If you allow him to grow up without this training, he learns to indulge natural, but annoying, bad behaviors like jumping on you, or grabbing you and pulling. He will not know key commands like come, sit, stay, and down, which are very useful in controlling the *adolescent personality* just around the corner. Your adorable puppy is one thing, but when he reaches the age of around seven months, which is almost full size and weight, you will need to have all your training skills in place so you can survive this difficult period, which may test your patience. Since a puppy must repeat any learned behavior many times, it's best to get started early and accept the fact that working with your puppy is a responsibility you took on when you brought the puppy into your life.

Leash Training

If you have followed the process of "Leash Bonding," your puppy is already a star at walking on the leash. (See Chapter 5, "A Short Course on Bonding," pp. 43–50 for an introduction.) If not, please regard the following paragraph as a further review, and get started immediately.

The Leash and Collar: We prefer a very lightweight, six-foot leash or even a show lead with a light-weight nylon choke collar about 14 inches long to start leash training. We find the lightweight leash allows you to communicate through the lead nicely to the puppy. However, the puppy first needs to get used to having a collar around his neck, and for this purpose a light-weight buckle collar is suitable. A Golden puppy is very accepting of a collar, and can wear a light-weight collar at seven weeks, but one thing you may notice is a tendency to sit and scratch the collar for the first few minutes until he becomes accustomed to it. I would not try to walk him on a leash until he is at least eight weeks and has had some time to bond to you so that he responds to your voice and wants to follow you.

We prefer that leash training in the eight- to twelve-week period be a gentle process, which we call leash bonding, as reviewed in Chapter 5, p. 49–50. If you start with a puppy that is well bonded to you and has had a chance to see a leash and play with it and perhaps drag it around for a while, you can then go into lead training the puppy. With the leash attached to the nylon choke collar, step forward and coax the puppy in your best high-pitched voice to follow you, saying "come on" or "let's go." At the same time get him to step forward by offering him a dog treat or a toy waved in front of his face. As he then steps forward, you say "Good Puppy" and simultaneously give him three gentle tugs. Once you get him going, keep going and encourage him with lots of praise. When he stops, start over with the toy or biscuit and the gentle tugs. We have found that it requires three gentle tugs in a row to get him to step forward. Each of the tugs gives him information about what you want. The tug gets his attention, and the release between tugs is a positive reinforcement for moving slightly forward. Do not haul the puppy or give a continuous long pull because the choking sensation will trigger his moving backward to escape being choked. You will most likely interpret that as being stubborn, which is not the case at all. With three short jerks he will soon be

Leash Training

walking forward. Thereafter, when the puppy starts to pull, give him three short jerks. He will soon learn to walk with you almost to the end of the leash but not to pull. A puppy taught to walk in this fashion will always be a joy.

Teaching Your Puppy to Sit

Probably the easiest thing of all to teach your puppy is how to sit. The little guy comes up to you and looks way up at you as you tower over him, but his neck becomes uncomfortable, so down goes the rear so he can take a better look at you. Meanwhile you have told him, "Sit." A happy meeting of the minds. You give him a piece of a dog biscuit and after a few times, he's got it. How proud you are, and he's pretty pleased, too (with all those treats—not to mention the way Mom coos over him). For now this is all you need to do. Later, with more official obedience training the sit will be tied to the heel command or the "Sit-Stay" command, but this is fine for now.

Teaching Your Puppy to Come to You

Teaching a puppy to approach you is probably the most mismanaged of directives. It is fairly simple, but human mistakes are so common that it becomes more an issue of what you should not do than what you should do. Basically, you give the command, "Come," then have the puppy come to you, followed by the reward (praise or a treat). It is important to start teaching this early because you want to instill the behavior pattern before the puppy establishes a pattern of not coming. The problem is that it is hard to set up the protocol situation—command, behavior, reward—because the puppy is not under your control or you would not be calling him. The very fact that you are calling the puppy is probably because he wants to do something you do not want him to do, which reinforces his going in the opposite direction when you command him to come to you. You need to keep in mind all the things you *should not do* as well as set aside some quiet time to go through the exercise of teaching him to come. Some of the things you should *never do* are as follows:

a. Never hit a puppy—neither with your hand, nor with a newspaper, nor with anything else. That is the first commandment. And in a similar vein—

b. Never punish a puppy when he comes to you, no matter what he did. Puppies only associate the immediate action with the punishment.

c. Never do something unpleasant with the puppy immediately after you call him, such as nail clipping, putting him in his crate, bathing, etc. But take a few minutes to reward the puppy for coming to you before you proceed with the unpleasant chores.

d. Never chase the puppy. This is one game you do not want to develop because it teaches the puppy to run away from you.

e. Never use the command "Come" over and over, and do not "reason" with the puppy about it.

f. Never change the command you are using. Do not use a high tone of voice when teaching a puppy. In other words, *never say please.*

One of the things that you *can do* quite automatically is to use the command "Come" every time you feed the puppy. Or you can use the command "Come" followed by the command "Sit" before you feed him. This is an easy way to make some progress with both commands. We usually carry dog biscuits when training a puppy, and will often call the puppy and reward him when he comes to us. I would recommend doing both things.

We have found that a dog in a fenced yard or pen for much of the day wants nothing more than to come to you when you return. It is the dog that is kept under much more control, say, in an apartment or town house, that learns to disobey if not taught early in specific training sessions to come to you. In a situation where a puppy is confined and controlled, one method of instruction is this: Take the puppy on a 20-foot line to a quiet area outside. Walk briskly away from the puppy, then call him once, and when the puppy moves toward you, begin praising him (by saying "Good Puppy"). If you drop quickly to the ground, kneeling, the puppy cannot resist coming to you. Much praise and a piece of a biscuit. You will often want to play with your Golden puppy; when playing with a ball or throw toy, the puppy becomes extremely bonded to his toy. Pitching the ball in the air or bouncing it will usually bring him back to you quickly when you are walking him off-lead in an unfenced area. However, you should still spend time practicing the command "Come."

It is also possible when dealing with a mature dog to use a throw chain (this is simply a short length of chain) to startle the dog to get his attention if he does not come after being called. I would be cautious about using this with a puppy.

Praise the puppy from time to time, even when walking. The puppy may help you understand his need for praise. He may slow down and look up to you, and you can bend over and pet him or reassure him, thereby reinforcing the bond. Sometimes after you have thrown his "toy," and he has returned it, he may run around, and not return directly to you. In that case, it would be best to let the puppy run around for now, but encourage him to return to you. Eventually, he probably will, and then you can repeat the retrieve to see if he's "got it." And then he will come to you every time.

Chapter 8:
Developmental Changes

Physical Appearance

The Golden Retriever puppy will grow, as all developing animals do, through several different stages. Many of the clues to what his adult structure will be like are present in the puppy. The shape of the eye, the distance between the eyes, the amount of stop, and the depth and squareness of the muzzle are there if one takes the time to evaluate the head. The color of the ear is a predictor of the color of the adult coat. There are also other indicators of the structure of the adult in the seven-week-old—such things as topline, angulation, presence of forechest, tail set, and the correctness of the front and rear legs.

The seven-week-old puppy is characterized by his full round face with a short muzzle. By nine or ten weeks, the face often acquires smoother, darker hair, while the hair on the skull remains fluffy. This gives the puppy the temporary look of a toy monkey.

Generally, the seven-week-old puppy's coat is rather fluffy and is close in quality to the undercoat he will have as an adult. The fluffy coat of the seven-week-old puppy is lost by nine or ten weeks—to be replaced by shorter, darker hair with less undercoat. This gives the older puppy a somewhat less appealing appearance. The coat change can first be seen as a broad stripe down the back, either very faint or pronounced.

The nine-week-old puppy is leaner and has longer legs than the younger puppy. Owners are often so enamored by the seven-week-old appearance that they unconsciously feed their older puppies more to retain that initial appearance. This is of course a mistake.

As the puppy grows, the different growth patterns that one sees, as in the twelve- or fourteen-week-old puppy, are less reliable as indicators. More importantly, the presence of a "weakness" may mean that one needs to make changes in his care. For instance, flat feet may indicate the puppy is spending too much time on floors and concrete and not enough time romping on grass. Similarly, a sagging topline may mean the puppy is too fat and the excess weight of the belly is pulling down on his back. Or it may simply mean that his hind legs have grown faster than his front legs, although the front legs will eventually catch up.

Other changes come quickly. While the leggier look is normal for the nine- or ten-week-old puppy, the ears at the ten- to 12-week-old stage have grown disproportionately larger. Never fear, the head will grow to fit them. The muzzle of the three-month-old puppy has gained a squarer, deeper look that is more like the adult muzzle than that of the seven-week-old, which is more refined. The tail of the four-month-old looks disproportionately long and with the short hair it appears more like a rope than a Golden tail. The feet begin to grow larger after seven weeks and by four months they have the shape of the adult foot. The wrist (carpal bone joint) of the four-month-old looks large because this is where the growth plates are located; as the legs continue to grow longer, the wrists become less prominent.

Through most of the period from seven weeks to almost four months the puppy retains its first set of teeth. Beginning at around four months, the baby teeth begin to be lost and the permanent teeth replace them—a stage that is usually completed by five months or shortly thereafter.

Behavioral Patterns

Many behavioral patterns set during the first four months will last a lifetime. Although dogs learn during their entire lives, early habits are hard to overcome. During the first year of a puppy's life, there are distinct developmental changes as well as environmental influences that need to be recognized.

The puppy is friendly and engaging, but frustratingly inquisitive. The puppy at this age will instinctively stay close you (his leader) and your home (his den). His dependency and friendliness is endearing.

At first Goldens will play with everything, and handle everything, with their mouths. Over time they will lose interest in many things, but the need to chew and their playful nature stays with them for almost their entire lives. Therefore, you must "Golden-proof" your house and yard. Golden retrievers are fun loving and see the house and yard primarily as their playground. You must put away things your puppy can chew on and keep them out of rooms they could damage. The yard too, or the part he is allowed in, must be made safe and free of things he can destroy or things that would hurt him. To be constantly stopping a puppy from what he is doing, or taking things away from him has a negative effect on your bond with the puppy. A puppy does not destroy things out of a sense of vindictiveness, but he is curious and has a natural inquisitiveness. It is the total responsibility of the owner to prevent the puppy from gaining access to things he can destroy. Puppies can learn what they can and cannot do. But it is a long process and requires constant monitoring for many months before the puppy will learn what is expected of him.

Isolating a puppy from other puppies or dogs, and bonding only with humans, may result in the puppy losing his canine identity. This is not desirable because an adult dog who is afraid of or aggressive toward other dogs—the two characteristics are related—is a nuisance to live with. The young puppy needs to have positive experiences with other puppies and dogs so that he remains comfortable with canine companionship.

PART III:

From Five Months through Eight Months

Chapter 9:
Developmental Changes

Physical Appearance

During this period the puppy no longer looks like the adorable little creature you have known and does not yet display the magnificence of the adult. At five months the puppy is growing rapidly and has not yet filled out. The coat is still short and relatively sparse. Males and females can look very much alike, although the male is somewhat larger and heavier headed. By eight months the sex hormones are beginning to produce changes. The male is acquiring greater musculature, which enlarges the head, and the coat of both sexes is becoming longer. I rarely differentiate between the male and female puppy but address them both as "he" because in many ways there is little difference between them and there is much overlap.

Behavioral Patterns

As the puppy matures he grows more confident and independent. With proper management and training, he is off to a good start. He has learned some of the basic commands and is becoming reliably housebroken, all of which is gratifying. Five months is a relatively peaceful period compared to the adolescence just around the corner. His independence may be a frustration, however, if he acquires a taste for running off to play with inviting neighbors. Good fences and equipment take the stress out of his management. He has become mature enough for puppy kindergarten classes. He should be exposed to many different experiences at this age, and this will have a life-long effect on his ability to handle new situations. An effort should be made to continue pleasant interactions with other dogs. As human bonds grow stronger, he may lose his identification with other canines if he does not experience positive canine interactions during this time.

Female puppies, and less often male puppies, of this age can exhibit submissive urination. This is seen in the more submissive puppies. You approach this problem indirectly by building the puppy's confidence (see "Submissive Urination," p. 142).

Mentally he is an exuberant puppy, has little awareness of hurting himself, and needs to be protected from doing too much. For these reasons he is at high risk for cartilage rips and tears and other trauma that could result in his developing hip dysplasia or other joint problems. He has a relatively short attention span, which makes him appear to be indifferent. He may exhibit little sense of concern for your mood or well-being (at least when compared to what he will have as an adult) and is most interested in play and other means of self-gratification.

As the puppy approaches eight months, when his sex hormone levels are rising, he has a new interest in investigating other dogs in order to discern their sex and social position. This period is generally considered to be the most difficult period for the owner. If a new owner is going to return a puppy to the breeder, this usually occurs around eight months. I have relocated several adolescents that were returned with descriptions of destroying the house, jumping unmercifully on their owners, and the like. After spending a few weeks with us, where no great training sessions are given him, but only kind, deliberate, caretaking, with other dogs to expend their energy upon, and limits set on their overbearing behavior, this same dog can be relocated with complete success to a new owner who later gives rave reports of a wonderful dog.

I remember one example of this a few years ago. A dear lady, whom I shall call May Day (a memorable name), bought a female puppy from me. She loved her puppy dearly, but as her puppy came into adolescence, May became concerned and annoyed with her puppy's exuberant behavior. One day she happened to meet a man who had owned one of my puppies, but who had returned the puppy to me because the puppy became "very destructive, destroyed the house, and was impossible to control." May called me, very concerned about whether her dog was perhaps also a "bad" dog. I checked my records and found I had re-located the dog reported by the man to May, and urged her to call the new people who now owned the dog, not really knowing what they would say to her. May called me back a few minutes later. Her tone was entirely different. She said, "Please explain to me how this can be, the first owner was so disgruntled and the second owner now thinks the dog is perfect." I explained to May that it was just the combination of the passing of time and a more experienced dog owner. May survived her Amber's adolescence and loved and enjoyed her dog for many years.

For those struggling through their puppy's adolescence, my role seems to be mainly that of counselor, listening while they ventilate their frustrations, and then offering words of patience, such as "this too shall pass." However, I believe the best strategy is that of preparing for adolescence by laying a good foundation of training beforehand.

Chapter 10:
Caring for Your Puppy

General Health Care

Vaccinations
At five months the puppy will have completed his series of vaccinations with the possible exception of rabies and Lyme vaccines. Kennel cough vaccine will normally be given, especially if the dog will be going to areas of high dog density such as parks, training classes, or boarding kennels.

Spaying and Neutering
It is usual at this age for the issue of spaying or neutering to be brought up by your veterinarian. Consider the issues carefully. (See Chapter 17, "Neutering and Spaying," pp. 177ff.) In my opinion such a procedure would be postponed until the puppy has completed his development.

Nutrition and Supplements
The five- to eight-month-old puppy is still growing rapidly. His stomach is now large enough for him to eat his required amount in a single meal each day. It generally depends upon the schedule of the owners whether that meal is in the morning or early evening. Some puppies do well on self-feeding of dry kibble. In this case the appropriate amount is added to a bowl or bucket once a day. Many Goldens would like to eat more than is appropriate for them and would consume all the dry food immediately. Eating that much dry food at one time is difficult for the puppy. He will often struggle with the food in his esophagus and may even regurgitate the food and then eat it again. In this case it is better once a day to feed the food moistened with water. Puppies

that are on the thin side, or puppies that spend a great deal of time in the cold, may need two meals a day.

A puppy of this age will continue to require more and more food each day. The five-month-old puppy may be doing well on three cups of food but by seven months he may need closer to six cups. It is imperative that you continue to evaluate the amount of fat on the ribs and the mass of the stomach in order not to allow the puppy to become too heavy.

The nutritional needs of a puppy at this age continue to be very demanding. A high-quality puppy food should be continued, as it will more closely meet the needs of the growing puppy. Supplements that may be helpful would be substances that are needed in especially high amounts by the growing Golden Retriever. Fresh meat added to the diet would supply additional protein. Antioxidants such as vitamin C or Superoxide Dismutase, for example, are important to the growing puppy. Glucosamine and Chondroitin Sulfate, the building blocks of cartilage, seem to be helpful in keeping the fragile joints sound. These are some guidelines. A dose of common sense should also be used when feeding your Golden.[23]

Exercise

The task facing the owner of a Golden at this age is to provide the puppy with sufficient gentle exercise to keep the muscles and bones healthy, but to prevent trauma or over-exercise that can result in damage to the joints and bones. Until growth is completed and the skeletal system is fully ossified, such an injury is common. The heavy bone of the Golden and the broad body puts him at high risk for such injury. Gentle exercise, on the other hand, develops the muscles, which in turn protects the puppy from such injuries.

One of the major contributions to the growth and development of a healthy puppy is his daily amount of gentle exercise. I like to speak of "free roaming exercise," mimicking that of the ancestral dog whose puppies came out of the den and played together on the grassy slopes. As they grew they tended to do the same thing every day. Muscles were used and strengthened as they wrestled together and moved about freely. The modern dog that is crated all day and taken out only briefly will have significantly less muscle mass to protect the delicate growing joints from injury during times of heavy exercise when his owner takes him to the Hamptons for the weekend, where he plays on the beach for hours with older dogs that push him beyond his limits. This is a recipe for trouble. Far better would it be to give the puppy gentle exercise every day and limit his activity in order to be consistent on special outings.

Grooming

The Golden Retriever is a beautiful dog. Part of this beauty is due to his lovely coat. Grooming a Golden consists of combing, trimming the feet, ears, and tail, as well as bathing. With a little instruction, grooming a Golden is not too difficult and can be a pleasant experience for both the puppy and his owner.

Grooming is best done on a grooming table. A table may seem unnecessary, but when the puppy is properly trained to the table, it makes the task far easier for two reasons: First, the puppy is at the proper height for you to see how to work on him. Second, once the puppy is used to a table, he is far better behaved because he is much more cautious about moving and struggling than when on the floor.

It is important to introduce the puppy early to the grooming process. Have a happy but firm attitude, always praising the puppy as you proceed through each step. Judge his patience and always end the grooming session on a successful step. Have someone help you by continually holding the puppy and petting him and even feeding him dog biscuits while you work. If you are struggling too much to control him, move quickly to a successful task so you can end the session on a positive note. The first time on a table may simply be a time where you pet him and praise him and feed him a few dog biscuits. The next session will go much better.

Combing

It is necessary to regularly groom the Golden. It is far easier to comb your Golden weekly in order to remove loose hair than to vacuum the entire house. Also, regular combing will remove loose hair before a mat can form. Mats are very deleterious since they are difficult to remove without leaving unsightly holes in the coat. To remove mats without inflicting pain on the dog requires a great deal of time and patience. I like to use a Greyhound comb that is seven inches long and has teeth one and a half inches long. A large "rake" is useful for removing dead coat without straining the hand.

Trimming

Feet. You trim the feet by picking up the foot; and then, from beneath, using sharp scissors, cut away the hair between the pads and as close as you can all the way around the pads of the foot. Then place the foot on the table, and, using thinning scissors, remove the hairs that stick up or protrude beyond the rest of the hairs. This "shapes" the foot. If you "back-comb" the hairs a bit, you can see the extra hairs and snip them away. Holding the scissors perpendicular to the top of the table, you can cut the hair around the foot to give it a round appearance. Hairs that stick up on the top of the foot should be trimmed flush with the rest of the hair on the foot.

Hocks. You trim the hair on the back of the hock by combing the hock hair straight out from the hock, and then trimming the hair at an angle from the longest hair at the top of the hock toward the foot in a straight line but at an angle to meet the back of the foot. You want to leave the hock hair rather long in order to keep the appearance of a short, heavily boned hock. I like to leave a finger's width of hair at the rear of the hock. One sign of a poorly groomed Golden is that of the hocks trimmed uniformly short so that the hocks look high and fine boned.

Ears. You begin trimming the ears by first combing out the ear, completely removing all mats underneath the ear. Then trim around the edge of the ear. Hold the ear away from the body and begin at the lower point of the attachment and trim closely around the edge of the ear and about half way up the upper side of the ear, and stop. The hair is moderately long at the upper point of attachment, which gives a natural look. The goal of trimming the ear is to give a neat appearance not unlike the look of a puppy ear. Next, trim the hair close at the base of the front of the ear. Beneath the ear remove much of the hair but allow it to taper naturally into the longer hair of the neck. Behind the ear the hair is long. It should be shortened slightly and then tapered from the longer hair to the very short hair at the edge of the ear. Trimming the hair on the outer surface of the ear is designed to give a layered effect. If you lift the hair with a comb and then hold the hair between two fingers as you cut, you can achieve this layered affect.

Tail. When you trim the tail, **remember to trim only the hair at the tip of the tail.** You start by completely combing out the tail. Then, with the tail hanging down, you comb the hair straight down. Next, with the scissors parallel to the table and perpendicular to the tail, and holding the tip between two fingers a fingers width beyond the bone on the tail, you make a cut straight across. You will thereby cut off two or three inches of the hair, and your fingers will have prevented you from cutting the bone at the tip of the tail. Then, when the tail is held straight out, it appears as if it is precisely tapered.

Bathing Your Older Puppy

The older Golden puppy should be bathed at least once a month, and if necessary, more frequently due to adventures in mud puddles, ponds, marshy areas, and the like. (The same procedure can be followed as in "Bathing Your Puppy," in Chapter 6, pp. 62–64.)

Owner Identification

Every dog should wear a tag with your current contact information, including your last name, address, and phone number. Tags can be ordered through pet supply stores or catalogues.

Dime and microchip implant (x 2.8)

It is now possible to have your puppy implanted, by your veterinarian, with an encapsulated microchip that will last his life-time. The implantation is as simple as any other injection. The microchip is implanted under the skin on top of the shoulders. It is about the size of a grain of rice and contains a tiny computer chip. The microchip contains a unique identification number, which is read by a scanner that shows that number after it sends a radio signal to the microchip. Most shelters, veterinarians, and municipal organizations now have such scanners.

Several companies have databases that store owner-contact information. One is PETtrac, which is for companion animals that have the AVID microchip. Another is the American Kennel Club's Companion Recovery (AKC-CAR) program for those with the HomeAgain microchip.

Environment and Cancer

With the seemingly higher incidence of cancer that occurs in dogs today as compared to the 1970s and even 1980s, you should be mindful of the cancer-causing agents (carcinogens) that are in the environment of the dog. This is a topic of great controversy, because there is so much we do not know about cancer and carcinogens; nevertheless, more is being learned all the time. What I was told was safe years ago is no longer considered to be safe. Of particular concern are: herbicides and pesticides, smoke, and contaminants such as PCBs and dioxin. It has been said that there are at least 82 different drugs, hormones, and other compounds that pollute our air and waterways, and even polar bears in the Arctic now carry these contaminants in their bodies. (For an in-depth discussion of the effect of carcinogens, see Chapter 21, "Perspectives on Cancer.")

A puppy is much closer to the environmental hazards than we are. He lies down on the grass and spends much time chewing on grass and sticks. For this reason we never use weed killer on lawns or in any areas where puppies or dogs may be present or where they may enter.

Chapter 11:
Training Your Puppy

Introduction

If the first four months have gone well, dealing with the puppy at this stage is now relatively easy. He and you, his owner, know his routine and things are going smoothly. All the advice and correctives are still applicable and, indeed, this is a period of reinforcement and consistency.

Crate Training
The puppy is now quite used to his crate and looks upon it as his den. He should be spending several hours outside each day, and when inside he will spend his nap times in his crate.

Free Time in the House
The puppy is free in the house as long as someone is watching him. It is best to have him loose when people are relaxing or watching TV. A rawhide or other toy to chew on will help occupy the puppy. Gentle retrieving games are in order and just having him in the room is important. Short training sessions will reinforce "come," "sit," and "stay." You should add "down" and "stand-stay." A "go-to-place" command (such as "crate" or "lie down") can be used to get the puppy to go to his crate or to lie down and relax. (It is also important that the puppy learns to relax and to sleep in a room with people. This will promote more quiet behavior.)

Teaching Important Commands

Training is an ongoing process, especially during his first year. It requires some specific training sessions where you teach certain commands, but it also requires that you observe your puppy thoughtfully to see when things are not going as you would like, and to make changes in how you handle your puppy to get the behavior you desire. Although your main technique is to reinforce the positive behaviors you want, you must develop an awareness of your puppy so that you can prevent undesirable behavior before it occurs.

You have already begun teaching your puppy to come to you, to walk on a loose lead, and to sit. You should continue to practice these commands, while adding some new ones.

The DOWN Command
It is easiest to begin with the puppy in the "sit" position (see pp. 85-86). Have a treat in your hand and say in a commanding tone, using first his name, "Charlie, down!" Take the treat from in front of his face straight down and then out to between his two front paws. He will follow you down. At this point keep him down by pressing on his shoulder and praise him and give him the treat. If he fails to go down at first, you can also move his front feet forward as you carry out the above. Repeat the command and procedure, and give him encouraging praise until he does the "down" without your physically positioning him. Increase the length of time you are keeping him down and then release him with the word "ok, good puppy." The "down" command is not as easy to learn as the "sit" command.

Teaching Your Puppy to STAY
The "stay" command is very useful. It can be used after the sit or the stay command. It teaches the puppy to be still where he is. There is a hand signal that is traditionally used to signal the "stay" command. It is the open hand, palm toward the nose of the puppy, stopping a few inches from his nose. Teaching this command is a matter of gradually

increasing the length of time that he remains still before you praise him and give him a food reward (that will release him). Food may make him too anxious to get the food; therefore, you may have more success if you start without food. As he begins to catch on, take a step back but return to him and praise him before he breaks. Every success will further his training. Gradually increase the time that he holds the "stay." If he starts to move, don't increase the time you are expecting him to stay and don't move away from him so rapidly. After the puppy masters the "stay" with the "sit," you can add it to your "down" command; in other words, "down stay." Try to practice these five basic skills (walking on a loose leash, come, sit, stay, and down) several times a week.

As the puppy develops these skills, use them in his daily routine. Ask him to sit and stay before you feed him, or when he meets strangers at the park. Practice at new locations, such as a friend's house, or on a walk about town. He will usually perform better outside of his own home. Combined with walking on a loose lead, these are the skills needed to have a well-socialized dog. However, you will also be giving the puppy lots of feedback about what is acceptable and what is not.

Checklist of Skills

The following is a checklist of the good-behavior skills your puppy should be acquiring:

1. Housebreaking: to relieve himself outside, and how to find his way out there.
2. No biting or rough play with people. No mounting of people.
3. Greeting people in a "stand-stay" or "sit-stay" without jumping on them.
4. Walking nicely on a loose leash.
5. Not playing or not chewing on certain things such as houseplants, curtains, furniture, trash cans.

6. Not begging or stealing food from tables.
7. Enjoying his crate as his bed and place to be when he cannot be watched or outside.
8. Remaining still for examination and when having his feet and tail handled.

These behaviors will not be accomplished without a lot of repetition, and you will need to monitor your puppy for the first year or even two years. Your negative sound or loud "no" followed by "Good Puppy" will be used over and over. Your teaching him to sit, stay, down, and come are the words needed to give the puppy an alternative acceptable behavior in order to positively reinforce his behavior. Your goal is to have a well-socialized puppy that is truly a welcome member of the family.

PART IV:

From Nine Months through Twelve Months

Chapter 12:
The Older Puppy

Developmental Changes

Physical Appearance

The nine-month-old Golden is in his adolescence. His cartilages and ligaments are still gaining strength, and he has achieved most of his height. His muscle mass is still increasing, and will do so for months to come, even into his second year, but his skeletal system has grown more rapidly than his muscle mass, and all of this makes him appear ungainly. He is somewhat high in the rear but, as the muscles develop, the angulation in the rear legs increases, which will drop his rear somewhat. His rapid growth has put him under considerable stress or strain, and he is also more vulnerable to injury at this time.

During this period there is a bloom of what is often called the second puppy coat. It is a very full, short, and thick coat but is more like the adult coat in quality than that of the fluffy puppy. It is a few shades lighter than the adult coat of three years of age and beyond. The fullness of this coat makes a very attractive picture. Puppies of this age can often do very well at shows. Such a puppy, in such a beautiful bloom, can often beat the adult winner and take the points. This is often very thrilling to the owner and gallery. It can be a win well deserved, but as a breeder, one has to wonder if that gorgeous puppy will turn out to become as beautiful an adult when the temporary second puppy coat has vanished.

And vanish it will, to the chagrin of the owner who must comb out bushels of hair, because sometime around the twelfth month there is a major shedding of this coat. Owners complain that they comb out bushels of undercoat. The twelve- to eighteen-month-old will not carry as much coat and is not as handsome as the nine- to ten-month-old for this reason. Never will there be a shedding as great as the shedding of the second puppy coat.

Behavior

The young dog of this age has much of his personality in place, but he is still a puppy, and as his size increases, he is more difficult to manage due to sheer size alone. There is an underlying tendency for him to continually test and retest the rules he has been taught and the limits of his strength, which can make him annoying at times. Physically, as he approaches one year, he is coming into equilibrium, so to speak. He will continue to mature in looks as his coat and muscles develop in the year to come. He still has much to learn, and indeed is capable of learning throughout his life. Now is a good time to start his higher education.

Serious obedience training is appropriate, and he should be strong enough and mature enough to handle long training classes. He is also able to handle the stress of going to dog shows for conformation classes.

As an adult, in the second and third year, a calmer temperament emerges. All your patience, love, care, and training will have paid off.

Training

This is the prime age to proceed with more formal training of your Golden. If you have worked on his early bonding and training and even attended puppy kindergarten classes, he will probably be doing pretty well, but there is a lot more satisfaction to be gained for you and your Golden if you go on with his training. There are several methods you can follow. You can do it yourself with the aid of obedience training books, or you can take your dog to obedience classes, or you can send your dog to a professional trainer, or you can work as an individual with a trainer. It is possible to train your dog yourself with the aid of books, but you will probably be more motivated if you join a class. Also, your puppy will, in addition to the training, learn how to behave around other dogs.

Standard Obedience

Equipment:

1. A nylon training collar, usually 21 inches in length and light in weight with a ring at either end.
2. A six-foot lead made of leather or webbing. It should not be heavy.
3. A long leash or line 12 feet to 30 feet for teaching the recall.

Heeling. In heeling, the puppy walks along your left side without pulling ahead or lagging behind, and he will sit when you stop. It is the first lesson you will learn in obedience. It is useful when you're walking your puppy in crowded or difficult situations, and is universally used. So, there is merit in adding the "heel" to your puppy's repertoire. He may at times be handled by strangers who will ask him to heel. This exercise is also important in changing the way you and your puppy relate to each other. It clearly defines the human as the leader.

Go into this exercise with a certain seriousness and be prepared to be firm. However, this does not mean you forget about praise and positive reinforcement. Keep the training period a happy experience. It should normally not exceed twenty minutes in length. Begin the exercise in a large area where the footing is even and firm. Dress appropriately so you will have no distractions or complications. There should be no distractions or interruptions while you are training. The puppy is on your left side. The nylon training collar goes across the top of the puppy's neck to connect to the leash. Hold the leash in your right hand. To begin, step forward with your left foot, and at the same time give the command "Heel" preceded by your puppy's name. "Charlie, Heel!" As you move forward, the puppy should quickly move with you. If he does not quickly move with you, give a sharp jerk on the lead. When you stop, put the puppy into a "sit" by pulling up on the leash with your right hand and pressing his rear into a sit position with your left hand. When things are going well, talk to your puppy in a cheerful way and praise him. Repeat the exercise and, as he begins to catch on to the "sit," you can simply pull up on the lead with both hands to glide him into a "sit" as you stop. Continue the exercise adding sharp right and left turns. As you turn right, give him a sharp jerk if he does not turn with you. As you turn left, deliberately bump into him if he does not react to your turn and turn with you. Although the heel exercise is a wonderful skill for any companion dog to acquire, it is not generally taught to dogs that will be shown in conformation. Both the "sit" and the closeness of gaiting to the handler are not acceptable in the show ring.

The Sit and Stay. If your puppy has learned to sit and learned to stay, training him in the "sit-stay" will be easy. Give the word "sit" in a deep and loud tone. With the puppy on lead, you would normally pull up with the lead at the same time. As the puppy sits, praise or reward him with food. While he is sitting, use the word "stay" while you bring your hand in a sweeping motion directly in front of his eyes, stopping just before his nose. Your hand should be open with the palm toward your puppy and with your fingers together and pointing down. Keep the leash taut to help hold your puppy in place. If he gets up, you should immediately go to him and put him back into the sit-stay position using the same commands. Then, reward him!

The Recall. Have you been working on the "come" command since he was a young puppy, by always rewarding him for coming, and by never chasing him or punishing him after he came to you on command? The recall exercise is a more formal version of the "come" command. It is performed from the Sit and Stay position. Leave the puppy and turn and face him. Stand tall. Remember that your body language is more important to the puppy than the spoken language. If you stand tall and still, he will be more likely to remain in his sit-stay position. Next, call the puppy using his name and the word "come." Say it clearly but with a happy, enthusiastic tone. At first, stoop down and open your arms to invite the puppy. A puppy usually cannot resist coming to a person that is low to the ground. Make eye contact with the puppy. When he gets to you, guide him into the sit position and reward him well. Start off by focusing only on the act of his coming to you and then overwhelm him with positive reinforcement. Make a huge fuss over him. There will be time later to polish the exercise. As you progress you can add more distance between you and the puppy. You will use your long line at this time. There are many good obedience training books that are available if you wish to proceed to higher levels with this exercise.[24] However, having a dog that comes when he is called is one of the skills most desired by a dog owner.

The Down. The second most desired skill is to have the puppy lie down when asked. Usually this is taught from the heel position. Begin by heeling and then stop. With the puppy sitting at your side, tell him to stay. Then, as you did with him as a young puppy, say "down" and point to the ground in front of his feet. If he does not go down, then move one of his legs forward while you press down on his back. Ease him down and praise him in a happy but low tone that will not encourage him to get up. Say "okay" before you let the puppy get up. Keep him down for at least thirty seconds before letting him up. You will need to repeat the exercise many times. As he gets better at it you can add the "stay" command. Eventually you can add distractions. Every time your dog breaks (moves) you repeat the "down" and "stay," followed by praise. Repeat the "stay" if the puppy shows any tendency toward rising.

Obedience Competition. Many people enjoy obedience competition. You will need help and should join an obedience club or a training group. As with other types of competition, it is best to start early. Puppy kindergarten classes are very helpful. They will also put you in contact with other people with similar interests, which can help you or point you in the right direction.

PART V:

Health Concerns

Chapter 13:
Vaccinations

Immunizations

Vaccines are given for the most severe of the communicable diseases of dogs, and for those diseases that are also transmitted to humans from dogs (zoonosis). These vaccines are updated in response to mutations that occur in the various disease-causing organisms. The vaccinations must be given according to a schedule, which will provide the best response of the puppy's immune system to these vaccinations.[25] Several factors impact upon the puppy's response and must be taken into consideration.

During the first days of nursing, the newborn puppy receives antibodies in the colostrum from his mother. These maternally obtained antibodies protect the puppy in the same way that they protect the mother. Whatever infections the mother is resistant to, the puppies are also resistant. As effective as these antibodies are, they are gradually lost and the puppy, to be protected, must make his own antibodies. In order to stimulate the puppy's immune system to begin making its own antibodies, you need to have the puppy immunized with vaccine containing antigens derived from the disease-producing organisms. However, before these antigens can stimulate the puppy's immune system to begin making antibodies, the antigens may form an antigen-antibody reaction with the maternal antibodies that are circulating in the puppy. This will cause removal of the maternally obtained protection—that is, the antibodies the puppy received from the colostrum—and cause the puppy to be vulnerable to the very diseases for which it was immunized. There is an interplay between the antigens contained in the vaccination and the maternally obtained antibodies, which often renders the vaccination ineffective. The problem is one of timing: In order to immunize the puppy, the vaccine must be given when the puppy no longer has any protection from the maternally obtained antibodies. Because this time is not specifically known, a series of vaccinations are given. The puppy receives his first vaccinations starting at approximately seven weeks of age, followed by an additional vaccination every three to four weeks until fourteen weeks. Once the immune system has been stimulated to produce anti-bodies to the antigens, it will make even more antibodies with the next vaccination. For this reason subsequent "shots" are often called "boosters." Studies have shown that almost all puppies will be fully immunized if the last vaccination is given at the fourteenth week.

In addition to the response of the immune system to the vaccinations, there are other considerations. It is important not to overload the puppy's immune system. As a puppy begins to play and investigate his surroundings in his new home, he will be inoculating himself with bacteria for which he has not yet developed any antibodies. It takes time for his immune system to respond. If at the same time the puppy has been recently immunized, he may not be able to make antibodies against everything at once, which may lead to an overgrowth of bacteria in the puppy's intestine. The bacteria are not being held in check by the puppy's defensive mechanisms (his antibodies). This bacterial overgrowth will cause an enteritis or diarrhea that can make the puppy very ill. I have observed that a healthy puppy given an inoculation of a rather potent vaccine is more vulnerable to becoming ill about three to five days after receiving the inoculation. Such illness, I believe, is a result of the temporary, short-term suppression of the white blood cells, which subsequently allows overproduction of the bacteria in the intestine. The puppy is presented with his first major health challenge in the form of a bout of diarrhea. (See also "Diarrhea" in Chapter 15, pp. 137–39.)

What to Vaccinate for and When to Vaccinate

There are certain vaccines that are generally given today to all puppies: These are vaccines for distemper, hepatitis, parvovirus, and rabies.

These are called core vaccinations. Canine distemper and hepatitis (caused by adenovirus) are less prevalent but serious diseases of the dog.[26] Parvovirus is a potentially fatal virus in all puppies, since they can be exposed to this deadly disease anywhere, most often in public parks or where sick dogs have been present. Rabies vaccine is required because of the possibility of exposure to wild rabid animals that could also transmit the disease to humans.

Distemper: Canine distemper is a widespread, often fatal disease, caused by a virus. At one time distemper caused the death of many puppies. Today, it is rarely seen because of the effectiveness of the vaccines. It is still prevalent in the environment and infects many different species of Carnivores. These wild or feral animals act as a virus reservoir.

Canine Adenovirus (CAV-1): Infectious Canine Hepatitis is a viral disease that affects primarily the liver. During the acute stages of the disease the virus is present in all body secretions. The virus can survive in the environment for long periods. Dogs contract hepatitis by oral or nasal exposure to infected materials, but most dogs will recover with appropriate therapy.

Canine Parvovirus or "parvo": This is a potentially fatal disease of the gastrointestinal tract. It causes a characteristic bloody diarrhea, fever, and dehydration because the virus attacks the lining of the intestine. As the integrity of the intestinal wall is lost, the bacteria from the intestine gain entrance to the blood stream resulting in a serious system infection. Even when vaccinated, puppies up through the age of 20 weeks are vulnerable. This is also a disease that is mutating rapidly. (**N. B.**: A mild false positive can show up in a parvo titer test 5 to 15 days after vaccination. This can lead to a faulty diagnosis of parvo in a puppy.)

Rabies is a fatal viral disease that can infect all warm-blooded animals and can be passed from other infected animals to humans. It is estimated that there are 50,000 to 70,000 cases world-wide, but only a few in the United States because of the stringent vaccination requirements. Puppies can be inoculated as early as two months, although they probably have maternal antibodies at that age, which would render the inoculation ineffective. Most townships require the rabies vaccine to be administered by six months of age. The initial immunization is good for one year. After one year of age the rabies vaccination is effective for three years. It is the same vaccine in both instances.

In addition to the above vaccines, there are others that are usually given as a "combined vaccine," although they may be given separately; but they are usually given after the above series, and are not always given to all dogs (except rabies vaccine, which is required of all dogs). In the combined vaccine, three doses of the vaccine spaced two weeks to four weeks apart are usually given. The last dose is given between 12 and 14 weeks of age. More than 90 percent of puppies will be immunized by that age. These vaccines include:

Canine parainfluenza, which is caused by a virus. Symptoms include coughing. It is part of the "kennel cough complex." Parainfluenza virus is one of the main causes of kennel cough, and the vaccine is a component of all multi-component vaccines that contain distemper, adenovirus, and parvovirus.

Leptospirosis, a bacterial (spirochete) infection that causes fever, vomiting, diarrhea, and depression. The bacterium infects many species besides dogs, including humans, and is therefore zoonotic. It is spread through the urine of infected animals. Rats can act as a vector by feeding and urinating on the puppy's food, if the food is left outside. *Leptospira* vaccine has a reputation for being hard on the immune system of puppies and is often given later in the series for that reason.

Canine coronavirus, a very contagious, gastrointestinal disease causing vomiting, diarrhea, and depression. It is normally not fatal unless combined with other infections, but is more serious in young puppies.

Giardiasis, a protozoan infection of the intestine. A vaccine is now available for giardia.

Bordetella bronchiseptica, a bacteria that also results in a respiratory disease often called "kennel cough." Like bordetella, all of the respiratory diseases are more serious if combined with other infections.

Lyme disease, a bacterial infection that is spread by infected ticks and can lead to seriously damaged joints, kidneys, and other tissues in dogs and humans. One does not usually vaccinate for Lyme disease when the puppy is under six weeks of age because of the interference of maternal antibodies that render the vaccine ineffective.

Lyme, giardia, and bordetella vaccines are also usually given after the initial series. Generally, the initial dose is followed in two weeks by a booster dose, and then an annual dose thereafter. These are often not given unless there is reason to suspect the organism is prevalent in the dog's area. *Leptospira* vaccine has sometimes been implicated in causing adverse reactions. Bordetella vaccine provides incomplete and short-term protection against a bacterial form of kennel cough. There are several organisms that cause kennel cough, one of which is Parainfluenza. Corona virus vaccine is sometimes considered to be unnecessary, since the infection is fairly mild in adults. Puppies, on the other hand, can become quite sick, so we include corona in our puppy immunizations.

The sum total of immunizations is now getting to be quite large, and there is some concern about the effect all these vaccinations can have on the overall health of the life of a dog—particularly on the immune system and the possible relationship to the early onset of cancer. To address this concern, there is growing support for the administration of vaccines at three-year intervals in adult dogs, unless they are exposed to large numbers of dogs such as in a boarding kennel or show situation. Tests are being developed that will measure the titer (amount) of circulation antibodies so that booster shots can be given only when definitely needed. These are called seriological testing (titer testing). At present, an animal's immune status cannot be reliably determined without further "challenge" testing.[27]

Adverse Reactions

Some dogs do experience adverse reactions to vaccines. These immune mediated reactions may occur within minutes to days following vaccination. The Golden Retriever is not a breed where this is common, but it is not unheard of. Vaccinations should not be given when the puppy is undergoing other stressful circumstances such as going on long trips. Puppies should not receive vaccine when they are suffering from any other illnesses.

Chapter 14:
Feeding and Nutrition

Feeding

The nutritional needs of a puppy are of great importance. Providing good nutrition is the key to having your puppy grow up to be the best dog possible as well as avoiding many problems that are diet related.

Developmental Overview of How Much Your Puppy Eats
The newborn puppy feeds hourly. As the weeks pass by, he feeds less frequently but is consuming greater and greater amounts of food at each feeding.

By <u>four weeks</u> the breeder as well as the mother are feeding the puppy, so he is eating six to eight times a day between the two.

By <u>six weeks</u> the mother's milk production is drying up and the puppy is relying on the caregiver to provide food at least every four hours during the sixteen-hour day.

At <u>seven weeks</u> of age the puppy is growing rapidly and still requires frequent feedings because his stomach is small and he cannot eat very much at each feeding. He will need to have access to food at least every four hours during the day. As the puppy grows he will consume increasing amounts of food. But as his stomach grows he will be able to eat more at one time.

At <u>ten weeks</u>, he is eating three meals a day, being fed all he will consume in ten minutes or so at each feeding.

Usually by <u>three months</u> the puppy will begin to become overweight if given all he wants and will need to have the amount he eats controlled.

He will continue to eat more each day and by <u>four months</u> he is usually being fed twice a day.

At <u>six months</u> one feeding a day is normally adequate, but the amount is still increasing.

At <u>nine months</u> your puppy will eat more in one day than he will ever eat in one day again.

These are general guidelines. You must evaluate your puppy's condition on a weekly basis by actually running your hands over the puppy and feeling the amount of fat coverage over his ribs and how heavy his belly is becoming. You need to make some changes continually in the amount you feed your puppy as he develops.

Choosing a Method of Feeding

There is more than one method to feed the puppy. One method is called "Ad Lib feeding" (*Ad libitum* or "at liberty"). With this method an indefinite amount of dry food (kibble) is added to the puppy's bowl once or twice a day, and the puppy eats small amounts frequently whenever he feels like it. One cup of dry food (more as he grows) poured into the bowl once or twice a day, whenever the food disappears, is all that is required.

Another method is the "wet meal," which is made by simply adding warm water to a portion of dry kibble in his bowl. Usually some sort of meat or canned dog food or milk or broth is added to improve the flavor. With the seven-week-old puppy one can prepare a meal that is "wet" or moist by mixing approximately one-half cup of dry kibble and a one-fourth cup of water. The mixture can be left to soak for ten minutes, or it can be warmed briefly in a microwave oven. Milk can then be added to the mixture, and a golf-ball-sized portion of the meat can be stirred in. This can be very appealing to a puppy that is not eating well. Feeding wet (moist) meals is often preferable, particularly when it is not possible to leave food out all day owing to the presence of other pets who might eat the food or children who might play with it. If wet meals are fed, then the puppy needs four meals a day at first. The puppy should be able to clean up the bowl in twenty minutes' time; thereafter, the food tends to lose its appeal and should be removed. The young puppy's need for frequent feedings makes "Ad lib" feeding attractive at that stage.

Whether one continues the "Ad lib" feeding as the days pass, or whether one feeds a moist meal or a combination of both, probably depends more on the owner's habits than on that of the puppy. Some people like the self-feeding approach; others do not. I usually recommend a combination of both methods in the early weeks and moistened meal feeding after three months.

The Basics of Nutrition

Good nutrition is one of the most important factors in raising a healthy dog.[28] Let us first look at what comprises the diet. The basic nutrients are those substances that are required to sustain life. They are: water, proteins, carbohydrates, fats and oils, vitamins, and minerals.

Water is the most important nutrient. Large quantities of water are needed on a daily basis to prevent dehydration. Puppies especially are very susceptible to dehydration and water should not be withheld. Generally, a puppy will drink frequently and drink only what his body requires. If water is not available, however, and the puppy becomes thirsty, he will drink water excessively when it becomes available.

Both the dehydration and over-consumption of water are deleterious to the puppy for different reasons. The correct water balance is necessary to maintain physiological functions. If a puppy becomes dehydrated, he runs the danger of his kidneys shutting down, of falling into shock, and even of dying. After the puppy drinks too much water he will look bloated. In the adult, this could lead to torsion of the stomach. In the puppy he will shortly urinate copious amounts of urine as his body attempts to re-establish the correct water balance. This will play havoc with his housebreaking schedule. It is necessary for the body to regulate water metabolism, because the correct balance of water and electrolytes is necessary for essentially all metabolic functions. It is far better to keep water available at all times. Also, one should always be aware when a puppy develops any diarrhea and immediately treat it because of the risk of dehydration that accompanies diarrhea. (See Chapter 15, "Common Health Problems," p. 139.) There are several other factors that affect water intake—such as heat, exercise, humidity, and food consumption.

Proteins are the main component of muscle tissue, connective tissue, enzymes, hormones, and hair—to name a few. As descendants from a wolf-like, carnivorous ancestor, dogs retained their need for eating a great deal of meat. They also ingested some vegetable food as they consumed the entrails of their herbivorous prey. The domestic dog, however, has developed a more omnivorous diet due to its long association with man.

Proteins are made of amino acids. Proteins, which are obtained from the diet, are digested and broken down into amino acids. There are 22 different amino acids found commonly in the protein of animals. The body can manufacture some of these amino acids. Others that cannot be manufactured by the body must be obtained from the diet; these are called "essential amino acids."

Considering protein's importance, there are a few important terms with regard to food that you should understand. One is the protein's *biological value*, which is a function of the food's composition of essential amino acids and is the percentage that is absorbed and used by the body. On a relative scale, eggs are given a biological value of 100; fish meal, 92; beef, 78, and soybeans, 68. The *digestibility* of a protein is the extent to which the gastrointestinal tract can actually absorb the protein. Some protein, such as hair, is less digestible because it is harder to break down than, say, meat protein. Another term is the *crude protein*, which would include all protein regardless of its digestibility. Protein is graded as either low or high quality. High-quality proteins have a high biological value (the percentage of the protein that is utilized by the body) and also contain many essential amino acids. Digestibility is one of the factors that determines whether a protein is high quality.

High-quality proteins are found in animal-source foods. Because the proteins from plant sources lack certain essential amino acids, they are not as complete a protein source. However, plant protein fed in conjunction with animal protein, which provides the essential amino acids, will meet the nutritional requirements of the canine. In my experience, high-quality protein diets produce the healthiest appearing puppies, and those that grow up with very few skeletal problems. I have fed between 25 percent and 32 percent protein with good success. When choosing a food, the ingredients are listed on the label in descending order by weight. The first three or four ingredients will tell you what the food is primarily comprised of. The Guaranteed Analysis tells you what levels of protein, fat, fiber, and moisture are in the food—in that order. However, these numbers do not tell you much about the quality of the food.

Carbohydrates are the group of nutrients that are based upon sugar; that is, simple sugars and the combination of sugars to form more complex molecules such as starch. Since the advent of agriculture, grains and sugars have supplied the majority of the calories of humans as well as their canine companions. Fiber is an essentially indigestible form of carbohydrate that adds a necessary bulk to the diet.

Fats and oils are fairly complex molecules. Fat is the form in which excess nutrients are stored in the body. Fat is composed of long chains of fatty acids. Fats are saturated or unsaturated depending upon whether or not they have a full complement of hydrogen atoms attached to the fatty acids. Oils are composed of unsaturated fatty acids. Fatty acids are needed for many biological processes. They also allow the absorption of fat-soluble vitamins, namely A, D, E, and K. Fats are a very concentrated source of calories.

Vitamins are molecules that are necessary for metabolic processes. The body cannot manufacture them, and they must, therefore, be obtained from the diet. This is true for both man and dogs, although this may not have been the case for man and dogs in the distant past.

The normally identified vitamins are vitamin A, C, D, E, K, and those of the B complex. Vitamins are either water or fat soluble. The fat soluble ones—A, D, E, and K—are stored in fat deposits and can have toxic effects when fed in excessive amounts. The water soluble vitamins—C and the B complex—are not stored and any excess is excreted in the urine.

Vitamin C had long been thought to have been manufactured

by dogs and therefore was not a necessary component of the diet. As a result of the dog's relationship to man, it has been suggested that the dog has also changed from the carnivorous diet to the omnivorous diet of man. Because the omnivorous diet provides vitamin C, there is no longer an advantage to the dog's ability to produce vitamin C. It may well be that dogs are losing their ability to make vitamin C, so that at times of stress, insufficient vitamin C is produced; thus, additional vitamin C must be obtained from the diet at that time. (Vitamin C is necessary in collagen formation, the main building block of cartilage, tendons, ligaments, and white fiber connective tissue.) A growing puppy would therefore have a need for extra vitamin C due to the body's demands for the production of collagen during this time of rapid growth. The puppy is constantly under stress as he grows, and there are some breeders who therefore propose that adding vitamin C to the diet may help prevent hip dysplasia.[29] (A beginning dose would be 250 mg/day.) Vitamin C may also be beneficial as an antioxidant (see p. 133).

Another reason for giving supplemental vitamin C is to aid in preventing bladder infections. Because excess vitamin C is excreted in the urine it will have the effect of acidifying the urine. Most bacteria that cause cystitis survive much better in an alkaline pH.

Minerals are elements that are needed by the body for many processes and are obtained from the diet. Some minerals such as calcium, phosphorus, sodium, potassium, iron, and zinc are needed in fairly large amounts but when fed in excess can have harmful effects. Calcium, for example, has been shown to be necessary for correct bone development, but, in excess, calcium will stimulate the release of hormones (calcitonin) normally involved in calcium regulation in the blood. This results in gross abnormalities of the skeletal system. Other minerals such as copper, iodine, and selenium are only needed in trace amounts.

Nutraceuticals

Nutraceuticals are dietary supplements with medicinal properties. They are not approved by the Food and Drug Administration (FDA) but are available over the counter. They are naturally occurring in food and are therefore similar in this respect to vitamins.

In the Golden puppy the most important of these nutra-ceuticals are Chondroitin Sulfate and Glucosamine. These have been used for many years in Europe, but have just recently begun to be used widely in the United States. They are the building blocks of cartilage and have been found to be helpful in cartilage regeneration and are therefore useful in relieving the pain associated with the bone-to-bone contact when the cartilage is damaged or deficient, as in osteoarthritis. They are also believed to replenish and renew synovial fluid, which is important in the lubrication of the joint.

Another group of supplements that are widely held to repair damage and promote good health are antioxidants. Antioxidants are substances that help remove free radicals and in doing so prevent these free radicals from causing cell damage. Free radicals are produced from chemical reactions within cells and from outside sources such as radiation and pollutants that act upon the cells.[30] Free radicals are found to be many times higher in the synovial fluid of an inflamed joint. They have been suggested to be part of the aging process and involved in the development of cancer. For example, cataracts can be caused by cellular damage from ultraviolet and visible light oxidation of the lens.

Vitamins B, C, and E as well as beta-carotene (a vitamin A precursor) are antioxidant vitamins. There are also many supplements available that are rich in antioxidants.

Preservatives in Dog Food
Preservatives are added to dog food to prevent the fats and fat-soluble ingredients from becoming rancid or oxidized. The preservatives are compounds that are called antioxidants, inasmuch as they prevent the oxidation of the food. There are both natural and artificial anti-oxidants. Natural antioxidants include vitamin E (mixed tocopherols) and vitamin C. The natural antioxidants are not as effective at ex-tending the shelf life of food as are the artificial preservatives.

Artificial preservatives are more effective than the natural antioxidants, but their use has been controversial. Ethoxyquin, butylated hydroxytoluene (BHT), and butylated hydroxyanisole (BHA) are the most commonly used artificial antioxidants. Ethoxyquin has been used in dog foods for over 30 years but in the late 1980s dog owners became concerned that ethoxyquin was related to medical problems in their dogs. The FDA recommended that the maximum amount of ethoxyquin used in pet food be reduced. BHT and BHA are synthetic vitamin E and are generally believed to be safe, but more research is needed in this area.

Choosing the Type of Dog Food You Should Feed

Young puppies grow rapidly, which places a high demand for a large amount of nutrients on the puppy. It has been stated that high protein diets promote "rapid growth," resulting in a greater incidence of problems such as hip dysplasia and panosteitis. In addition it has been suggested that these faster-growing puppies are more likely to sustain soft tissue (ligaments, tendons, and cartilage) injury during play or exercise.

It is clear that Golden Retriever puppies are prone to developmental growth problems, and a fourteen-year study recently completed by the University of Pennsylvania School of Veterinary Medicine in conjunction with Purina Ralston Company shows a correlation between rapid weight gain and an increased incidence of HD. No correlation between dietary protein levels and such growth problems were included in the study and therefore does not substantiate the claim that high protein alone causes these developmental growth problems.[31]

My experience indicates that the approach of feeding a low protein, less nutritious food that could insure "slow-growth" is, however, incorrect—a conclusion verified by the experience of at least one eminent veterinarian.[32] My experience has been that the better balanced the nutrition, with a relatively high level of protein to foster the greatest muscle mass, the more likely the puppy is able to grow and develop to its fullest and finest potential. Therefore, I think it behooves one to buy the best puppy food that is available.

Currently one hears a great deal about the raw food diet for dogs and puppies (otherwise known as the B.A.R.F.—bones and raw food—diet).[33] Those who use this diet claim excellent health benefits for their dogs. Concerns for bacterial contamination may be unwarranted in view of the fact that canines are often scavengers. In the raw food diet, vegetables are added to the meat, which is in keeping with the canine being historically accustomed to digesting the gut contents of other animals in the wild. The diet is consistent with the origins of the canine as a carnivore. My personal observation is that dogs and puppies relish raw meat, which seems to agree with them. I have always fed some raw meat as a part of their diet.

The physical appearance and health of your Golden is your best measure of whether you are feeding the best diet.

Chapter 15:
Common Health Problems

Introduction

In this chapter, I am reviewing some of the health problems that I have encountered in the past thirty years. Although this review is not intended to replace a veterinarian's advice, it will help you recognize what you are dealing with. Many times it is important to "nip a problem in the bud." Other situations are best given "a tincture of time" before going to the veterinarian.

Diarrhea

Puppies frequently suffer from diarrhea. Diarrhea can occur with or without other symptoms of illness and may occur in apparently healthy puppies. Or it may be symptomatic of another illness. Diarrhea should never be ignored, because the fluid loss in the fecal material will result in dehydration that can be potentially dangerous. Puppies with diarrhea do not grow well and have an unthrifty appearance.

There are many causes of diarrhea. One cause is an adverse reaction to what the puppy has eaten. Other causes of diarrhea include viral infections, intestinal parasites, small intestinal bacterial overgrowth, stress, and diet.

Puppies have a natural tendency to eat almost everything they come in contact with. Unless they are constantly supervised, they will eat many inappropriate things. Any new or inappropriate material a puppy eats has the potential of causing diarrhea. When the puppy eats something he shouldn't (this is called a "dietary indiscretion")—such as other animal feces or spoiled food that contains bacteria, or plants or fungi, which can be toxic—this disrupts the puppy's normal intestinal action, and may lead to diarrhea.

There are three physiological actions of the intestines that are important in understanding the mechanisms that cause diarrhea. First, the secretory process is the action whereby fluid that aids digestion is normally secreted into the small intestine by the intestinal epithelium. Second, the absorption phase is the process whereby nutrients and, more importantly, the excess fluid are absorbed as the digested material (chyme) passes through the large intestine. The third action is the motility of the intestine or the overall speed that food moves through the intestines. If the material moves quickly, insufficient water is absorbed and diarrhea results. To summarize: the secretion of fluid, the resorption of fluid, and the motility of the intestine will determine whether a formed stool or diarrhea results.

Bacteria are normally found in the intestinal tracts. There are good species of bacteria such as lactobacillus, and harmful bacteria such as *Salmonella* and certain strains of *E. coli*. Bacteria that are consumed by the puppy may grow and disrupt the normal intestinal flora. Because of their immature immune system, puppies can easily have diarrhea as a result of ingesting such foreign bacteria, for which they have not yet developed resistance to prevent such bacterial overgrowth. Puppies are especially vulnerable because they are under a certain amount of stress as they adjust to their new home. In response to this stress, their immune system is compromised in its ability to respond to these new bacteria. This was discussed in Chapter 6, p. 65, as part of the "fight-or-flight" mechanism. The hormones that are released in response to the stress can result in a stimulation of the motility of the intestine as well as the suppression of the immune system. Without antibody production there occurs an overgrowth of unfavorable bacteria. This condition is known as small intestinal bacterial over-growth (SIBO).[34] In addition, protozoans such as coccidia or giardia are opportunistic and will proliferate under these conditions. These protozoans live in, and irritate, the epithelium of the intestine, thus increasing the speed with which food transverses the intestine, which does not allow sufficient time for the absorption of fluid from the intestinal material.

Diarrhea is also caused by bacterial and viral disease—such as parvovirus, corona virus, and distemper—by increasing the secretory action of the intestine. Fortunately, today's vaccines largely prevent these diseases. Parasitic worms will cause a tendency for loose stools. A stool sample should be checked if there is a recurring pattern toward loose stools.

Another cause is a change in diet, which alone is capable of causing diarrhea. Digestive enzymes are somewhat altered in response to the diet. When the diet is changed, the enzymes are no longer appropriate to digest the new food. In addition, other new factors in the changed diet—such as the amount of fiber or salts—will also disrupt the activity of the intestine.

If the new puppy develops diarrhea—even diarrhea with a little bit of blood, but which otherwise seems normal—an approach based on my experience of many years would be to give the puppy immediately Albon and Flagyl and a long rest.

If the puppy is vomiting and seems depressed, he may be dehydrated. Dehydration is extremely serious in puppies and can cause death largely through the loss of bodily functions, one of which may be the shutting down of the kidneys. Puppies that have signs of dehydration have a thin look to their face. Their skin will be slow to return to its normal .position when stretched. Puppies that seem depressed and lethargic, are vomiting, and, when defecating, are producing little fecal material, or only mucus, need immediate attention. It has been my experience that puppies with diarrhea that are treated with antibiotics such as amoxicillin, or Albon and Flagyl, will recover quickly. I would not attempt to entice the puppy to eat, but I would leave his normal diet available, usually dry, so that he can eat if he becomes hungry. Generally, a puppy with diarrhea has little appetite. Keep water available. Some puppies prefer to drink an electrolyte replacement fluid such as Pedialyte®.

It is important to let the puppy rest. Handling and taking him places are harmful to the exhausted puppy. In my experience, if the situation does not improve after a long sleep and the administration of antibiotics, the puppy should see a veterinarian.

Intussusception

On rare occasions, a puppy will become ill with vomiting, diarrhea, and abdominal pain that is caused by what is termed an intussusception, which is a telescoping or invagination of a portion of the intestine into the lumen of the adjoining part of the intestine. Although the exact cause is unknown, it is associated with a hyperactive bowel; anything that irritates the intestine, such as enteritis or a foreign object, increases the chance of such an occurrence. Intussusception is most commonly seen in puppies under three months of age. The symptoms are diarrhea and vomiting. If a puppy exhibiting these symptoms does not respond quickly to antibiotics, I would be immediately concerned that an intussusception may be the cause of the problem. The puppy needs immediate veterinary care and corrective surgery.

Megaesophagus

Megaesophagus is a condition where there is an enlargement and hypomotility (slow movement) of the esophagus that leads to regurgitation or vomiting. The puppy may be debilitated by the condition. There has been concern in recent years about the occurrence of megaesophagus in some Golden puppies. Although I have not personally experienced puppies with megaesophagus, the condition is suspect in puppies with symptoms of vomiting.[35]

Cystitis

Cystitis, an infection of the urethra or bladder, is a problem that is seen frequently in puppies. It is usually first noticed when the puppy apparently has lost the ability to control urination. At other times one may observe frequent urination. The puppy squats frequently and passes only dime-sized amounts of urine. Sometimes there will be a drop of blood in the urine. The urine has a strong or unusual smell. The infection is caused by microorganisms that have over-grown and irritated the bladder and urethra. The bladder normally has a balance to the bacterial flora so that no bacteria or yeast overpopulates and causes disease. In many ways cystitis is not unlike the problem of diarrhea in the new puppy. As with the intestine, if bacteria are introduced for which the puppy has no resistance, time is required for the young puppy to develop antibodies to the over-populating pathogens. In cystitis, organisms entered the urethra from the outside when the puppy was lying on the ground or pavement. Because the puppy is small and lies on the ground, the organisms gain easy entrance. This is one reason why cystitis is more common in female puppies. Larger puppies, or adults, will usually have their leg under them when they lie down, a position that protects the opening to the urethra. Males have a longer urethra, which usually protects them against the ascending microbes.

Another reason why the female puppy, or neutered female, is more prone to cystitis relates to the lack of estrogen. Estrogen has a positive, perhaps protective effect upon the cells of the urinary tract. Once the female puppy has been through a season she will no longer have a tendency to develop cystitis. For this reason I refer to the cystitis in this early period as "juvenile cystitis."

Cystitis is often self-limiting. Apparently the puppy develops resistance to the microbes that have overgrown, and after a few days the urination returns to normal. If a puppy with cystitis is treated with an antibiotic such as Clavamox, the symptoms usually disappear quickly. However, it is not uncommon for the symptoms to return as soon as the antibiotic is stopped after a few days. Often a cycle of antibiotics, which cures the symptoms, followed by a recurrence of cystitis once the antibiotics are stopped, followed by more antibiotics, and so on, will be experienced. The problem does not appear to be structural; rather, it seems to be related to the difficulty in reestablishing the correct bacterial flora. For this reason I like to taper off and gradually reduce the dose of antibiotics, rather than stopping the antibiotics abruptly. Also, I usually give a thousand milligrams of vitamin C per day, which may help acidify the urine and prevent the growth of bacteria. Cranberry pills also are effective and are supposed to help prevent bacteria from adhering to the wall of the bladder. Scrubbing the surfaces upon which the puppy is lying is helpful in preventing cystitis.

Submissive Urination

Not to be confused with cystitis is the natural tendency for puppies to urinate when they are acting submissive to other dogs or people. The more submissive individuals will be more prone to this. I would approach this problem by building the puppy's confidence. This is done through praise, never scolding, and distraction with toys or food at times when the puppy is likely to go into her submissive urination behavior. As the dog matures this behavior will almost always stop.

Skin Irritations:
Puppy Acne or Dermatitis, "Hot Spots"

Generally a seven-week-old puppy will have perfectly clean and blemish-free skin. Underneath, the belly will most often appear gray due to his natural dark pigmentation. It can also be white or slightly pink without signs of irritation.

When that puppy is brought out of the house, he may come into contact with bacteria on the grass, dirt, or pavement for which he does not yet have resistance. The result may be what is known as "puppy acne," a skin irritation that appears as little red blotches, small red pustules, and even large carbuncles that can be as large as marbles under the skin. These carbuncles rapidly come to the surface in a matter of days, and discharge their greenish contents, heal over, and disappear, but may cause a depigmented white spot that will last for a few weeks before eventually disappearing. These skin irritations will be seen on the inner surfaces of the thighs and belly. They will heal and reappear until the puppy's immune system is sufficiently mature to fight off this superficial skin infection. Although the puppy will eventually outgrow the condition, it is better not to ignore the symptoms.

As with human acne, the goal of the treatment is to reduce the germ level, generally staph (staphylococcus bacteria), on the skin. Puppies that are inside in their clean pen will not have this problem. I thoroughly disinfect the surface where the puppy is lying and prevent the puppy from digging and lying in the dirt. This problem is much more common in warm weather. Perhaps the puppy will need to stay inside for longer periods. Also, when it rains, germs that have been previously dormant proliferate on the outside, moist surfaces. In addition to the soil, a concrete surface harbors many bacteria that appear to be activated in wet environments. Puppies that are outside during and after rainy periods should be rinsed off, if not bathed, when they are brought in. The condition of a puppy's skin will be much improved during dry weather, as opposed to rainy weather. Skin suffers more in the summer because warm moist surfaces harbor many more bacteria.

Treatment. Ideally, the puppy should be bathed in order to clean the skin and reduce the bacterial population. Any antibacterial medication designed for superficial (topical) use can be helpful. A bath alone will usually make a significant improvement in clearing up the irritation. If the skin does not respond, however, the oral administration of antibiotics by a veterinarian will probably be effective.

The first approach to the problem, nevertheless, should be that of good hygiene and the superficial treatment of the skin. Many of the products used in the treatment of human acne will improve the puppy's skin condition. In any case, as the puppy matures and the immune system makes more and more antibodies to the bacteria in the puppy's new environment, the puppy will be less prone to this condition. I have used furacin spray for years for the treatment of superficial skin infections in puppies and dogs, with good results.

Ear Infections

The ear canal should be clean and white inside, with no redness or black wax. If the ear contains a great deal of black wax or is red, or has pus or flaky material in it, then the ear should be medicated for a few days and then washed. Mineral oil, baby oil, or a medicated otic ointment or ear cleaning solutions are some of the effective agents that can be put in the ear canal to soften the wax debris. There are several medications available for the ear that are used to clear bacterial or yeast infections. Panalog® ointment, Tresaderm®, and Topagen® ointment are commonly prescribed by your veterinarian. They should be used for a few days, until such time as the ear no longer appears to be irritated.

Sometimes there are ear mite infections, which can be treated easily. Some of the flea, tick, and mite killing products that are applied to the skin will also kill ear mites. After a few days of treatment, the ear can be bathed as directed above. (See Chapter 6, p. 64.) Usually the ear of the puppy is free from any signs of infection, and a simple cleaning with soapy water is all that is needed. Clean water must be flushed into the clean ear canals to remove all the soapy water and any remaining debris. Finally, the ear canal will need to be re-acidified since the normal acid pH of the canal has been destroyed by the alkaline pH of the soapy water. Unless the acidity is restored, undesirable bacteria and fungi will flourish and cause the ear to become irritated. Therefore, ear maintenance products can be used for this purpose of re-acidifying the ear, such as OTO-Care B or 3 drops of white vinegar.

Many years ago I was told of a formula for an ear cleaning and drying solution that we have used ever since. We have found it to be exceptionally effective and as a result we have no dogs with ear inflammations. The maintenance solution that I use can be made by mixing:

> 1 pint of isopropyl (rubbing alcohol)
> 2 tablespoons of boric acid powder
> 16 drops of 1% topical gentian violet solution
>   (purchased through a pharmacist)

I pour this mixture into a small plastic bottle with a long nozzle, and squirt a few drops into each ear. This solution is used to reacidify the ear after the bath and to clear up bacterial or yeast infections.

The Eye

In humans it has been said that the eyes are the windows to the soul. In dogs it is certainly true that by observing a puppy's eyes you can often gain some insight into a puppy's physical and mental well-being. The normal puppy eye is dark in color. If one raises the eyelid, the conjunctiva appears so white that it is almost bluish. There will be no squinting or tearing or rubbing of the normal eye. And there should be no sign of pus or infection.

On the other hand, a "listless" look in the eye—that is to say, a dullness or lack of liveliness—may indicate that the puppy is not feeling well. Also the eye itself may "not look right," because it may be infected, or in other ways need attention. In addition, there are other problems involving a Golden's eye that are common enough, and a discussion of some of these conditions is in order.

Tear Staining
Tear staining in a puppy is seen as a darker color to the hair running down from the inner corner of the eye toward the nose. There are several causes of tear staining in a puppy, but in each case tears are spilling out of the eye and running down the face. Most of the time the cause is due to a temporary shape of the lower eyelid of the growing eye, so that the tears only spill out of the eye for a time and the condition is later outgrown. Some puppies may have a small tear duct and are thus prone to the tears spilling out. Sometimes tearing only occurs when the dog eats and his face is tipped down. In many such cases, as the puppy grows the staining becomes less noticeable. An-other temporary cause of tearing is excessive wind or dust in the air, or even brushing against littermates in a large litter. Another cause may be a

reaction to such foreign matter in the environment as smoke or the aromatic compounds in cedar chips.

Other causes may be infections such as conjunctivitis (see below) or an infection of the tear duct itself. Structural problems, such as extra eyelashes pointed toward the eye (districhiasis) or entropion (where the eyelid rolls inward toward the eye, see pp. 147–48), can cause tearing. Another cause may be the result of an injury as with corneal dysplasia, where a puppy has injured the cornea by running into a pine needle, branch, or even another puppy's toe nail. Sometimes there is no apparent cause. It may be a swollen or over-filled tear duct or a minor infection or immune-system response.

Treatment. Often nothing needs to be done but to allow a tincture of time. However, if you see what seems to be an unusual amount of tear staining, the eye can be flushed with saline solution, or eye drops could be put in the eye. There are also products that can remove tear staining. Since tears oxidize the hair, and tear staining does not go away by itself, the stain remains until the hair is replaced. If the products that can lighten tear staining are used consistently for a number of days, they will remove the tear staining.

Foreign Elements in the Eye
When you notice something unusual about the eye, you should immediately examine it for foreign objects. Hold the puppy on your lap or on a grooming table if the puppy is squirming. If the puppy is squinting, draw open the eyelid and observe the appearance of the eye, and flush out the eye with a saline solution. It would be unusual to find something in the eye, because the puppy's immediate reactions would remove something from his eye. If the conjunctiva (translucent mucous lining) above the eye appears red (the normal appearance is a bluish white), I suggest putting an ophthalmic ointment into the eye; this ointment will lubricate the eye and have an antibacterial effect.

Conjunctivitis
An infection of the conjunctiva of the eye is known as conjunctivitis. The white of the eye appears red and the capillary blood vessels are evident. There is usually a cloudy discharge from the eye.

There are three kinds of conjunctivitis: bacterial, viral, and allergic. Conjunctivitis, which can arise from a bacterial infection, is characterized by a more profuse discharge. Viral conjunctivitis, on the other hand, usually causes little discharge and cannot be helped by antibiotics, and although not too serious in and of itself, it can lead to complications and therefore should not be ignored. The third type of conjunctivitis, known as allergic conjunctivitis, is caused by a foreign substance (an antigen such as pollen or dust) that triggers an immune response in the eye.

Treatment. The eye should be treated with an antibiotic ointment applied several times a day. This should remedy the problem, but if it persists you should see your veterinarian.

Muscle Spasm

It is not uncommon for puppies to experience some spasm of the muscle that surrounds the eye. For instance, cold winds may cause the puppy to squint. The squeezing of the muscles may bring the hair of the face into contact with the cornea, irritating the cornea of the eye and causing tearing. In severe cases the muscle spasm will result in what is called entropion (see below).

Also, you should be aware that, if you pull down on the lower eyelid of the puppy, the puppy may resist you by squeezing its facial eyelid muscles, and the overcompensation may cause the eyelid to brush temporarily against the eye. This would not be true entropion.

Entropion

The eye problem known as entropion is a condition whereby the eyelid rolls in so that the hairs of the cheek touch the cornea. Entropion can occur as a result of changes in the puppy's facial development, which sometimes makes the puppy more prone to it than at other times. Conjunctivitis, cold weather, dusty winds, or other irritants can initiate a series of events that result in entropion. As the puppy squints as a response to the eye irritation, the muscle involved will grow larger (hypertrophy) and perhaps go into spasm. This will cause the lower eyelid (rarely, the upper lid) to roll in. Once the lid is rolling in, it tends to stay that way. The muscles remain overgrown due to the constant squinting. I have seen this condition far more frequently in the winter, attributing it to the effect of cold winds blowing into the puppy's eye.

If entropion is spotted early enough, ophthalmic ointment can be used to soothe the cornea and allow the eye to relax, quieting the spasm reaction.

If the entropion becomes well established, however, breeders of some breeds where this condition is more common than in Goldens have developed skills in tacking the eye. Tacking is a method whereby the lid is pulled away from the eye for a 24-hour period by a suture being placed from the eyelid to the cheek. This pulls the lid away from the eyeball, allowing the spasms to relax and the hypertrophy of the muscle to retract somewhat. Then the tack is removed and the entropion is no longer there. In Goldens, this procedure is not, to my knowledge, generally done.

Treatment. If the puppy cannot outgrow the entropion, or if treated with ophthalmic ointment for some weeks but the treatment is unsuccessful, then the eye can be surgically corrected by a veterinarian. A cut is made just below the lower eyelid and the edges are slid past each other slightly and then sutured. This changes the tendency for the eyelid to roll in.

Uveitis

Uveitis is by definition an inflamation of the uvea of the eye and provides much of the blood supply to the inner parts of the eye. The uvea is located primarily in the middle part of the eye and is composed of the iris, the ciliary body, and the choroid layer. The iris is in front of the lens, the ciliary body supports the lens and the iris, and the choroid layer supports the ciliary body and continues around the inside of the eyeball.[36]

Uveitis in Goldens is most likely an autoimmune disease of the eye. Because the eye is formed very early in embryonic development, the antigens of the inside of the eye are considered to be foreign by the dog. When there is injury or infection involving the eye, the immune system may be sensitized to the inner-eye antigens and the production of antibodies to these antigens will begin. These antigens will slowly attack the eye, which will lead to inflammation, scaring, and even glaucoma. I have never seen this condition in a puppy, but I mention it here to emphasize the fact that any infection of the eye should be aggressively treated so that the dog's immune system will not become sensitized to the inside of the eye.

Treatment. The disease is probably not curable but can be suppressed through the use of anti-inflammatory agents for the eye. You should see a veterinary Opthalmologist.

Teeth

A puppy constantly explores its world, discovering how to interact with its environment and to determine its social position in the pack, by using its most important tools for survival—its teeth. A young puppy has small, sharp, baby teeth that can inflict painful nips, which can even break the skin in some cases. This is not an unusual occurrence and the behavior must be understood, and your reaction not exaggerated, because the offending nip is probably never intentional but is a result of its normal playful pack behavior. Goldens *are* very oral (a trait selected for because they're hunting dogs). They are also very playful, and even though they have no intention of hurting you, when they bump into you with their sharp teeth it can be very painful. The teething process tends to exaggerate the puppy's mouthing behavior, but this will normally diminish in time. A positive approach must be adopted and the non-nipping behavior reinforced. Correct your puppy with a sharp "no" or "settle down." When he stops, the correction must always be followed by praise, "GOOD PUPPY." (This topic has also been discussed at some length in Chapter 7, under "Nipping," pp. 74–77.)

Teething

One of the more difficult times in a puppy's development takes place as the puppy explores its world during the first four months of its life. It is a time when teeth underneath the "baby teeth" are growing, causing the puppy's gums to swell and causing irritation that at times may be rather uncomfortable for the puppy. (A puppy has a total of 28 teeth: 14 on the top and 14 below.) At around four and a half months these small, deciduous teeth will begin to fall out and be replaced by the permanent teeth. The baby teeth will lose their nourishment and may gradually turn dark or greenish. Also, at such time, double teeth may appear: The retained deciduous teeth and the permanent teeth are both present. (There are a total of 42 permanent teeth in an adult.) When the baby teeth do not immediately fall out, the permanent teeth will grow alongside the baby teeth. This is not necessarily an uncommon situation, and a chew toy may help the process along, but if it bothers you, you may want to have the "offending" baby teeth pulled.

Time will invariably help you out anyway, when Nature takes care of it herself. There will probably not be any misalignment as a result of a "double" tooth taking its time before falling out.

Missing Teeth

The complete set of teeth normally erupts around by six months, but Goldens can and do have missing premolars on occasion. This is an undesirable condition with a strong hereditary basis; however, it does not seem to affect the dog in any way.

Tooth Maintenance

Although dogs are thought to have more resistance to tooth decay and gum disease than humans, it is true that, without proper care, by the time the dog is seven or eight years old, the teeth will have accumulated lots of tartar, discoloration, and receding or irritated gums. As time goes by, black areas of decay will appear and teeth will eventually be lost. You can regularly brush a puppy's teeth in order to prevent the formation or build-up of tarter. There are pleasant tasting products available for this, or you can use ordinary baking soda. You should start the training early and cautiously, praising the puppy for submitting to this procedure. If the puppy starts to struggle, you must be firm and at the same time gentle, maintaining control until he relaxes. Praise him as he becomes quiet and relaxed. Constantly stroking his breastbone will help. Be sure he is quiet and calm before pressing on to continue the job at hand. If you start early and praise the puppy while being firm, your puppy will gradually learn to accept tooth brushing. In any case, if tarter is building up on the teeth it should be removed with a tooth scaler. You start at the gum line and scrape toward the end of the tooth. If you do this periodically, the Golden's normal chewing will complete the teeth-cleaning process. If this is not done, your dog may well need professional cleaning as he ages, and may even need tooth extraction by your veterinarian.

The enamel is normally perfectly white, but there are occasions when the puppy's enamel is not white, where the teeth have a brownish cast. The cause is a result of the puppy having been ill during the early months when his teeth were forming below the gum. (In the past, when distemper was common, these were called "distemper teeth.") If tetracycline or related antibiotics are administered to the puppy at this crucial time, or if he eats meat from an animal contaminated with tetracycline, they will also cause a brown staining of the teeth. These antibiotics are therefore not given to a puppy until his teeth are fully formed.

Coprophagy (Stool Eating)

This is a very unpleasant habit for the puppy owner, and an unhealthy one for the puppy. A stool-eating puppy will probably have a greater tendency toward diarrhea, a loss of appetite, and poor growth. The habit may begin as early as five or six weeks, but can start at almost any age. When puppies are crowded together in their whelping box or pen, the warm stool becomes attractive. Or if the puppy is isolated with few distractions he may eat the stool first out of curiosity. Once a puppy acquires a taste for it, the puppy may behave in an excited and enthusiastic way when a stool is being produced, and the puppy will quickly go for it . . . and eat it.

As with most bad habits, it is far better to prevent the habit from the start, rather than to correct it. If it does happen, you need to be even more vigilant and immediately remove the fresh stools quickly. Be prepared with either a pooper scooper or a paper towel to quickly pick up that stool before the puppy gets to it. That may be difficult so it may be best to remove the puppy from the area and then clean up the stool.

In a puppy practicing coprophagy, there is overabundance of certain bacteria in the intestine, producing an unhealthy state in the puppy's digestive tract, which seems to further accentuate the puppy's desire to eat more stools. When there is a bacterial overgrowth in the intestine, protozoans, which are said to be opportunistic, will also proliferate. Giving the puppy mild antibiotics, such as Albon or Flagyl, seems to be helpful. The Flagyl probably inhibits a bacterial overgrowth, such as *E. coli*, and the Albon mainly suppresses coccidia, which is the most common protozoan offender.

The standard treatment for coprophagy is to add an enzyme product, such as Forbid™, to the diet. This product has a bitter tasting amino acid in it that appears in the stool and changes the flavor of the stool to one that does not appeal to the puppy. Another approach is the addition of enzymes that help break down proteins in the stool that may add the attractive flavor. I have found, however, that neither of these approaches is as effective or successful as giving Albon or Flagyl for five days and practicing good hygiene. If I do this, rarely do I see this behavior continue.

This kind of behavior in a puppy does not seem to be related to stool eating in adult animals. My experience with adults is that there are certain individuals that will acquire a taste for stool eating, and these are not necessarily the ones that were stool eaters as puppies. You need to police the ground where they exercise in order to pick up all animal droppings. Often stools appeal to many dogs when the temperature is below freezing, but they do not appeal to dogs at warmer temperatures.

Cryptorchidism

Both the testis and the ovary of the embryo develop within the abdomen. Normally the testes pass through the inguinal canal sometime after birth. In the Golden puppy the testicles generally appear at about six weeks of age. If they are not there by ten weeks there is a high probability that they will never descend, but I have known cases where the testes did not descend by ten weeks, yet did appear by six months. By that time, however, the inguinal canal generally closes. It also seems to be the case that occasionally one of the testes will ascend after previously having descended and not reappear. It may well be that the testicle is able to move freely through the inguinal canal for a time, but as the canal narrows the testicle is trapped within the abdomen. I have also observed a higher incidence of undescended testicles among fat puppies, and it may well be that the fat pads in the abdomen somehow prevent the testicle from descending.[37]

To have one or both testicles missing is a disqualification with regard to the American Kennel Club shows. Dogs with only one testicle are fertile but are generally not considered to be breedable in this country. Dogs with both retained testes (i.e., undescended testicles) are not fertile. It is generally recommended that dogs with undescended testicles be castrated because there is a reported higher incidence of testicular cancer <u>in later years</u> in dogs having retained testes.

Hip Dysplasia

Hip dysplasia is the most prevalent disorder of the canine hip and the most important cause of discomfort, abnormal gait, and structure, especially in the rear of the Golden Retriever. Although almost all breeds are at risk, hip dysplasia most commonly affects large- and giant-breed dogs. It is prevalent in the Golden and therefore of great concern to the Golden Retriever breeder, as well as the owner.

Hip dysplasia is first seen as an instability of the hip joint, which occurs as muscle development and maturation lag behind the rate of skeletal growth. The first three or four months of life are the most critical period for the developing structures of the hip. When stress and weight exerted at the hip joint exceed the strength limits of the supporting cartilages and ligaments, joint instability results. This instability will lead to damage as the exuberant Golden puppy is often very active, thus leading to more severe hip dysplasia.

Diagnosis of hip dysplasia is based on both the physical examination and the radiographic evaluation of the hip joint. Lameness of the hind limb and abnormalities of the gait especially after exercise are indicative. Joint laxity can be felt when you place your hand on the hip as the femur moves. The click or popping is known as Ortolani's sign. When radiographs are taken, proper positioning is critical in the puppy to ensure a correct diagnosis. There are also both non-surgical and surgical approaches to the treatment of hip dysplasia. (See Chapter 22, "Perspectives on Hip Dysplasia," for further discussion.)

There are two conditions that determine whether a puppy will have hip dysplasia: (1) The genes the puppy inherits, and (2) the environment in which the puppy is raised. It has also been established that the development of the hip is influenced more by environmental factors than by genetic endowment.[38] The impact of genes represents about 20 to 40 percent of the outcome of the hips in the Golden; the remaining 60 to 80 percent is due to the environment. This information is based upon heritability studies. (See Chapter 22, pp. 240–41.) To summarize: Whether or not hip dysplasia is exhibited in a puppy can be attributed to two conditions: the genes and the environment that the puppy experiences.

The Genes

What can we say about the role of genes? First of all, the genes necessary to produce large and giant breeds are implicated in hip dysplasia.

In large breed dogs, the genes that have been selected to make such a large dog are also genes that render a dog susceptible to hip dysplasia. These genes produce the rapid growth that is necessary if the dog is to attain its large size during its growth period. Because of this rapid-growth period, a large-breed puppy is vulnerable to hip dysplasia. If one were to breed a Golden Retriever that was not susceptible to hip dysplasia, such a dog would need to have the structure of one of the breeds that do not commonly develop hip dysplasia. Such breeds are the smaller breeds or the narrow-structured large dogs such as the greyhound, borzoi, or wolfhound. These breeds are relatively free of hip dysplasia because they have a narrow pelvis, and their hips are closer together than the hips found in Goldens or other breeds susceptible to hip dysplasia. Because the weight of the abdomen is partially suspended from the hips, the farther apart these points are from each other, the less stable the hip is. Overweight puppies have a lot of weight in their abdomen, which is an additional burden in their developing hips.

There are probably additional desirable characteristics large dogs share that make them susceptible to hip dysplasia—such as the amount of bone in the legs, the broad head, even the gentle, lazy temperament, which could be related to less musculature and greater amount of body fat. There are, on the other hand, genes that could be selected for that could decrease the risk of hip dysplasia. Such genes are those for increased muscle mass, a stronger type of muscle fiber, greater ligament and cartilage strength, and perhaps a slower growth rate; these may afford additional protection against CHD. These characteristics are part of the puppy's genetic endowment. In other words, to breed a Golden Retriever that is completely free of the tendency toward hip dysplasia is an impossible task. Such a dog would not have the desirable body type we know as the Golden Retriever. If this were not so, hip dysplasia would have been bred out of the breed years ago. But the fact is that thirty-six years of OFA evaluations of hips in these susceptible breeds has not eliminated the condition, nor even lowered the incidence, according to OFA evaluations over eighteen years.[39] Gerry B. Schnelle, VMD, Vm. D.H.C., the person who first identified hip dysplasia, said twenty-five years ago that you will not change the susceptibility of hip dysplasia without changing the breed.[40] This is as true today as it was then.

Are all Goldens then genetically alike? Almost genetically alike, but not quite. It is quite obvious that there are some differences. Therefore, selection for breeding stock with perfect hips is not to be discounted. We are now in our tenth generation of breeding dogs from

OFA certified parents. This means that phenotypically we are only breeding individuals that have perfect hips—dogs that are probably in the upper 15 percent or better for the breed. In my thirty years' experience, I have seen hips greatly improve, and the same observation has been reported to me by other long-term breeders. It is impossible to say, however, that we are breeding a line of Golden Retrievers that is genetically free of dysplasia. Whether our methods of rearing puppies are responsible for the improvement, or whether the nutritional advances in modern dog food are responsible, has not yet been determined. I do believe that we have about as stable a structural configuration that one can have, and still have a high-quality Golden; however, breeders cannot control the environment in which every puppy is raised after it is in its new home, so it is impossible to say hip dysplasia will never occur.

The Environment

What are the environmental factors that lead to hip dysplasia?

　　1. Diet: Most important are nutrition and total calories. The ratio of muscle mass to total weight is also very important. Good nutrition that is high in protein will foster muscle mass, which is essential to support the developing skeletal system. Vitamins, antioxidants, and the cartilage precursor can all impact upon the proper development of the joints. (See Chapter 14, "Feeding and Nutrition," pp. 129–33.) Puppies, dogs, and humans are all more prone to joint problems when they are growing, especially if they are overweight.[41]

　　2. Lack of Proper Exercise: Insufficient exercise does not produce muscles that adequately support the skeletal framework. On the other hand, over-exercise damages joints. Only gentle exercise is beneficial because it develops the muscles that help protect the hip.

　　3. Trauma: This is probably most often the immediate cause of hip dysplasia.

　　Contrary to what some orthopedists have been known to say, puppies that come from a breed with a susceptibility to hip dysplasia should not be retroactively deemed unfit for sale, the reason being that the environmental component largely determines the condition.[42]

Do's and Dont's

Do's:

• Do allow your puppy playtime everyday to exercise freely on grass surfaces.

• Do avoid all trauma to the joints.

• Do avoid running your puppy for long stretches, and never on hard surfaces, until fully grown. Avoid slippery surfaces such as linoleum or ceramic floors and rocky areas.

• Do avoid having your puppy leap or jump from elevated surfaces.

• Do not neuter your puppy until he is fully grown. He does not need the added stress of surgery during his rapid-growth period and hormones play a role in his development.

• Do not panic if the puppy limps. Give him time to rest and heal, but change your methods of handling him. Limping is a red flag indicating that he may have injured himself, or you may not be managing him properly, or he may be simply going through a difficult growth period. (See also "Panosteitis," p. 158.)

• Do know that orthopedists at the University of Pennsylvania School of Veterinary Medicine have stated that most orthopedic surgery on a puppy should never have been done.[43]

• Do know that the success rate after adopting the Conservative Approach for Goldens varies between 70 percent and 95 percent and few Goldens have long-term discomfort, but even that discomfort can be managed. Euthanasia is never an option.[44]

• Do know that Chondroitin Sulfate and Glucosamine have been shown to help repair damaged cartilages.

Dont's:

• Don't buy a Golden Retriever puppy if you are not willing to raise him carefully.

• Don't feed your puppy poor quality food. Good food fosters good development. A high protein diet does not cause hip dysplasia.

• Don't allow your puppy to get fat. It has been estimated that two-thirds of Goldens are too fat.

• Don't keep your puppy crated long hours at one time. Muscles atrophy. Circulation is impeded. Posture is altered.

• Don't X-ray a non-symptomatic puppy. Under anesthesia, without muscle support, the joint is fragile. Looseness can be felt as clicking (Ortolani's sign) when you place your hands on the moving hip. Such clicking will usually disappear by twelve months. Some looseness may be necessary in the six-month-old puppy—to allow for growth; however, loose hips are more likely a sign that you are giving the puppy too much ligament-stretching exercise. We recommend only gentle, free roaming exercise.

There is a great deal of diversity of opinion about the causes of hip dysplasia and what should or should not be done for a dysplastic puppy. For a more in-depth discussion of Hip Dysplasia, please see Chapter 22, "Perspectives on Hip Dysplasia."

Panosteitis

Panosteitis is a painful condition affecting the long bones of the young puppy quite often about four months of age. It is characterized by lameness and usually seen as limping in the front. It may shift from one leg to another. Puppies often walk as if their front feet hurt. It is said to be self-limiting, meaning that it will eventually go away. In my experience it usually goes away in a few weeks and responds well to rest and to not exercising on hard surfaces.

Osteochondrosis

Osteochondrosis (OCD) is a disturbance that arises in a joint during the ossification process in bone development. It is characterized by sep-aration of the articular cartilage from the underlying epiphyseal bone (the end of the bone where growth occurs). The upshot is that the cartilage may float freely in the synovial cavity and give rise to inflam-mation (synovitis) and pain (more commonly in the shoulder but can be elsewhere as in the elbow). Two additional conditions that recently are more frequently brought to the attention of puppy owners are osteochondritis dissecans and elbow dysplasia. Although I am relatively unfamiliar with the technical differences of these conditions, my experience with Goldens has been that with time and rest they are corrected; however, I can report what the concerns are and refer the reader to the descriptions.[45]

Osteochondritis Dissecans

In osteochondritis dissecans, the chondral (cartilage) fracture separates the growing cartilage from the bone and a flap is formed, causing the inflammation and pain. The condition usually appears from the age of four to eight months, and causes lameness. The cause has been attributed to excessive nutrition and too rapid growth, trauma, and biomechanical stress or pressure on the affected areas, thus precipitating the clinical signs. The inheritance of the predisposing factors (muscle mass, size of dog, rate of growth) is unknown. Restricting exercise and resting the puppy from four to six weeks usually results in recovery.

Elbow Dysplasia

With elbow dysplasia, the "incongruency" of the elbow joint is apparently related to abnormal developmental growth rates, or cartilage development, and stresses or trauma to the joint. The joint is formed by the coming together of the upper arm bone, the humerus, with the two bones of the forearm, the radius and ulna. These bones must grow in concert with each other to avoid misalignment and wear and tear in the joint. In addition, the end of the ulna (called the anconeal process) that comes in contact with the end of the humerus is a separate bone in the puppy. The anconeal process begins to fuse with the ulna starting at three months of age, and is normally completely fused by four or five months. The term elbow dysplasia includes several problems in the elbow joint. One problem is the ununited anconeal process (UAP). Another is osteochondritis dissecans (OCD) of the end of the humerus. The third problem is a fragmented coronoid process (FCP), the coronoid process being another outcropping of the ulna forming contact with the humerus. All these problems are probably related. Stress to the elbow can cause breaks in joint cartilages. Elbow dysplasia is characterized by lameness, pain in the elbow joints, and muscle atrophy. Detection and grading of the condition is performed by the OFA. Again, early surgical treatment is often recommended, but in my experience any pain in the front limbs has always been self-limiting if given time and rest. (See "Panosteitis," p. 158.)

Chapter 16:
Parasites

External Parasites

External parasites such as fleas, ticks, mites, and lice are a common parasite of most mammals. It would be astonishing to realize how many are present on each individual of our own species alone (and perhaps fortunate that many are invisible to the naked eye). Sometimes we are bitten by many of them, often without even realizing it. So, it should not be surprising that, yes, our beloved companions have them also. Although some parasites are relatively innocuous, there are those that take a toll and are decidedly unfriendly. Still, it is most important that you know what you are dealing with.

Fortunately, all can be managed fairly easily, and there are many products for treating external parasites. Newer products are continually being placed on the market. Therefore, your veterinarian can test or recognize the culprits and prescribe the correct remedy.

Still, the eternal dilemma will remain, which is that, as has often been proven to be the case in nature, the elimination of one organism leaves that niche open to a new organism or a newly mutated organism (see also p. 164). The struggle for existence, the evolution of parasites, and the response of a canine's protective immune system are taking place all the time in various ways and in places unseen and unknown.

A Word about Scratching
Puppies sit and scratch with a hind foot whenever they feel something on their coats. Whenever a puppy scratches, it is a signal that the puppy should be examined closely. Don't panic. Just remember that there are other common reasons for a puppy scratching besides the presence of parasites: A first-time collar, rain, dew or a healing irritation will all cause a puppy to stop and sit and scratch.

161

Fleas

Fleas belong to the insect order *Siphonaptera*, or "wingless siphon." They have mouthparts that allow the flea to pierce the skin and insert a sucking tube to feed on the dog's blood. The flea is encased in a hard outer covering and compressed laterally so that it can easily move among the hairs. Fleas have the ability to jump almost a foot high and two feet horizontally.

Today the problem of fleas is much less common than it was in the past, thanks to new anti-flea products. Any time a puppy scratches, however, he should be examined for the possible presence of fleas. Fleas move quickly, and you cannot expect to see one easily. Because fleas rapidly evacuate the area you are searching, you are more likely to see just the black, irregular granules of their fecal material. This material is often left in one particular area, such as the base of tail, along the back and on the neck under the ears, or under the front legs. To determine the presence of fleas, part the hair and search along the skin; any black specks observed are probably (but not always) flea dirt. Earth or organic debris, such as leaf mold, may be present if the puppy has been outside, but such debris is usually browner in color. During a puppy bath, however, the soapy water can "narcotize" fleas, and it is easier to spot them. Once the fleas are located they can be picked off and flushed down the drain. A flea comb is very useful.

If fleas are located, the source of that flea must then be considered. If there is more than one flea, there is a strong likelihood of those fleas having laid eggs. Thus, the sleeping areas of the puppy should be promptly and properly treated. Bedding should be washed and the floors where the puppy has been present should be vacuumed or scrubbed.

The Flea Lifecycle. You should be familiar with the life cycle of the flea in order to understand how a flea problem can be solved. The adult flea usually remains on a puppy or dog throughout the flea's adult life, ingesting blood as its food source. Female fleas are noticeably larger than male fleas. After mating, the females store sperm for use as needed. Feeding stimulates egg-laying and a flea can lay more than 2,000 eggs in its lifetime. Every day the mature female lays several eggs, which fall from the coat wherever the dog goes. These flea eggs hatch into larvae, which live in the cracks of the floor or in the bedding and rugs. The larvae eat any dead organic material they come across. Depending upon conditions, but usually in about three weeks, they develop to a point where they spin a cocoon and are transformed into pupae. The flea remains in the cocoon for protection, emerging as an adult only when conditions are favorable. The pupa hatches into an adult flea, which will then wait for the first warm-blooded animal that happens to come along and jumps on it because the adult flea possesses jumping legs that can catapult it a great distance in proportion to the size of the tiny flea.

There are a couple of points that are important to note with regard to these various stages in the development of the flea. First, the length of time spent in the larval and pupa stage is variable. In a warm, moist climate the flea can develop from egg to new adult in a matter of a few weeks. On the other hand, during cold seasons the process is very slow, which tides the flea over the winter months only to pupate in the spring and start the next flea season. Fleas can survive months without feeding, and can survive freezing for a year and then revive. Second, the larval flea is much more vulnerable to routine cleaning than either the pupae or the adult. Therefore, if fleas are suspected, it behooves one to run the vacuum frequently everywhere the dog has been present.

Disease. Fleas have the potential to carry disease, including bubonic plague. However, fleas are considered to be more aggravating than deadly. Dermatitis (atopy) is the most common complaint. Dogs commonly become allergic to flea saliva. One bite will then cause itching for several days.

Getting Rid of the Flea Problem. At one time insecticide sprays were used if there was a flea infestation. This is no longer the primary recommendation. There are now many products to address the flea problem that are less dangerous to all that inhabit the house. Some of the newer medications that are available are topical products. These substances are absorbed into the skin and kill the fleas when they ingest the material. Such products are Advantage®, which contains Imidacloprid; Frontline®, which contains Fipronil®; and Defend®—all of which will rapidly kill any fleas present. Other products—such as Program®, which is a pill containing lufenuron—prevent the production of viable flea eggs, thus affecting the fertility of the flea and thereby controlling the flea population, but not killing the adult flea. Newer products are continually being placed on the market. These products have greatly eliminated the flea as the main external parasite of the dog. As mentioned in the beginning of this chapter, and as has often been proved to be the case in nature, the elimination of one organism leaves that niche open to a new organism, and so, as fleas decline one can expect to see more lice and mites taking their place.

Ticks

Ticks are also ectoparasites (that is, they inhabit the host's skin) and are found on most terrestrial vertebrates. There are some 850 different species known and they are all blood sucking. Ticks are large mites and are not insects; rather, they are arachnids, related to spiders and scorpions, having eight legs as adults. (As larvae they are called seed ticks and have six legs.) There are four developmental stages: the egg, larvae, nymph, and adult. Ticks are brown to gray with oval-shaped hard bodies. They are flat before feeding but become plump when attached and feeding. Ticks vary from pinhead size to the size of a lima bean when engorged with blood. In temperate zones there is often just one life cycle annually. In a colder climate, two to four years are required by most species. Ticks can live for months, occasionally even years, without food. Most species have a three-host cycle, which means each stage feeds on a specific host. If a preferred host isn't available, ticks can feed on other hosts that are available. Ticks spend only around ten percent of their lifetime on the host.

Ticks are of concern because they can transmit infectious agents that cause several diseases in both man and dog. For instance, the brown dog tick, which is probably the most widely distributed species of tick, transmits blood parasites and viral infections including canine ehrlichiosis. The Lone Star tick, found in the Southern United States, transmits Rocky Mountain spotted fever, tularemia, and Q-fever, and may cause tick paralysis. The Rocky Mountain wood tick, which is found throughout the Western and Northwestern United States and Canada, is a vector of Q-fever and Colorado tick fever, and the chief cause of tick paralysis in humans and animals. The American dog tick, which is found throughout the Western and Northwestern United States and Canada, produces tick paralysis, and is a chief vector of the agent of Rocky Mountain spotted fever. The Northeast "deer tick" feeds primarily on mice and deer and can transmit Lyme disease bacteria to dogs and humans. Ticks can harm their host not only by causing anemia but also by introducing toxins from their salivary glands and opening the skin to secondary bacterial infections.

Petting your puppy daily should include running your fingers around the head, neck, and underjaw and underarms of the puppy in order to feel for the presence of ticks. Also, ticks do not immediately attach themselves to the skin of a dog, so that after every walk the head and back of the dog can be observed for walking ticks that have not yet attached themselves. During the bath any ticks that are present will be easily seen and can be removed by grasping the body of the tick and gently pulling the head away from the skin. You do not want to jerk or yank the tick away, because the mouth parts may then break off and remain imbedded in the skin. The foreign mouth parts imbedded in the skin, however, represent foreign material that may trigger a complicated rejection process. It is preferable to pull the tick off so that the mouth part pulls a small amount of skin away from the puppy, as this small wound will quickly heal. Ticks are also treated with several chemical products. (See the Table on p. 175.)

Mites

Puppies can, and often do, have mites. Although it is probable that there are some mites on most puppies and dogs, mites are not acceptable in large numbers.

There is more than one kind of mite that causes problems in

dogs. Ear mites, for instance, live in the ear canal and cause intense itching of the ears. Mange mites are found on the skin, and there are three different kinds: (1) the Sarcoptic mange mite, which is also called Scabies; (2) the Demodex mange mite that lives in the hair follicle and causes demodectic mange; and (3) the Cheyletiella mite that causes "walking dandruff" and is characterized by flaking skin. Veterinarians generally do skin scrapings to identify the species of mite under the microscope.

Flaking skin, however, may have several different causes: Sarcoptic mange mite; the healing of bacterial infections; and the Cheyletiella mite. In puppies, the most common mite is the one that causes Sarcoptic mange. Symptoms indicating the presence of Scabies mites are scratching and flaking skin; the skin may also have blotchy pink patches. Also, since scratching can have several causes, the flaking skin can be more diagnostic; however, a few weeks after a skin irritation from a superficial bacterial infection, there can also be a resultant flaking of the skin as in the healing process. The Cheyletiella mite also may be a cause of flaking skin. Therefore, knowing the history of a problem is helpful. When the flaking and itching is severe, it is probably prudent to treat the puppy for mites. Today there are a number of new products that are applied to the skin to make the eradication of mites far easier than the before. (Demodectic mange does not manifest itself in young puppies.)

Treatment for Mites. The old methods for treating mites are giving way to newer methods and products:

<u>The Old Way</u>: Bathe the puppy thoroughly. After the rinse, place the puppy in a bucket of warm water, where, following the directions, the appropriate amount of insecticide, often called "dip," can be added. This product is labeled for the treatment of Scabies mites and is available in feed and pet stores. Products containing pyrethrins or the synthetic form, permethrin, are useful. The treatment solution should be put on every part of the puppy's skin. The directions usually say that the solution is to dry on the puppy, not be rinsed off, but one does not dip dogs without becoming concerned that there will be a negative effect on the puppy's immune system. Therefore, you should not dip a

puppy without just cause, and then only when the puppy seems to be in a very healthy condition. If the puppy is having other major stresses in its life, the treatment should be postponed.

The New Way: Today there are a myriad of products that are directly applied to a spot on the dogs skin or are taken internally. Some of these products are combined with heartworm prevention such as Ivermectin, which kills many external and internal parasites. Some products are more specific for one type of parasite as opposed to another. (See the chart at the end of the chapter for a summary of the "Products and Ingredients in Common Pesticides," p. 175.)

Lice

Lice are wingless, flattened insects usually less than two millimeters long. Their legs are adapted for clinging to hairs, and their mouthparts are adapted for chewing skin or sucking blood. They spend their entire life cycle on the host, feeding on the outer layer of the skin. Lice cement their barely visible, oval translucent eggs to the hair shaft. The eggs hatch to release a nymph that resembles the adult (although smaller in appearance and habits). The nymphs mature through three stages before becoming adults, and the entire life cycle takes about three weeks. Lice are very host specific, which means that dog lice are not contagious to people and vise versa. However, they are highly contagious among dogs. Grooming tools that have been used in direct contact with an affected dog, should be soaked in a pyrethrin solution to kill any eggs, nymphs, or adults.

Symptoms of the presence of lice are: intense itching, scratching, hair loss, and skin irritation and skin infection. If there is a heavy infestation of the blood-sucking lice, there can be an anemia from the blood loss. If you comb an affected dog with a flea comb, the lice and nits (eggs) will be collected by the comb and can be seen and felt as the dog is combed.

Treatment for Lice. Treatment has been mainly done through the use of dips, sprays, or dust. Pyrethrins are effective and are currently the treatment of choice. Other insecticides that are used to kill fleas and will also kill lice are: dioxathion, rotenone, methoxychlor, lindane, diazinon, and malathion. These are, however, toxic to people as well as to puppies and dogs. Today, topical applications of pyrethrin such as Frontline® are now available and effective. The current popular treatment is through topical applications.

Internal Parasites

I'm often asked questions about the presence of parasitic worms. It seems that people often are so surprised that their dog could have worms. As a professor of Biology I used to tell my students in "Principles of Biology" that, if everything in the world magically disappeared, except for Nematodes (the group to which the common parasitic roundworms belong) you would still be able to deduce where almost everything had been merely by the presence of the different kinds of roundworms. Roundworms are found in our yards and parks and trees and soils, and in most living organisms including you and me. Indeed, because the eggs and larval stages persist, even for years, roundworms are everywhere.

Our dogs are also prone to worms because of their oral nature. Just as our dogs have evolved in response to the benefits of association with mankind, so have their worm parasites gained entrance into the dogs' bodies mostly by taking advantage of dogs' dependence on using their mouths to pick up and carry objects, to taste, test, and explore their world. Most parasites release their eggs or reproductive cysts into dogs' digestive tracts so that they pass out in the dogs' feces. It is easy to see how the parasitic worm eggs in the soil or on the grass are easily ingested, since a puppy eats and chews on just about everything in the yard. In addition, the parasitic worms have also evolved mechanisms whereby the pregnant bitch passes on tiny immature worms to her offspring. Encysted larval stages lay dormant in the tissues of the mother dog until the time of her pregnancy and lactation. Then high hormone levels trigger the migration of these larvae into her puppies either through the placenta or, later, through her milk.

For this reason, puppies are generally and routinely de-wormed when they are quite young, before they are weaned. Then they are de-wormed again several times during the early months. Diagnosis of the presence of roundworms, hookworms, and whipworms is made through a microscopic identification of the worm eggs in the fecal floatation test. Correct diagnosis of the presence of worms is important in order to use the best treatment, since this varies with each different kind of parasite.

For your reference, I want to briefly review the various internal parasites common to all canines:

Roundworms

Roundworms (Ascaridoid nematodes: *Toxocara canis*) are the most commonly found worms in puppies. The adult worms live in the puppy's or dog's intestine. The female worms are larger than the male worms, are spaghetti-like in size and color, and have a tendency to curl up into a coil. The adult worms release eggs into the feces of the dog, and these eggs will form a cyst that will remain viable in the ground for years. Later when the cyst is ingested by another dog, it will mature through several different larval stages before it becomes an adult. The larval stages migrate through the body; that is, from the stomach they pass through the stomach wall into the blood stream and then travel to the lungs where they pass through the walls of the capillaries into the bronchioles. Then they are coughed up to the trachea and are swallowed, where they complete their development in the dog's stomach and intestines. Here the worms reside, reproduce, and release their eggs, which then pass out of the body. In the bitch, some of the migrating larvae will encyst in the tissues and lay dormant until pregnancy triggers their maturation and migration to the host's intestines, or other larvae will cross the placenta to the fetal puppy's blood stream and migrate to their intestines. Others will pass through mammary circulation into the ducts of the milk gland, and then are ingested by the puppies as they nurse. Thus, the worm has successfully been passed on to the next generation.

Treatment for Roundworms. The most common substance used to remove adult roundworms is pyrantel pamoate. Because of the nature

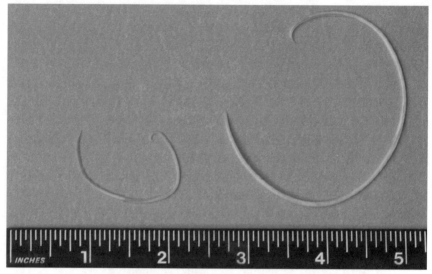

Roundworm: Male (left); Female (right)

of the life cycle, it is necessary to repeat the worming in three weeks to remove any immature larvae that have matured since the previous treatment.

Hookworms

The hookworm (*Ancylostoma caninum*) that infects dogs is characterized by the three hook-like teeth used to anchor the worm to the lining of the gut. Hookworms feed on the blood of the dog and can cause anemia, especially in the puppy. Adult hookworms residing in the small intestine release eggs that pass out of the body with the feces, and these can persist for months in the soil. They can enter a dog's mouth or burrow through the dog's skin. If the larvae enter though the skin, they will migrate through the blood stream to the lungs. The larvae then move up to the bronchioles and are then coughed up to the trachea to be swallowed; then they go to the intestine where the larva matures into an adult. Puppies can be infected before birth by larvae that pass through the mother's circulation to the puppy. The puppy can also be infected soon after birth by larvae that travel from the mother by way of her milk. Adult dogs can harbor larval stages in their tissues for years.

Treatment for Hookworms. Pyrantel pamoate is effective in removing hookworms.

Whipworms

The whipworm (*Trichuris vulpis*) is a small worm that has a long, slender anterior portion and a thicker posterior third; thus, they resemble a riding crop. The worms are found in the large intestine attached to the lining. The mature worm releases eggs in the feces and these mature in the environment to an infective stage where, if ingested, they further mature in the intestine to the adult stage. There is no infection during pregnancy or through the milk, as can happen in the case of roundworms and hookworms. The coat of a Golden infected with whipworms often has a dry, dull appearance.

Treatment for Whipworms. Diagnosis is made through microscopic examination of the feces. Treatment is usually successful with Panacur® (fenbendazole), which is mixed with the food on three consecutive days, or with Drontal Plus®.

Tapeworms

The tapeworm (*Dipylidium caninum*) is a flatworm (Cestode). One characteristic of the tapeworm is that its reproductive cycle always involves an intermediate host. There are several species of tapeworms that commonly infect dogs. *Dipylidium caninum* is acquired by eating fleas. In several species of the *Taenia* genus, a rodent is the intermediate host. Tapeworms are species specific; that is, you will not get a tapeworm from your puppy; however there is one potentially serious public health concern involving humans as accidental intermediate hosts. If eggs are ingested by a person, a highly pathogenic condition (alveolar Hydatid disease) results from the development of the cyst stage in humans. (As mentioned earlier, when a disease organism affects more than one species it is known as zoonosis.)

The tapeworm is composed of a head, or scolex, which is attached to the lining of the intestine. The rest of the tapeworm is composed of segments that are continually being produced by the anterior portion of the worm. As these segments (called proglottids) are being generated, they form the long ribbon-like worm that can reach a length of several feet. The ribbon of segments receives its nutrition by absorbing the host's digested food. Each segment has reproductive structures, and as they mature they become full of eggs. Each segment breaks off and wiggles its way out of the anus and becomes attached to the nearby hairs. Alternatively, the segment comes out on the stool where it can be observed as a moving, flat, fluke-like worm about a quarter of an inch in length. In either case the segment soon dries and breaks open, releasing the eggs. The eggs are then ingested by an intermediate host. Fleas or rodents are the common intermediate host of the dog tapeworm. Once inside the intermediate host, the eggs hatch into a larval stage that is encysted in the intermediate host's tissues. The puppy or dog must eat the intermediate host tissues to pass on the larvae, whereupon the larvae invade the small intestine of the puppy or dog and develop into adults attached to the wall of the intestine.

Puppies or dogs infected with a tapeworm can appear un-thrifty. Often the exiting segment will cause an itching of the anus and an adult dog will often drag its anus along the ground with its front feet. After the attached proglottid dries, it resembles a grain of rice. A positive diagnosis can be made by observing the segments either on the stool or on the hair around the anus.

Treatment for Tapeworms. The medication often used to remove tapeworms is Droncit® (praziquantel, manufactured by Bayer).

Heartworms

The heartworm (*Dirofilaria immitis*) is a filarial nematode, which is several inches long in the adult stage and lives in the heart and the pulmonary arteries of the dog. The adult worms discharge microfilariae into the bloodstream, where they remain for one to three years. The microfilariae can be ingested by a mosquito at this time and transported to another dog as it feeds. When they are about two to four months, they migrate into the right ventricle. The worms reach sexual maturity after an additional two to three months and begin to release microfilariae to the circulation. The adult worms impede blood flow, which leads to inflammation of the heart. The worms can also cause blood clots, which can damage the kidneys. Dogs infected with heartworms often show exercise intolerance, difficulty in breathing, lethargy, coughing, and even weight loss and sudden death. The accepted preventive approach to heartworm disease is to administer one of several products that prevent the maturation of each microfilaria.

Diagnosis of the presence of adult heartworms is based on the presence of the microfilariae in the blood as well as other tests such as radiographic findings and tests for the presence of adult worm antigens. Dogs are generally treated by destroying the adult worms. Since the treatment is toxic, the dog must be monitored by a veterinarian who will be on the lookout for developing problems. Following treatment, exercise should be restricted for four to six weeks. Dead and dying worms can lead to clots and shock. Microfilaricidal treatment should follow the destruction of the adults, and then preventive treatment should be used.

Treatment for Heartworms. Accepted preventive measures are based on the oral administration of diethylcarbamazine, Ivermectin, or milbemycin oxime. These compounds, which arrest development of the larvae, prevent the parasites from reaching the heart. Products such a Heartgard™ are now widely used. Other products, such as Interceptor®, which are the combination of several compounds, will prevent adult heartworm infestation as well as some other parasitic worms.

Ingredients in Common Pesticides

The following discussion and chart are a summary of the ingredients in some of the products mentioned in the text:

Pyrethrins are an insecticide, but are currently considered to be relatively safe. It is a naturally occurring compound that is extracted from chrysanthemum flowers. As an insecticide, it has been used for over 100 years. It affects the nervous system of the insect, resulting in its death. Pyrethrins do not affect a dog's nervous system, however, and are readily destroyed by stomach acids if ingested.

Permethrins are synthetic compounds that are similiar in chemical structure to pyrethrins. Permethrins are slower in action than the natural product and are not degraded so fast. They have a longer action but may not be as safe as the pyrethrin.

Insect Growth Regulators (IGRs) include fenoxycarb and pyrioproxyfen; they are both present in the product called Nylar®. Methoprene® is another insect growth regulator, which acts as the insect hormone called juvenile growth hormone. The continued presence of this hormone prevents the larvae from molting into adult fleas. Eventually the larvae will then die. Because the insect hormone has no effect on mammals, they are considered to be very safe.

Another class of compounds, called Insect Development Inhibitors (IDI), interfere with the formation of chitin, which is the material that forms the exoskeleton of the flea. Lufenuron is one such chemical; it is stored in the fatty layer of the skin of the dog and is ingested by the flea when it feeds on the dog.

Imidacloprid is another chemical specific to an insect's nervous system. It blocks the transmission of impulses, which results in paralysis and death of the insect, but it does not affect the nervous system of the dog and is therefore considered to be safe. The insecticide is stored in the hair follicles and is slowly released.

Amitraz® is a drug used for the treatment of ectoparasites including the Demodex mange mite. It inhibits certain enzymes and is toxic in dogs and people in high doses. It is used in some products to kill ticks.

Ivermectin is another neurotoxic drug that is used to kill many parasites, depending upon the dose.

Milbemycin oxime, also called milbecycin, is an antiparasitic drug that is similar to Ivermectin. It also affects a parasite's nervous system.

Pyrantel pamoate (Nemex®, Strongid®) is an antiparasitic drug that blocks neurotransmission in the parasite. It is used in puppies as their first de-wormer.

Table of Products and Ingredients
in Common Pesticides*

External Parasites

Brand Name	Active Ingredient(s)	Action
Advantic□	Imidacloprid, Permethrin	Kills fleas, ticks; repels ticks and mosquitoes
Advantage□	Imidacloprid	Kills fleas in 12 hours
Biospot□	Permethrins, Nylar□ IGR	Kills fleas, ticks; repels mosquitoes
Capstar™	Nitenpyror	Kills fleas in 4 hours
Defend□	Permethrins	Kills fleas, ticks, and mites
Frontline□	Fipronil	Kills fleas, ticks, and lice
Frontline Plus□	Fipronil, Methoprene	Kills fleas, ticks, and lice; breaks life cycle of fleas
Ivomec□	Ivermectin	Kills many internal and external parasites
Preventic Plus□	Amitraz□, Nylar□ IGR	Kills ticks; sterilizes fleas
Program□	Lufenuron	Kills flea eggs
Revolution□	Selamectin	Kills fleas; prevents heartworms, mange mites, and ticks

*See your veterinarian for appropriate treatment.

Table of Products and Ingredients in Common Pesticides*

Internal Parasites

Brand Name	Active Ingredient(s)	Action
Capstar™	Nitenpyram	Kills fleas in four hours
Droncit®	Praziquantel	Kills tapeworms
Drontal Plus®	Praziquantel, pyrantel pamoate, and febantel	Kills tapeworms, hookworms, roundworms, and whipworms
Heartgard™	Ivermectin	Prevents heartworms
Heartgard Plus™	Ivermectin, pyrantel pamoate	Prevents heartworms, kills hookworms and roundworms
Interceptor®	Milbemycin oxime	Kills heartworms, roundworms, hookworms, and whipworms
Ivomec®	Ivermectin	Kills roundworms and also external parasites
Nemex®	Pyrantel pamoate	Kills roundworms and hookworms
Panacur®	Fenbendazole	Kills whipworms
Piperazine	Piperazine Dehydrichloride Piperazine adipale	Kills roundworms
Sentinel®	Milbemycin oxime/ lufenuron	Prevents heartworms; kills fleas, roundworms, hookworms and whipworms
Strongid-T®	Pyrantel pamoate	Kills roundworms and hookworms

*See your veterinarian for appropriate treatment.

Chapter 17:
Neutering and Spaying

Introduction

Whether to neuter your Golden or not, and when to do it, is a little more complicated than one first imagines. If you don't want to use your dog for breeding, then why deal with the seasons and the dog's desire to breed? These are the main difficulties of leaving the male or female intact. So, why not have the puppy neutered as soon as possible? Many veterinarians, generalizing for all breeds, will feel that this is the best path to choose. By the age of six months, the puppy is sufficiently large so that he can undergo surgery without any great difficulty, and the timing is such that it will precede the development of any sexuality. These considerations alone seem to dictate the time to neuter or to spay.

I believe early spaying and neutering may be unwise if all the ramifications are not evaluated. I would build a case for allowing the puppy to fully mature before undergoing this surgery, because, when the ovaries or testes are removed, you are of course removing the sex hormones, which affects a puppy in many ways.

It is important to understand that the development of the skeletal system is under the influence of the sex hormones in both sexes, and so, if the gonads are removed, you are altering the natural development of the skeletal system, which affects the look and function of the dog. The sex hormones have an effect on the closure of the growth plates of the long bones. Because of this delay in closure the bones continue to grow and the dog becomes taller than the normal Golden. Also, the sex hormones foster the greater development of the muscle mass. The muscles ensure the proper alignment of the developing skeletal system as well as help protect the puppy from injuring himself.

177

(For the relevance of muscle development, see Chapter 22, "Perspectives on Hip Dysplasia," p. 246.) The dog is still growing rapidly at six months, and will continue to do so for several more months. I do not consider a Golden fully grown and mature until eighteen months.

As long as the Golden puppy is growing, he is relatively fragile, although robust in behavior and appearance. The effect of the anesthesia, surgery, and being away from home are all major stressors for the young puppy. My major concern for the puppy at the age of five to six months is to prevent anything that might initiate hip dysplasia. Any trauma is risky, for cartilage is easily damaged, inflammation in the hip joint will follow, and hip dysplasia may ensue. For these reasons, my advice is to postpone surgery until the most critical age for the development of hip dysplasia is past. This susceptible period exists at six months, even though it may begin earlier. The most important reason for postponing spaying and neutering a Golden Retriever puppy, therefore, is to avoid anything that can disturb the development of the puppy and thereby trigger the development of hip dysplasia. Any complication of the surgery has a greater impact on the growing puppy than it would have on a mature dog. Why take any unnecessary risk?

Neutering the Male

The change in appearance and structure of the male is the main reason to postpone neutering the puppy. Without the testes, there will be no secretion of testosterone. A lack of testosterone will prevent the development of the secondary sex characteristics—the broader head, the fuller ruff, and the more muscular body—that would negate some of the reasons why you chose the male in the first place. If a dog is neutered at six months, before any of these secondary sex characteristics develop, he appears feminized. Without the earlier closure of the long bones, the dog continues to grow in height and becomes unusually tall, but without the normal muscle mass. The masseter and frontal muscles of the skull do not become as large. (The masseters and frontal muscles contribute to the look of the masculine headpiece, which is very broad through the skull.)[46] This results in the head having a prominent occiput and a bony ridge down the center of the head, because the skull is not covered by the musculature. And finally, the dog's coat is more refined with fewer furnishings.

On the other hand, the neutered male is generally quieter, somewhat less active, has no interest in sex, and does not exhibit territorial behavior or stimulate any such aggressive behavior in other male dogs. Thus, the neutered dog makes a most trouble-free companion. I am in favor of neutering the average male companion dog; my concern is only one of timing. I recommend the procedure be done no sooner than eighteen months of age.

Spaying the Female

The changes in appearance that occur in the female when she is spayed are less noticeable than in the male. Without the ovaries, which produce estrogen, the body responds to the lack of estrogen by producing hormones from the adrenal glands. These hormones belong to a group of androgens called 17-keto steroids, and so the female dog is somewhat masculinized. The spayed female thus has a longer coat. Once the ovaries are removed, there is no cycle and no fluctuation in the levels of the sex hormones. With constant hormone levels, the spayed female does not have a periodic loss of coat that would result from the periodic fall in hormone levels. With this loss of periodicity in the spayed female, the coat tends to grow longer and longer, giving the spayed female a characteristic but not unattractive look.

There is often a high incidence of urinary tract infection (called UTI or cystitis, see pp. 140–42) in the female Golden puppy, which disappears by the first season. This is because the female puppy has low estrogen levels until her first season; she is therefore susceptible to UTI. At the time of her first season, when the ovaries mature, she will produce more estrogen; therefore, if you wait to spay the female until after her first season, you reduce significantly the occurrence of urinary tract infections. This is because the structure and the chemistry of the urethra is changed positively under the influence of estrogen. (The absence of estrogen—owing to the absence of ovaries—produces a greater tendency toward cystitis and incontinence as she ages after she is spayed.)

There are also behavioral differences between the spayed female and the unsprayed female. The *spayed female* has a tendency to be more aggressive toward other dogs, and she may lift one leg slightly off the ground when urinating; she may even have a tendency to mark, because she has predominantly more male hormones. As I already mentioned, because of the periodicity of the female cycle and the higher levels of androgens that come from the adrenal glands, the coat becomes much longer. The spayed female evidences masculine traits due to the preponderance of male hormones. The *unspayed female*, on the other hand, has a higher metabolic level, so she is less energetic and less "trouble." Her personality is no different, but the energy level is lower, and she will therefore tend to gain weight if the caloric intake is not decreased. An ideal weight can be maintained if food consumption is reduced. If she is allowed to become overweight, she will become less active and thus more prone to becoming overweight. This cycle may be difficult to turn around.

Sexual behavior is eliminated in the spayed female, and that makes her much easier to manage, especially when there are children in the family. This is truly the main reason you neuter a dog or spay a bitch. There is no reason to breed a dog unless you are seriously undertaking the responsibility of producing quality offspring and are willing to invest the necessary time and energy to insure that puppies have a good home. You are ultimately responsible for the welfare of the dogs you do produce.

Longevity and Cancer

The cancers sensitive to sex hormones that a dog can develop would not be stimulated after neutering or spaying due to the lack of estrogen or testosterone. With regard to the effect of neutering or spaying, respectively, on longevity and cancer, there are pros and cons. On the one hand, cancers that *are* dependent on sex hormones will be diminished. With the neutered male, you would not expect to find cancer of the prostate or testes. With the spayed female, there is less probability of cancer of the mammary glands. On the other hand, females that have had a litter or more may be less susceptible to other kinds of cancer and may be somewhat protected from them due to the positive (albeit not fully understood) effects on the immune system of a successful pregnancy and lactation. Whatever benefits come from breeding must be weighed against the risks; however, there is no reasonable basis for breeding a female based on the belief that it would be an efficacious event that would increase her lifespan.

Neutering/Spaying Later in Life

There is no reason why a dog cannot be neutered later in life. It does not need to be done only in the young animal.

Breeding vs. Neutering/Spaying

I would certainly postpone any decision about spaying or neutering as long as there are some thoughts about breeding. One needs to collect all pertinent data—for instance, hips, eyes, and heart issues—before you make a decision about breeding. Certainly the true status of the hips and eyes cannot be ascertained at six months.

While weighing the pros and cons of breeding, I would think in terms of the contribution of that individual to the gene pool. The individual dog represents a collection of genes—genes that many breeders of the past have committed a great deal of time and energy to preserve and to pass on to you. To remove that individual with so many wonderful traits from the gene pool does have a negative impact on the breed at large. I would certainly postpone any decision about neutering a great dog as long as there are some thoughts about breeding. However, if the dog is primarily a companion, the needs of the owner or family must be considered because of the great deal of work and responsibility that breeding entails. Breeding is not something that can be entered into lightly.

PART VI:

Additional Training for Specific Purposes

Chapter 18:
Beginning Show Training

Introduction

If you have an interest in possibly showing your Golden, or having your Golden shown by a handler, there are some things you can do as you socialize your puppy that will make it much easier. Many of these things are useful even if you are not going to show your dog. They can also be thought of as a game to play with your dog that develops his attention span and his ability to look to you as his leader.

The Cookie Game
Early on you can play the cookie game with your puppy. This will lead to "free baiting," which is an important part of ring showmanship. This can be done on or off lead. The puppy should be in a space free of other distractions, either inside or out. If the puppy is outside and off lead, the game should be played in an enclosed space. With a pocket full of dog biscuits or liver "bait," one should call the puppy and tell him to "stand, stay" and immediately give him a tidbit. Now that you have his attention, do it again. He will tend to move toward you and jump on you, or he will sit. If he jumps on you, correct him by blocking him with your knee, and when he is standing give him a tidbit. If he sits, use your foot to lift him gently onto all four feet and then give him a reward. Keep repeating the process until he learns to stand and stay. Next, try to step back and lengthen the distance between yourself and the puppy without his moving. You need to be sensitive to what he is doing and thinking, and you will reward him for staying before he moves. If he moves, say a stern "no" and start over. After a while he will be an expert at standing still and will not move even if you move. Keep your hands together and held slightly above the level of your

185

waist. He will stare intently at the food in your hands. If you move your hands toward the puppy you can guide him into the correct position of his feet. For example, move your hands to the left and he will lean in that direction and reset his right foot. The more you do the better you will become at positioning him in a correct stance. Having him stand motionless with his tail wagging and his eye intent on you is your goal.

Playing Catch

Once the puppy has learned to stand-stay, you could go a step further and teach him to catch in place. Instead of handing him a tidbit, you can pitch it to him so that he can learn to catch. Some dogs are better at this than others but with practice they can all learn to catch. Popcorn can be useful because its light nature causes it to float through the air and be easier to catch.

Gaiting Your Puppy

After you leash train your puppy, trot with him on a show lead. Do not keep him at your side but encourage him to move four to six feet in front of you. Hold the puppy in the trot, but correct him with a jerk of the lead if he starts to gallop. If he starts to sniff things or stop, keep him moving by jerking the lead. Keep using your voice in a high-pitched animated way to encourage him and to make him look happy. Your goal is to have him travel at a steady trot in front of you with his head and tail up on a loose lead. When you start off, use a high-pitched excited voice saying something like "Come on, let's go boy." Hold the leash high, and pat him under his chin as you step off. Travel about 20 to 30 feet. When you stop, have him stop and stand still and look at you before you reward him with a tidbit or praise. (See "The Cookie Game," above). You are developing the pattern of gaiting a dog for the show ring.

The Grooming Table Game

If you intend to show your puppy, he must learn to be happy on the grooming table. Even if you do not show him, it is ever so much easier to groom or examine your puppy while he is on the table. He will also be much more cooperative when he has to get up and stand on the veterinarian's examination table. Without an early start or some pleasurable experiences on the grooming table, the puppy will find a table very traumatic. In addition to starting him early, one of the best ways of getting a puppy used to a grooming table is to feed him a few times on the grooming table. You can also distract him from his fear of the table by having someone feed him tidbits of dog biscuits while you groom him on the table. While someone is feeding him, you can set his feet in the proper position under him. This is the beginning of "stacking your dog"—one of the most important things your puppy must learn as a show dog. Soon you will be able to position his feet and then give him a piece of a biscuit while you pick up his tail. All the time you are saying "stay" and "good puppy." In a similar fashion, you will be able to groom your puppy and cut his toenails. If you run into resistance, have someone help you by feeding him tidbits. In everything you do with the puppy, try to remain in control. Correctly predict when he is getting to the end of his patience and stop and reward him before he objects to what you are doing. Use a lot of praise and always end on a positive note. Each session will be better and can be longer.

Using the Crate

If you are going to show your puppy, it is almost mandatory that he be quite comfortable in a crate. Dog shows are often all-day affairs, and in between the times a dog is actually doing something he can be sleeping peacefully in his crate. Many people are already using the crate with the puppy so the basics are established (see Chapter 6, "Crate Training," pp. 51–57). A puppy should also spend time in a crate in a vehicle. If a puppy spends a few nights in the crate in a van, and is also fed in a vehicle, he will get over his apprehension of being in a car. This will also have the added advantage of preventing the puppy from becoming carsick.

Developing Confidence and Charisma

The hallmark of a great show dog is confidence in every situation and a friendly attitude to all he encounters. This cannot be instilled in a puppy without his having a variety of happy experiences in his early formative months. He needs a strong human bond of trust. It is imperative that you take him many places where he can greet many people. Shopping Centers, parks, playgrounds, and sporting events are such places. Nothing makes a Golden happier than his interaction with children. Control will come with time, but the charismatic mind of a puppy can only be formed with many happy early experiences with people.

PART VII:

Special Topics
for New Owners

Chapter 19:
Your Puppy's First Visit to the Vet,
An Interview with
Jean H. Cunningham-Smith, VMD

(This interview was conducted by R. Ann Johnson on Saturday, July 24, 2001 and updated in October, 2003. Jean Cunningham-Smith has been breeding Golden Retrievers since the early 1970s and is part-owner of the Bloomsburg Veterinary Hospital, Bloomsburg, Pennsylvania.)

RAJ: First question. Jean, what are you looking for when a Golden Retriever owner brings a puppy to your office for the first time?

JHC: The thing I like to see most is a puppy that is outgoing, friendly, gregarious, and not afraid of people. The next thing I like to see is a puppy with a bright, clear-eyed look, not thin, but with a nice, shiny coat, and good conformation—definitely looking like the puppy is having a good start in life. Often, puppy purchasers, who are new to buying a puppy don't know what to look for, and they tend to buy on impulse. The impulsive choice leads them to a puppy that may be shy or retiring, or perhaps ill, because they feel sorry for it.

During the physical exam, I usually start with the nose and work back. I like to see puppies with a cold, wet nose, bright eyes without any discharge, ears that are clean and not showing any sign of ear-mite infestation, fungal or bacterial infection, and no lice or external parasites, such as fleas or ticks. I usually check their lymph nodes to see that they're not enlarged, and I feel their bone structure, making sure that their chest is nicely developed.

I palpate the abdomen looking for any lumps or bumps that

191

shouldn't be there, such as inguinal and unilateral hernias. Next, I listen to their hearts, and I'll check their temperature. Often I will take a direct smear of fecal material even if the clients have brought in a stool sample. Sometimes you will pick up parasites with a direct smear that you will not see on a fecal floatation. Tapeworms, for example, will often not show up on fecal flotation but will sometimes be observed on direct smears or segments one can observe around the anus.

RAJ: What tests do you routinely do on your new puppy exams?

JHC: The fecal floatation is one test. We always ask the owner questions about the puppy's history. Because roundworm and hookworm infestations are zoonotic diseases, the veterinary community recognizes this and recommends that puppies be de-wormed, even if the fecal sample is negative. Puppies coming from pet shops are more likely to have coccidia and giardia, and we routinely screen for both. In our area we rarely see giardia as a problem. Usually if we see signs that the puppy has diarrhea and it doesn't respond to the usual treatments for diarrhea, we often will treat it as if it is giardia. The fecal flotation test can be falsely negative because the oocytes [the reproductive cells of the coccidia] are shed periodically and, therefore, can often be missed.

If puppies are born during the winter, we don't routinely test them for heartworm until they are six months old. If we see a puppy that has been born during the colder months, we'll go ahead and get them started on Interceptor®, which has antihelmentic properties as well as the anti-heartworm properties, and then we won't test for heartworm for a full year. Actually, we don't test puppies for heart-worm routinely until they are at least four- to six-months old anyway, just because of the life cycle of the heartworm. We would not be able to find any before that time.

RAJ: What are the most common internal and external parasites that you run into in your examination?

JHC: In our area, we find more hookworms and roundworms than anything else. Since the advent of using heartworm preventatives, the incidence of seeing heartworms has gone down tremendously. We do see a lot of tapeworms because fleas are still a problem, and the flea, being one of the hosts for the tapeworm, has not been affected by Interceptor® (Novartis) or other heartworm preventatives. Occasionally we see a light coccidia infestation in a puppy not coming from a pet store and not having any diarrhea. I often don't think this is a problem and only request a recheck sample at the time of the next visit. The protozoa are gone by then. If the puppy originates from a pet store or a kennel, and we see any coccidia, we will go ahead and treat the puppy. Occasionally we see lice on puppies, but not that often, and fleas, of course, which are ectoparasites. With the advent of topical once-a-month flea preventatives, we're seeing a lot fewer cases of flea infestations.

RAJ: What effect does the stress of leaving the litter have on a new puppy prior to your seeing it?

JHC: When puppies are taken out of a litter situation and moved into a household, they often are over-stimulated. We usually advise people with new puppies to take it easy for the first day or so and let the puppy make the adjustment. Moving from a litter to a new environment is a stressful situation for a young puppy. Puppies will get over-tired and over-exercised and over-stimulated, and all these things, just as in humans, can result in vomiting and diarrhea and also result in outbreaks of coccidia. Being an intestinal protozoan, coccidia will oftentimes be in any dog's intestine without causing any problem, but when a stress situation occurs, it alters the whole mechanism and the coccidia start to reproduce, and when this happens, they actually break out of the wall of the small intestine, causing a great deal of irritation and diarrhea. Once you get to the diarrhea stage, the puppy is not feeling well and doesn't eat. One thing leads to another and you have a pretty sick puppy.

RAJ: How do you treat a puppy that has been diagnosed with coccidia?

JHC: If the puppy is presented with diarrhea, and the only thing we find on the stool sample is coccidia, we usually treat it with Albon

(Pfizer), but we oftentimes will use Flagyl (metronidazole) along with it, especially if the puppy obviously doesn't feel well.

RAJ: For how long a period of time would you treat this puppy?

JHC: We always begin with a ten-day dosage routine and ask the owner to let us know at the end of that time if they still are having any problems or if they are fine. Usually our experience has been that in three or four days things are resolved, and the puppy is feeling much better, but because of the life cycle of the coccidia organism we feel it's a better idea to keep them on medication for at least a week to ten days. We can also use an oral electrolyte product that you substitute instead of water, and it often has a very positive effect on puppies when they have an upset stomach or loose stool. Other than that we will instruct our clients to maintain the puppy on a steady and probably slightly bland diet for a couple of days until the diarrhea resolves itself. Generally, we always try to recommend that people use a good quality dog food, and not give puppies dairy products and not switch around from one thing to another, and not give them table scraps and left-overs, but rather keep them on a basic diet, especially when their bowels are upset.

RAJ: Jean, can you tell us how you approach the problem of hookworm, whipworm, and roundworm intestinal parasites?

JHC: We try to encourage all of our clients to put their dogs on heartworm preventatives. Our usual procedure is to start the puppies/dogs on Interceptor® (Novartis) on their first or second visit. If they are showing any sign of worms, we routinely worm them if we feel that it is necessary. Our favorite product is either Panacur® (Hoechst) or we will use Drontal® or Drontal Plus® (Bayer). What we've found is this: If we start these puppies on Interceptor® at eight weeks of age, and then repeat it at twelve weeks and then again at sixteen weeks, weighing the puppy every time, and then start them on a monthly routine for heartworm prevention, we are in effect treating and eliminating their parasites. I wouldn't rely on Interceptor® to be the end all, so therefore, if we find that a puppy actually presents itself with a heavy load of roundworms or hookworms, we will go ahead and de-worm those. We use Nemex® or Strongid®. If it's just roundworms, we will often just use Piperazine® or in the case of treating them in the office, we'll oftentimes give them a dose of Strongid®. If they present with whipworms, then we use Panacur® and/or Drontal®, which also gets tapeworms. But the real honest truth is that since we've been using or encouraging people to use heartworm preventatives, we've found that this has been very successful in treating and controlling hookworms and roundworms, which are the two main intestinal worm parasites we see in our practice.

RAJ: How frequently do you find heartworm infestation among the dogs of your clients?

JHC: You have to understand that Bloomsburg has a very low incidence of heartworm disease, and of all of the dogs that we test for the disease, which generally speaking each year averages more than a thousand, we probably see one or two cases. So, heartworms in the Bloomsburg area are not really a severe problem. People tend to be very mobile these days, however, and the chance of heartworms becoming a problem certainly exists. We feel that testing is a good thing to do, and we try to encourage heartworm prevention, or heartworm prophylaxis. But we're going to try to prevent heartworm because once you get the disease, the treatment is a lot worse than the prevention. We stress the zoonotic problems of intestinal parasites and use this to encourage heartworm prevention.

RAJ: Jean, tell us about the tests that are available for Lyme disease.

JHC: There is a new test by Idexx called the 3DX, which we are currently using in our practice, that screens for heartworm disease, Lyme disease, and erlichiosis. Erlichiosis is another tick-borne disease.

Surprisingly, when Idexx was test marketing this kit in New Jersey, they found about a six percent incidence of erlichiosis. I think they picked the New Jersey area because they expected to find a high incidence of Lyme disease, which they, in fact, did, but the other test was just a bonus for people who were developing the test kit. If you have a positive on this test for Lyme disease, it means that the spirochete, which is the little critter that causes Lyme disease, is, or has been present, in the liver of the animal that you are testing. If this test is positive, it means the dog had contact with that spirochete. Cornell has found a nine percent false positive. Because of this we confirm the positive with Cornell labs before we treat. In Bloomsburg, we see only a few positive tests, and all of these dogs were non-symptomatic. They all seemed fine, but they tested positive for Lyme disease. However, just south of us, actually, about the level of the Appalachian Mountains into the Lehigh Valley, the incidence has been much higher, and I'm sure in the New Jersey area it has been very high also. Again, this isn't something for which we would be testing a young puppy—in other words, before six months of age—because we would be running this concurrent with a heartworm test. Even with the false positive, it is a convenient screening tool.

RAJ: Jean, could you tell us more about the treatment of the ectoparasites that you are coming across in your practice?

JHC: There are a number of different products on the market. The primary product that we use for fleas and lice is Advantage® (Bayer). Advantage® is actually topical; therefore, it's not really absorbed into the body; it spreads across the skin, probably through the lipid layer, and within an hour it will kill fleas and probably also lice. It works very rapidly.

Frontline® (Merial) is also a flea and tick product. It is actually absorbed into the sebaceous glands of the dog. The tick must actually bite the dog and the flea also actually must be in contact with the dog for a little while. Advantage® is a lot faster but doesn't kill ticks.

There is a new product on the market called Capstar® (Novartis), which works within an hour; however, it lasts only about twelve to fourteen hours. For example, if you have an animal that has a heavy infestation of fleas coming into the hospital or the kennel and you want to get rid of the fleas, you can use Capstar®. It's a little less expensive than Advantage® if you just want to treat the dog initially and get rid of the fleas that are on the dog. It does not work on ticks.

Revolution® also exists. Revolution® works for heartworms and fleas. It's not as fast for fleas as Advantage®; it takes 24 to 36 hours to really get them under control. But it also has an interesting sideline of getting Sarcoptic mange and also ear mites. So it has its own little niche. Revolution® used with Capstar® can be effective.

Novartis also has a product called Sentinel®, which is a combination of their Program® and Interceptor®. Program® contains lufenuron, which is a growth inhibitor and which controls fleas by preventing the eggs from developing and hatching. It's another option. If you have a flea problem and you want to use Program®, that's fine, but you may also want to use something like Capstar® or Advantage® to get rid of your adults and get your problem under control a little bit faster. Program® and Capstar® are systemic and appeal to people who are worried about getting drug residues on themselves.

Some people still use house and carpet sprays in the home, and they're somewhat effective, but I think that the beauty of all the topical products is that it gets you out of the dipping and the powder and the spraying and exposing your body to all the insecticides.

We usually recommend that people put Advantage® or Frontline® on the dog in the evening before they go to bed, and by the next morning most all of it is absorbed and/or diffused over the dog and isn't a problem for clients getting it all over themselves.

RAJ: What is your opinion about the concerns people may have with regard to the toxic nature of these drugs?

JHC: If people are worried about residues, they can always use the

Novartis line of products. Capstar® is a pill and is given by mouth. It can be given once a day or every other day for five or six doses in order to get rid of adults while you start Program®.

Program® is a growth inhibitor that's absorbed; that is, it's taken in by the dog orally and travels in its bloodstream to its sebaceous glands where it's shed in the sebaceous excretion and acts to inibit the development of larvae, thus breaking the flea life cycle.

Where you have small children, Advantage® and Frontline® need to be applied in the evening after the kids go to bed and by the next day the puppies or dogs are probably safe as far as the hugging and all of that goes on. As far as people are concerned, the LD_{50} of these products is extremely high, and I don't know that there have been any reported incidences, at least that I'm aware of, where anybody has had a toxicity problem. Every once in a while you'll get an animal that will get a spot of hair-loss at the site where you applied the topical product.

What we used to do to prevent fleas and to treat fleas in dogs was so dangerous, with all the insecticides we dipped ourselves in, with dips and sprays and powders that just left residues all over the house. House and carpet sprays were used constantly, and I just can't even begin to think of what we actually exposed ourselves to, without really intending to. What we have today is so much safer and so much more aesthetically pleasant, that it's like a whole other concept in the treatment of these matters.

RAJ: Jean, would you tell us about your program of inoculations in your practice?

JHC: Our vaccination program varies a little depending on the age of presentation of the puppy. Basically we vaccinate every three weeks for distemper, adenovirus, leptospirosis, corona virus, and parvo virus— using a high titer vaccine until the puppy is 16 weeks old. We vaccinate for rabies at 12 weeks. We recommend vaccinating for bordatella and Lyme disease. If people will be traveling and/or camping or have a tick problem, we prefer to do the vaccination series when the puppy is eight to nine weeks of age. If we start earlier, which we will do if puppies do not have much maternal immunity, we occasionally will see some diarrhea and depression in puppies six- to seven-weeks old.

RAJ: How often do you find puppies with heart murmurs on your initial exam and what do you suggest to do in regard to these puppies?

JHC: If we pick up or detect a heart murmur puppy and the puppy is about seven weeks old, and if the murmur is slight and basically a systolic murmur, we note it on the record card, tell the owner about it, and have them come back in three weeks for their next checkup. A good percentage of the time these murmurs will disappear and everything will be fine.

If we detect a machinery murmur, which is indicative of a Persistent Ductus Arteriosus (PDA), that is a completely different matter and something that is more specific. Often, subtle murmurs are really hard to pin down what is going on, because puppies are happy and wiggling and panting. And it's better, before making any snap decisions, to wait until they are another three of four weeks of age and then listen to them again. If this is a puppy that has been purchased to be a future breeding dog or a show dog, we will refer the owners to a cardiologist for a work-up if the murmur is still in existence at their second exam. If it's a puppy that was purchased as a pet, and the murmur is not such that we think it's going to be a life threatening or life-shortening situation, we usually discuss with the owners what their options are. We can do an ultrasound cardiac work-up, with a consultation via telemedicine, or we can refer them to a cardiologist for a work-up. Often people will just elect to do nothing about the situation, and we'll follow the heart murmur through the puppy's life. I would say 95 percent of these puppies live full and productive lives and have no really serious problems. But people have the option. If they would like to go further, we can certainly send them to a cardiologist for an echocardiogram or whatever is necessary to work it up and make a diagnosis. Then they can follow the recommendations of the cardiologist.

RAJ: Do you have any thoughts on SAS (subaortic stenosis)?

JHC: I know what an SAS should sound like, but I cannot say I have actually diagnosed one. We are doing a lot of referrals via the ultrasound and telemedicine, as I said before. Adults are much easier to listen to than wiggly, panting puppies. I will be the first to admit that I am not a cardiologist, but I just wish owners would allow puppies to grow a little before becoming alarmed when slight murmurs are detected, because some are artifacts and do disappear.

RAJ: Jean, what pertinent ingredients do you look for in a dog food for a puppy Golden Retriever?

JHC: When I examine a new puppy and the owners ask me what it is that they should be feeding, I do not often try to promote one brand or another. I do tell them what they would be advised to look for in a dog food: one that has a high protein/high fat content and is supplemented with vitamins and minerals that the dogs need for everyday growth. I do tell them what I do myself, which is to feed Eukanuba (an Iams product). I have been doing this since 1972. Before there were all the different varieties of Iams, I always used the Eukanuba Premium Performance, which is the old hot pink bag that has 30 percent protein, 20 percent fat. I used to use this for my puppies. Now that Eukanuba has a line of puppy foods, I will have to admit that I use the Eukanuba small puppy, bite-sized pieces for getting puppies started and then I tend to switch directly to the Premium Performance rather than going to the large-breed puppy, only because it's convenient for me; and, having read the two bags, I don't really think that there's all that much difference. The Iams people would disagree, but it works for me. I think the important thing to tell our clients is: You get what you pay for. When you're spending a little additional money for a puppy, you should spend a little bit additional to get them a good, high-quality puppy food, not the store special or one of the cheaper foods, simply because protein is what you're paying for.

RAJ: How do you advise people about the way a puppy will eat everything in sight in the early weeks—from grass to toadstools to sticks and things. How dangerous is this?

JHC: I think you need to be somewhat careful because there are plants and things out there that are toxic and will cause problems, and toads for sure will cause problems. The problem is that you cannot follow your puppy around trying to take things out of its mouth all the time. I think that you just have to use common sense.

It is important to know which plants and bulbs are really toxic. Rhododendron and mountain laurel are poisonous.

Sticks are a concern. I've seen cases where dogs have run sticks into their mouth and had bleeding abscess tracks develop simply because you can't find all the splinters.

Certain kinds of toads are very poisonous. Some toads will just cause drooling and a lot of salivation, but there are others that will cause very serious illness and sometimes death.

Chocolates are dangerous also. You can't let a puppy eat chocolate because of the theobromine in it, which is toxic to dogs.

I really think it comes down basically to knowing what in your yard is poisonous. A little grass isn't going to hurt anything, but you have to be somewhat vigilant about your puppy or dog chewing and swallowing rocks. Although there are those animals that seem to eat rocks on a regular basis and do just fine, I see them as foreign bodies that need to be removed surgically. I think just monitoring what's out there and what the puppy is chewing on and making sure it's still there is important. Puppies are like children: They're going to take chances, and they're going to take risks. I think that, being a puppy owner, just as being a parent, you have to let them explore, but then you also have to be aware of what they're doing and try to prevent them from doing harm to themselves. And if harm occurs, respond as fast as you can seeking veterinary care.

RAJ: Why do puppies sometimes seem to have a liking for rabbit droppings and other animal excrement?

JHC: If I could answer that question I would make a million dollars. However, I think you need to understand and go back to the times when dogs were wild, when there actually was nutrition in that kind of material that wild animals do utilize. Just as in our society, we're feeding a well-balanced dog food, so in our minds we question why they might want to do that. But in fact I do think there is a nutritional component. Those animal excrements they're eating, like rabbit droppings . . . well, the rabbit digestion systems are different and these animals are oftentimes herbivores, and I think that the products of their digestion, the bacteria and all that are left in the droppings, probably historically added nutritional value to dogs' diets, and dogs do seem to seek this out. Why they seek it out with such relish I don't think we'll ever know. I think that if the dog-food or cat-food companies could come up with an answer to that, and then incorporate it into their pet food, they would probably sell a lot more pet food.

RAJ: So this would also apply to puppies that are determined to eat their own stools?

JHC: I think that there is some validity in that. When people come in with this complaint, I have suggested that they try a couple products on the market: one is called Deter®; another is called Forbid®. Both are supposed to impart a nasty taste to the stool, and since it tastes so bad to the puppy, it will supposedly stop this behavior before it becomes just a bad habit. One has to think that they're seeking something, and I guess the question is: What? I don't know the answer to that. I think that perhaps they or their bodies must sense some nutritional problem and they're just trying to find whatever it is they're missing. What is hard to explain is that when you're feeding a good, high-quality dog food, what is it that they could be missing? I don't think anyone knows the answer to that. I do suggest to owners that they get out there and pick up the stools as fast as they can, or on a very regular basis. At least make it so hard for them to find that perhaps it will break the actual habit formation that's about to occur. But if there is something they're seeking, I certainly am not sure what it is. All we can do is practice really good hygiene and provide the best nutrition we can.

RAJ: How dangerous are mushrooms and toadstools, that are in your yard, to your new puppy?

JHC: Again I don't know all of my types of mushrooms and toadstools, but the *Amanita* sp. are dangerous and they are definitely around. Those are the ones with the reddish color to their caps. We do have dogs come in that are sick, with vomiting and diarrhea, and the owners will report that the dogs have taken, chewed on, or were eating mushrooms or toadstools. The ones that seem to pop up in the grass, the little white-capped ones, I have always felt were not particularly toxic. Unfortunately, when people come in and report that the dog has been chewing on toadstools, they don't see what the dog was eating. I think that you should probably refer to a book on toxic plants. Be vigilant and prevent ingestion. If you see the puppy/dog eat a mushroom or toadstool, try to recognize it. If they become ill, it might help the treatment. Clinically, you might see drooling, vomiting, diarrhea and/or incoordination. Then it would be necessary to get veterinary care. Fortunately, no puppy or dog has ever died at our practice from confirmed mushroom/toadstool ingestion.

RAJ: So what are the cardinal signs that a puppy needs immediate veterinary attention due to eating some toxic plant or material?

JHC: They may become a little uncoordinated, they may drool, they vomit, sometimes they could even collapse. I know with toad poisoning, for example, they can actually collapse. Any time any animal shows signs of severe distress, possibly respiratory distress, and have an anaphylactic kind of reaction where they actually just collapse, you need immediate attention. If you actually know the item or product the puppy ingested, poison control can be a valuable source of antidote information. If something has been chewed on but not ingested, and you just see a little drooling and the puppy seems perky otherwise, you can always try just rinsing out the mouth and just waiting a little while. I think that if there is ever a question, you should probably consult with a veterinarian or emergency clinic.

So, if it's just a situation where there is a possible suspicion of chewing on some sort of toxic kind of thing, and the puppy is fine, bright, alert, and the only thing that has happened is that it has maybe drooled a little bit, maybe it's thrown up once, but seems otherwise fine, active, or playing, it's always good to alert someone when there might be a problem, because that way, if you have to call a couple hours later, they're not angry. I think that you should always go by what your professional tells you. At our hospital, when someone calls, and the animal seems to be fine in every other respect, except perhaps it has vomited once, maybe a little salivation, but it seems lively and its not acting like it's in any kind of crisis, we will often tell the owner just to keep it quiet and withhold water for a little while and just see what happens. If it starts to deteriorate or seems to be getting worse, if the vomiting is persistent, if the salivation is getting more severe, if the animal seems to be having problems with coordination or vision, then we have them bring it in. If it's something really specific that they know—for example, daffodil bulbs, which are toxic, and/or the mushrooms that we know are poisonous, and/or toads—then they will have to bring the puppy or dog in right away, where we'll hospitalize it and watch it so that if it starts to deteriorate, so we can get it started on supported therapy as soon as possible. The most important thing is not to take a chance, but to consult your veterinarian and follow instructions.

RAJ: What kinds of cancer do you see in your practice that are more specific to Golden Retrievers than to other breeds of dogs?

I think, universally, in Golden Retrievers we're seeing more hemangiosarcomas and lymphomas and lymphosarcomas than any other specific types of cancer. Those stand out, and we're seeing these cropping up sometimes as young as three years, but more often older than that. The hemangiosarcomas are often presented when the dog is actually dying. The sarcoma has ruptured and the dog has collapsed and is bleeding internally. Hindsight, which is more perfect knowledge, tells us that when you look at these dogs they are often "not quite right," as the owner calls it, but I don't think that we actually see them enough in advance to diagnose that there's a problem. One of the biggest problems with hemangiosarcoma is in diagnosing it, in my opinion. You won't see a whole lot on your serum chemistries, which will mislead you. With ultrasound we can actually start to look and see splenic lesion: Is the dog sick enough when we see them, or "not quite right" to warrant an ultrasound? If you're looking at the spleen, for example, and there is a hemangiosarcoma, you can actually really visualize this with ultrasound. I think now about the cost factor, and what the client really wants to do becomes a factor, because often the clinical signs these dogs exhibit are very subtle. The question is: Is the dog just getting older, or showing some signs of age, or in fact is there some problem going on? We'll do lab work and very often there is not a whole lot of indication to let us think that we have to go further. And it seems you don't want to just be suggesting to a person that they spend a lot of dollars doing an ultrasound without a really good reason. So, hemangiosarcomas tend to be a little frustrating and even if you do find them, 95 percent of the ones that we have had experience with, when we go in surgically and do exploratory surgery, you'll find that they've metastasized to many sites in the abdominal cavity, in which case there really isn't a whole lot you can do, so I think ultimately you have to try to figure out how to find them when they're just in the spleen and be able to do a spleenectomy. This is a challenging area that we have not yet completely conquered.

And lymphomas and lymphosarcomas in Goldens . . . we definitely are seeing these, and we've had some moderate luck with chemotherapy, and there are some protocols we've been using, where we've been extending the life of some of these dogs. There are more and more things coming along, and I suspect it won't be too long until we may actually be able to treat them fairly successfully. Right now our batting average has been that we're able to extend the lives of some of these dogs for about a year. Sometimes even longer than that, and they've had a fairly decent quality of life, and that has been very satisfactory to the client, but with the advent of a lot more diagnostic techniques and perhaps DNA studies and all, we're going to be able to do more for those dogs. A lot of exciting work is being done out in Colorado, the Veterinary School in Colorado, on different types of cancer in all breeds of dogs. We're seeing some really interesting advancements in osteosarcoma; and just as with any cancer therapy, with humans as well as animals, I think lots of things will be coming in the next few years that I hope will result in positive outcomes for the dogs that are afflicted.

RAJ: In trying to prevent cancer in your puppy, starting with your puppy, do you think there is a correlation between cancer and certain environmental factors such as cigarette smoke, industrial pollution, lawn herbicides and pesticides, and even the dog food preservatives?

JHC: I think that what we're finding in humans and in animals is that the more we gain experience with these different kinds of cancers, the more we are finding that there are many things that are affecting all of us, causing genetic mutations and/or errors to occur that are leading to cancer becoming a more common diagnosis. When I started practice back in 1970, we actually saw tumors and cancer, but not that often. Over the years we see them more, and more often in younger animals, and I think that, as with the human population, we're seeing cancers more and more in younger children—clusters of leukemia and what have you—and often these can be traced back to some sort of environmental influence. There was a definite correlation, for instance, between leukemia in children and the insecticides that some of the lawn-treatment companies were spraying. At this time I'm not really sure, but I would assume that some of the lawn treatment companies are no longer using what they were using in those days. But I do know that there was an absolute definite correlation between leukemia in young children and lawn chemical treatment. I can't help to think that over the years of dipping dogs for fleas and using things like chlorpyrifos and some of the other chemicals that we have been using—I can't help but think that that has been an important factor in the increase in the number of cancer cases we're seeing.

I also believe that farming techniques and crop-raising techniques may be worth looking at. I think we're beginning to see and realize that a lot of this stuff we're spraying on crops and feeding this stuff on a regular basis is not in our best interest, and I think that this is going to spill over and add to the environmental pollution that's out there. I think that, when you're talking about preservatives in food, we try to do the best we can with what we have, and I think that the best thing to do is to try to provide your pets with good solid, clean, nutrition and again try to use the best type of parasite and ectoparasite control that you have at your disposal. What we don't know, just like we didn't know when we were using such things as dichlorpyrifos, is what the long-term effects are of Advantage® and Frontline® and the Interceptor® products and all of those things. There is no way to know that until the years go by and we actually start to see some of the results. It seems to me, though, that what we're trying to do today is better than what we were doing ten years ago, and is also less pathologic to the animal. I think that in our pets' lives, as well as our own, we have to try to provide the best environment that we can give them as well as to give ourselves. I think that each person has to come to grips with what he or she thinks is the right thing to do. Our country does the best job at policing residues and stuff that is offensive to our bodies. Unfortunately, in our society today, we all want to have watermelon in December and grapes in December, and we want to have all these things that are being imported from South America, and who knows from where else. Those countries don't have the rules and regulations that we do, so you just have to realize that when you're buying those things that are pleasing to the palate, you may also be buying insecticides that aren't controlled by the EPA. I think the import requirements need to be tightened in order for certain items to be imported into this country. In the meanwhile, we must realize that the foodstuffs imported into the country may not be as good for us as we think.

The same thing holds true with dogs, which is another reason why you might consider buying a better quality pet food—one that has been standardized so that you're not just shopping around for any protein source that has been put on the commodities market. You might have to pay a little bit more for it, but you'll also want something that you know has been standardized. If organic makes you feel good, then that's what you should do, because that probably ultimately is as good as you can get.

RAJ: Jean, I know that you could write a book in itself on hip dysplasia, but do you have any comments that would be helpful to every new puppy owner?

JHC: First of all, I think it's important to realize that most of the people who come to our practice are just pet owners, and we don't really have a lot of breeders that we deal with. Of the breeders we know about, we always recommend that they radiograph their animals for hip dysplasia, and we recommend that they try to use OFA normal animals in their breeding stock. We ourselves are not certified to do PennHIP, but the reason is only that there are just not many people in our area who are really interested in pursuing this, so that we felt it was not worth our while to do it. We can refer those to another practice, which has somebody that is trained and certified in PennHIP. We rely mostly on the OFA, and I would say that, in general, most of the radiographs we send, most all of them pass, because we're pretty good at screening out the bad ones and we generally just advise people that, to us, they're showing radiographic abnormalities, and that they not bother to send them to the OFA, because it's not really worth spending the money. We can tell them that the dog has a problem, and we can tell them whether or not it's a fairly decent batting average, whether it's going to be mild, moderate, or severe. So when we do send X-rays to the OFA, we've been getting a pretty good percent of OFA numbers, again, mostly because we're pre-screening them at the hospital stage. Basically, if we have a puppy owner who has purchased (or is going to purchase) a purebred puppy, we recommend purchase from a handler who has made an effort to use OFA normal stock. It's something that I think we'll always strive to encourage: to try to lessen the impact of the genetic component by selecting the best bitches and males that you can find.

As far as orthopedic problems that are related to the hips, our practice tends to be a very conservative practice. We do a lot of counseling, and if a person is coming in with a large-breed puppy, and they're feeding this puppy way too much food, and it's getting fat, and their puppy seems a little sloppy behind, and let's say there's no known history on the hip status of the parents, which in our particular location is a very common thing because there is a lot of backyard breeding going on, we tend to counsel people to try and regulate the puppy's exercise, and control the amount of racing and running and jumping. We're also trying to counsel them to maintain the weight to an acceptable level.

We try to keep these puppies fit with moderate exercise and a moderate amount of food, and prevent getting them overtired or overstressed to the point where they're actually causing themselves some injuries. We often will suggest, again, a well-balanced dog food, providing all the protein and nutrients they need, and sometimes we will use supplements like Fresh Factors™, which is made by Springtime Inc., just because it has a little Glucosamine in it. We're certainly not opposed to people who want to supplement with some kind of Glucosamine or Chondroitin Sulfate. I think the important thing is that people with puppies just need to realize that these puppies are young, rapidly growing individuals, akin to a youth going from fifteen or sixteen years in their first year, and their little bones and joints are very easily stressed and damaged, and that owners just have to take it a little easy with these guys, and let them grow at their own rate without damaging themselves.

If we see puppies having a lot of acute pain at six or seven months of age, we will explain to the people what is happening: that the puppies often get microfractures in the top of their acetabulum, and this is causing pain. We will radiograph puppies or young dogs that have a lot of pain or discomfort and try to advise the people, and sometimes just put these animals on some sort of nutritional and exercise program, to make sure they continue to move, but that they're being cared for. If they need pain therapy, we will treat them for pain, while trying to supplement them nutritionally and allow their cartilage to heal. It has been our experience that many of these puppies will go on and live totally fruitful lives, without the need for extensive surgeries.

Occasionally we will get a person that wants to be referred to an orthopedist, and we always provide them with this option. We also tell them what's probably going to be involved and the expense in doing some sort of reconstructive surgery of the hip. Most of our clients will opt just to use conservative therapy. We always tell them that if worse comes to worse, they can always do a femoral head resection. Most dogs do very well after that surgery and are comfortable and functional.

Very rarely do you have a puppy that ends up having to be put to sleep because of hip dysplasia. We try to not put the fear of death and alarm in our clients' heads. We try to counsel them that it's something that we can hopefully manage and make the puppy a nice productive member of the family and the dog can lead a happy life—without having to go ahead and subject the puppy to a huge surgery and spend thousands of dollars in the process. Again, in the long term, you don't know what the outcome of these surgeries is going to be. Now that more data is available on the success of surgery, I don't think the surgery results are any better than the conservative approach.

A lot of time has gone by since veterinary orthopedists have been doing TPOs (triple pelvic osteotomies). Most of the time we don't need to do this, and the dogs will do very well with some counseling and some care. Again, we start out by trying to care for the large-breed dog, any large-breed dog—Goldens, Labs, Newfies—and point out the fact that these dogs are growing exponentially so much faster than a little terrier, and try to help the owner understand things they can do at home that will help this puppy develop in a better manner without a lot of wear, tear, and stress. I think that you can actually alter the course of how much discomfort and pain this animal might be subjected to as it matures. As I said, the most important thing is the actual management. I believe that you try to improve upon the genetic component through selective breeding, but now we need to stress the education of the owners themselves managing puppies correctly. I think this is of major importance in a puppy's development.

RAJ: Thanks so much, Jean.

PLATE 1. The author with puppies.

PLATE 2. Mother and five-week-old puppies being supplementally pan fed.

PLATE 3. Six-week-old puppies ready to go.

PLATE 4. When selecting a puppy, you can evaluate the head if two puppies are held side by side.

PLATE 5. Robin Meirs (left) with eight-week-old puppies. Ann Johnson (right) with a ten-week-old puppy.

PLATE 6. Craig Westergaard holding six-week-old "Lacy,"

PLATE 7. A puppy "stacked" for evaluation.

PLATE 8. Bart and seven-week-old son at Southern California Luau party.

PLATE 9. Six-month-old female enjoying her new home. (Photo: Eric Weiss.)

PLATE 10. Doll Daisy on the lake.

PLATE 11. O'Brien in the lake.

PLATE 12. Puppy in action. (Photo: Richard Speedy, Hopewell, NJ.)

PLATE 13. Puppy enjoying a day on the beach.

PLATE 14. Seven-week-old
Royal MacDuff puppy.

PLATE 15. Seven-week-old puppy (Ace x Georgia), sleeping.

PLATE 16. Nine-week-old puppy in sleigh: Gold-Rush Hobson. (Photo: Lana and Paul Goldberg.)

PLATE 17. Five-week-old puppies (Ace x Georgia).

PLATE 18. Nine-week-old Bart puppy: Gold-Rush Jettsetter ("Riviera").
(Photo: Jean Ettinger.)

PLATE 19. Six-week-old puppy at attention.

PLATE 20. Six-week-old puppy on grooming table.

PLATE 21. Kim Johnson with three-month-old puppy at match show.

PLATE 22. Three-month-old puppy, after the show.

PLATE 23. Seven-month-old Gold-Rush Cover Girl ("Naomi"),
during her W.C. test.

PLATE 24. Nine-week-old puppies sired by Ch. Copper Lee Gold-Rush Apollo.
(Photo: Anna and Terry Moore.)

PLATE 25. Gold-Rush Spencer Tracy being hand-fed at eight weeks of age.

PLATE 26. Gold-Rush Spencer Tracy at nine months.

PLATE 27. Can. Ch. Spencer Tracy at two years of age.

PLATE 28. (Left) Gold-Rush Kelly of Braemoor at eight weeks. (Photo: Barbara © '94.)

PLATE 29. (Middle) Gold-Rush Kelly of Braemoor at twelve months.

PLATE 30. (Bottom) Can. Ch. Gold-Rush Kelly of Braemoor at eighteen months.

PLATE 31. Gold-Rush Ivy of Braemoor at six months,
one frosty morning in Canada.

Chapter 20:
Developmental Biology and Your Puppy, A Scientific Approach

The Importance of Understanding Development in Young Puppies

If one stops to think about it, the task of any embryo or young organism as it grows into an adult is mind-boggling. To become an embryo you have to build yourself from a single cell. As a young organism you need to have form or a gut before you can respire and digest; you need to form a brain before you can think. And you need to build bones and walk on them at the same time. No machine has ever been made to function before it was built.

As you raise your new puppy, you are entering the realm of Animal Development. Developmental biology is one of the fastest growing fields of biology. As the molecular mechanisms of animal development are becoming better understood, developmental biology is assuming a unifying role in the biological sciences. It integrates molecular biology, genetics, embryology, physiology, cell biology, anatomy, cancer research, neurobiology, immunology, ecology, and evolutionary biology. The study of development has become essential for the understanding of every other area of biology.

Biology, like any other science, does not deal solely with facts; rather, it deals with evidence. The first and weakest type of evidence is correlative evidence. Here, correlations are made between two or more events, and there is an inference that one event causes the other. This type of evidence is weak because you cannot say with certainty that one event causes the other. There could be other causes causing both events, or the simultaneous occurrence of the two events could be simply coincidental. It is the provenance of the scientific method and the use of experimentation to provide greater evidence and to support cause and effect relationships that elucidate the mechanisms in biological systems.

The dog world today seems to look at the dog only through the eyes of the geneticist. There is an underlying assumption that every problem has a genetic basis. If you've got a problem it must be in the genes. Therefore the genotype is at fault. Nevertheless, it is the embryo that mediates between the genotype and phenotype; development involves the inherited genes and also the impact of the environment upon those genes as they are expressed. As Helena Cronin says, "There is no such thing as 'the' phenotypic effect of any gene. Phenotypes are always the result of an interaction between gene and environment."[47]

All of the above is relevant to our better understanding of the puppy and the importance of how we raise our puppies. For instance, nothing is more important to the growing Golden puppy than good bone formation. When one is dealing with a large breed puppy, the genes that make the puppy large also make him prone to growth problems. Yet some puppies have problems and others do not. It is here that the environment—the effects of nutrition, exercise, stress and trauma, for example—has a major impact upon the genetic endowment.

To gain a little more understanding of what is involved in bone formation in the puppy let us look a little more carefully at osteogenesis or the development of bone. There are two major ways in which bones are formed. In one type, pre-existing tissue is converted into bone directly. This is seen in the bones of the skull and is of little concern to the puppy owner. The one exception that I am familiar with is the temporary bony growth that occurs when a puppy repeatedly bumps his head (such as when going under a table). The other type is where undifferentiated tissue is changed to cartilage and the cartilage is later replaced by bone. The cartilage is a model for the bone that follows. The skeletal components of the extremities are formed in this way. Since the Golden puppy is known for growth problems in his legs, let us look at this process carefully.

The process by which cartilage is formed and then replaced by bone cells is called endochondral ossification. The process coordinates cartilage production (chondrogenesis) with bone growth (osteogenesis). In the embryo, the precursor cells are stimulated by surrounding cells to change into chondrocytes. These cells secrete the proteoglycans and collagens that form the cartilage matrix. Cells in the center of the shaft of cartilage grow large and change their extracellular matrix to that of collagen and fibronectin. This allows blood vessels to enter. The blood vessels bring in the osteoblasts (bone-forming cells) and as the cartilage matrix is degraded the osteoblasts secrete bone matrix on the partially degraded cartilage. This explains how bone is formed on the pre-existing model of cartilage, but how does one account for the growth of the bone?

At either end of the bone the cartilage changes to epiphyseal growth plates. The cartilage at the ends of the bones contains chondrocytes that proliferate, which accounts for the new growth before they, too, hypertrophy and, in a similar fashion as in the center of the bone, form secondary ossification centers. Now we see the crux of the Golden puppy's problem. The developing skeletal element is simultaneously bearing a load, growing in width and responding to local stresses, and growing at its ends. Is it any wonder that large breed dogs can have periods of pain and limping as they go through this process?

Another point of interest is that the epiphyseal growth plate cells are very responsive to both growth hormones and sex hormones. Sex hormones are responsible for the cessation of growth. At the end of puberty, high levels of estrogen or testosterone cause the remaining chondrocytes to die and are replaced by bone. Without any further cartilage, growth of these bones ceases. It is for this reason that the early neutering of the male Golden causes him to be taller than he would have been had he not been neutered. Without the sex hormones the growth plates continue to grow and the bones become longer.

It is clear to the developmental biologist that the instructions for development do not reside wholly in the genes. The organism is sensitive to cues from the environment. This makes the organism vulnerable to environmental changes that can disrupt development. For instance, it has been estimated that from one-half to two-thirds of all human conceptions do not develop successfully to term. Many of these embryos become abnormal so early that they fail to implant in the uterus. About five percent of all human births have a recognizable malformation.

In view of this why do we expect dogs to be without defects, many of which are caused by environmental factors? As one becomes aware of the complexity of development, one must realize that development is critically keyed to the environment. The exploration of environmental regulation on development is just beginning.

Selection is a powerful tool at the disposal of the breeder. Moreover, I contend that an understanding of the science of development is important not only to the breeder, but especially to the puppy owner, because you cannot change the genes your puppy inherited. What you can change is the environment, which affects the expression of those genes.

The question often posed to dog fanciers is: "Which is more important, the genotype or the phenotype?" My answer, of course, is: "For the breeder, the genotype is more important. For the pet owner, the phenotype is clearly more important." Pet owners are not usually interested in breeding their dogs, but are interested in a healthy, long-lived pet. There are around 52,000 Goldens registered annually with the AKC, and only 200 to 250 become champions each year.[48] Most Goldens serve as pets.

The answers that the new owner is seeking lie not so much in the realm of genetics as in the realm of developmental biology. Proper care can make the difference between a healthy and an unhealthy puppy in most cases. What the pet owner needs to know is the answer to the question: Given the genes that my puppy has, how can I raise him so that he is healthy? The answer is: You need to raise him very, very carefully.

Chapter 21:
Perspectives on Cancer

Introduction

A current topic among dog breeders today is that of the high incidence of cancer in dogs. Cancer causes more deaths than any other disease. It is a topic of great controversy because there is so much about cancer that has yet to be understood. For Golden breeders and owners the specter of cancer weighs heavily on our emotions because it strikes down our cherished Golden, sometimes prematurely.

It may seem out of place to speak about cancer in a book about puppies, but since every dog has the potential to die some day of cancer, it is never too soon to look at what we know of the causes of cancer in order to do all we can to avoid the premature loss of our faithful Golden.

Some thirty years ago, when I was new to the Golden Retriever World, I was talking to Joe Dainty, one of the founders of the Garden State Golden Retriever Club, who was also a popular Golden judge for many years. At that time I was concerned about hip dysplasia in the breed, and I remember well his saying to me somewhat impatiently, "Goldens don't die of hip dysplasia, they die of cancer."

With exceptions, notably Gold-Rush Charlie, who died of acute pancreatitis at age twelve, my experience has been that most Goldens do die eventually of cancer, if they don't die of something else beforehand. From studying the breed these many years, I know that cancer is nothing new, but it does seem that Goldens are often succumbing at an earlier age.

As someone trained in the biological sciences, and as a lover of Golden Retrievers, I have been interested in the subject of cancer for many years. I have talked about it with veterinarians, cell biologists, geneticists, biologists, toxicologists, dog owners, and dog breeders, and have read current articles in the scientific literature. I do not claim to be an expert, but I do want to share information that is relevant to the discussion. However, I do so reluctantly because there is so much we do not know about cancer and carcinogens (cancer-causing agents), and new information is being presented almost on a daily basis. Nevertheless, I do feel a responsibility to convey some personal reflections on this matter.

At the beginning of any discussion about cancer, it might be wise to marvel at how uncommon cancer is in the human species as well as in canines when compared to the huge number of cell divisions that occur in an orderly fashion. In fact, it would be a commonplace observation to say that the incidence of cancer is a rather infrequent occurrence when compared to the vast numbers of cells that divide every day. The embryo grows from one cell to approximately ten-trillion cells in the adult. Many cells die and are replaced by others. All of these cells are equipped with genes that turn out products essential to their division and other genes that signal those genes to stop making this product when local conditions indicate that the tissue is mature and no additional cells are currently needed. Growth of cells and cell division are controlled processes. Most of the time they occur in a normal fashion. When these systems fail, the result is often cancer. To understand the information about cancer that is in the literature and in the news media one needs to know some of the basic definitions and concepts of cell biology as well as some of the history of our understanding of cancer.

Definitions and Concepts

Cancerous cells are cells that grow and proliferate, as all cells do. What cancer cells lack are the processes that inhibit their growth so that they grow continuously.

When the factors that regulate cell death (apoptosis) and cell division are changed, as is the case when there is a change (mutation) in one of the genes that normally control growth, or make it unable to respond to conditions that normally control growth, then a mass of abnormal cells arises. This mass is known as a tumor. A *tumor cell* is an altered cell that reproduces and grows without control by the host. When a normal cell is changed to a tumor cell, a change has occurred that allows the tumor cell to determine its own activities of growth and division. This newly acquired property, known as *autonomy*, is the most important single characteristic of tumor cells. A second characteristic is that of *transplantability*. When tumor cells are removed from a host and implanted into an appropriate host, they develop again into tumor growths. When tumor cells closely resemble the normal cells of the tissue they inhabit, they are said to be *well-differentiated* and may even function normally. Such tumors that usually remain localized at the site from which they originated, and cause no harm, are said to be *benign*. When tumors are comprised of cells that have lost their resemblance to the original cell type, these cells are said to be *undifferentiated* and have a greater likelihood of spreading to other parts of the body.

Tumors that can eventually cause the death of the individual are called *malignant.* Another important characteristic that distinguishes malignant from benign tumors is the ability of the malignant tumor to invade underlying tissues and to detach small groups of cells from the tumor that move, or metastasize, through the blood vessels and lymph channels to distant sites where a new tumor will be formed. It is this capacity of malignant cells to become widely disseminated in a host that makes cancer such a dangerous and often incurable disease. However, it is also true that tumors do not have to metastasize to cause the death of their host.

The capacity to invade and metastasize is often acquired relatively late compared to the first sign of the tumor. In general, tumors have been shown to go through several stages. This ability is called the capacity for *autonomous growth.* These changes have come to be known as *tumor progression.* The growth itself has many gradations—from very slow to very rapid.

In multistage tumor development a chemical carcinogen may convert normal cells into tumor cells that do not at first proliferate into a tumor growth. Such tumor cells require another type of chemical, which has been called a *promoter* or a co-carcinogen, to stimulate the incipient tumor cell to develop into a *neoplastic growth* (cancer).

Each stage in the multistage process may be facilitated by specific chemicals that may not be active as promoters at other stages. There are also instances whereby a normal cell is transformed into a rapidly growing tumor cell in apparently a single step.

It is usually impossible to determine if a tumor is benign or malignant by its outward appearance. When a small sample of the tumor is surgically removed (called a *biopsy*) and a small section of the tumor is studied under the microscope, the cells of a benign tumor will closely resemble the normal surrounding cells—with the exception that the tumor cells will be seen to be undergoing the process of cell division more frequently. Malignant tumor cells can be distinguished from benign tumor cells, or normal cells, because the malignant cells are predominantly in the process of dividing. In addition, they usually have an abnormal number of chromosomes. Benign tumors are usually encapsulated by fibrous tissue, which makes it easy to remove the entire intact tumor. Malignant tumors are encapsulated only in their early stages and in later stages possess no clear boundaries. Death is usually due to the metastatic spread of the malignant tumor cells to other organs rather than the effect of the original tumor.

Growth of a tumor is dependent upon the development of blood vessels for support. Metastatic tumors usually secrete chemicals that induce the formation of blood vessels. This process is called *angiogenesis*. Primary (original) tumors secrete chemicals into the blood stream that inhibit angiogenesis and, therefore, the growth of the secondary sites. When the primary tumor is removed, the growth of the secondary sites are no longer inhibited and the metastatic sites are then able to grow. Other dog breeders have told me, as an "old wives tale," that if one leaves a tumor alone the dog is not seriously affected. If, however, the tumor is removed, it was believed that the effect of exposing the tumor to air caused the tumor to spread so the dog soon succumbs to the metastatic cancer. In the light of recent understandings, I now believe that it is more likely that it is the removal of the inhibitory factors secreted by the primary tumor that allow angiogenesis and growth of the cancer cells that have already spread throughout the dog's body.[49]

Some tumor cells are controlled by the environment in which they are growing. These have been called *conditional* or *hormone-dependent tumors*. Conditional prostate or breast tumors, which may be highly malignant, grow only as long as the appropriate hormonal stimulus is present. When the specific stimulus is withdrawn, the tumor stops growing. Many conditional tumors undergo progression to a *hormone-independent state* and then become true tumors.

In normal cells in animals (and plants) there are mechanisms whereby cell division and cell death are directed. It had long been observed that carcinogens interrupt those regulatory mechanisms so that certain cells become cancerous and grow out of control. There is usually no single element or condition that causes cancer; rather the cause can be attributed to numerous factors or events that interact. For this reason cancer occurs with a higher frequency in older individuals where the passage of time has allowed for the series of events to occur that transform a normal cell into a cancer cell. These events are referred to as "risk factors," i.e., those factors that have the ability to affect the genes within a cell.

Classification of Cancers

Cancers are classified according to the primary body site where the cancer originated, such as skin cancer, ovarian cancer, or lung cancer. The type of cancer from which the tissue originates also is the basis for their classification. There are two main types: carcinoma and sarcoma.

Carcinomas are derived from epithelial cells—that is to say, the cells that form the outer and inner surface layer of organs. Epithelial tissue arises from the embryonic endoderm. Probably because these tissues are more exposed to the external environment, most cancers are carcinomas.

Sarcomas arise in connective tissue. This tissue, which is from the mesoderm of the embryo, forms the inner supporting material of organs and structures such as bones and cartilage.

Lymphoma and leukemia, which are cancers of the lymph system and blood stem cells, respectively, are sometimes classified separately from carcinomas and sarcomas.

Kinds of Cancer in Golden Retrievers

The more common cancers in Goldens are lymphoma, hemangiosarcoma, mast cell cancer, and osteosarcoma. These cancers are, however, less prevalent in young dogs than in older dogs. Dogs also seem to be more vulnerable at certain ages for a specific kind of cancer. While the number of puppies that die of cancer is very small, such mortality is not unheard of.

Lymphoma is a cancer of the lymph system. It is first noticed by the presence of very enlarged lymph nodes in the neck and chest. They can be felt as round growths large as marbles. This disease can be found in the young Golden, but is most commonly found between the ages of three and seven years.

Hemangioscarcoma is commonly seen in Goldens around age seven. The tumors involve the circulatory system and are filled with blood. The disease usually strikes suddenly when a tumor ruptures, causing an internal hemorrhage that leads to the collapse of the dog. The disease is devastating and recovery is usually only temporary.

Mast cell tumors are carcinomas that are not uncommon to Goldens and are the most common malignancy in dogs—occurring in about 20 percent of canines. They range from being relatively benign to being extremely aggressive and leading to death.

Osteosarcoma is a cancer of the bone. It is more commonly found in large breed dogs, including the Golden, but in my experience it is seen less frequently than the other cancers mentioned above.[50] The age of onset seems more variable than other cancers; however, the frequency of osteosarcoma seems to increase with age. A tumor of a leg can be removed (often along with the leg) and sometimes the life of the dog is thereby extended.

A Brief History of Our Understanding of Cancer

When the war against cancer was declared in 1971, biologists did not know what the cancer-causing mechanisms were. The conventional wisdom was that cancer was not a single disease but a collection of disorders involving tumor formation. It was thought that there were many causes, most of them external. From the beetlenut-chewing Indians who developed cancer and the boy chimney sweeps in England who developed scrotal cancer to the Asbestos and Cigarette law suits more recently, external carcinogens have been demonstrated to cause cancer.

It had already been shown, in 1909, that a chicken with a form of cancer called sarcoma could pass the disease to a healthy chicken. This discovery led to the Nobel Prize for Peyton Rous, the discoverer, and the virus is named for him. These viruses that cause cancer are called oncoviruses, and by the 1960s many cancers, such as cervical cancer, were shown to be at least partly caused by viral infection.

By the 1970s it became apparent that there were many cancers identified whose causes involved viruses as well as numerous other biological, chemical, and physical agencies.[51] In the mid-1970s it was discovered, by sequencing the virus from the Rous sarcoma, that the oncogene (a gene that can cause cells to grow, and only causes cancer when it gets permanently turned on, i.e., "jammed on") was also found in chickens, mice, and humans. It was believed that the Rous sarcoma virus had stolen its oncogene from one of its hosts.[52] By the end of the seventies, DNA taken from three kinds of tumors had been used to induce cancerous growths in mouse cells. Thus, a case was being built that cancer is a disease of cells involving the genetic material. However, the cells involved are not the cells of the egg or sperm (i.e., the germ line) passed on from generation to generation,[53] but are the genes of the cells of the tissue containing the tumor. In 1989, J. Michael Bishop and Harold E. Varmus made the discovery that a virus was only the indirect cause of the cancer. It triggered the cancer by modifying the normal gene (proto-oncogene) to produce the cancer. Ultimately, our own altered genes were seen to be doing the damage; they became the oncogenes.[54]

Proto-oncogenes are normal genes that promote cell growth and division. These genes are required during the development of the individual and subsequently to promote new cell growth during normal replacement of old cells or damaged cells. Our cells possess such genes so that we can grow from an egg into an embryo and child and adult, and so that wounds can heal later in life. If these proto-oncogenes are damaged by mutation, they become oncogenes, which are abnormal genes.

Oncogenes are genes that encourage cells to grow, but what is different about them is that they do not respond to the chemical signals that normally turn them off when cell division is no longer needed. It is as if they are "jammed on." With the trillions of body cells, and cells being continually replaced, there are plenty of opportunities for oncogenes to be jammed on during a lifetime, even without the effect of mutation-causing cigarette smoke, or other carcinogens.

It was soon discovered that there are other genes, called tumor-suppressor genes, that can recognize a tumorous cell (containing a jammed on oncogene) and arrest that cell in its growth cycle. If, however, the tumor-suppressor gene also fails ("jammed off"), the tumorous cell will continue to grow.[55]

As it turns out, there are other safeguards. There are, for example, some defects in the genetic material (DNA) that can be repaired. If these fail, another gene detects, and is switched on by, the abnormal behavior of a cell that leads to the production of chemicals that directs different genes within that tumor cell toward cell death (apoptosis).

While many cancer studies have focused on the behavior of cells, they have done so in cultures away from the dense fibrous network of proteins and sugars that normally envelops them. More recent studies have examined the behavior of cells in their natural environment—that is, the environment attached to the intracellular matrix. It has been found that the components of the matrix proteins, such as laminin and fibronectin, bind to specific molecules known as integrins (there are twenty or more) that are attached to the cell surface. Through these attachments various signals are given to the cell that regulate the activity of certain genes and thereby determine which genes within the cell are active. These genes in turn determine whether the cells grow, migrate, become specialized, or even die. The large number of integrins indicates how large the matrix control is on the cells. Investigators have found that cells from very different organs and tissues become almost indistinguishable when grown outside the body in culture on glass or plastic surfaces. When specific matrix molecules are added, only then do the cells begin to behave like specialized tissues. Clearly, chemical signals from the environment of the cell will determine its behavior and specificity.

Researchers then began to explore the effect of such chemical signs from the environment on cancer. For example, it was shown that, when antibodies to integrins that block their function are added to malignant cells, the malignant cells become normal again. Cancer researchers now believe that the cancer cell's altered connections to its surroundings are just as important as the internal changes in the cell that spur its excessive proliferation. This information leads one to believe that we have just begun to understand the complexities of cancer and also leads to new areas of research and ultimately cancer therapies that establish normal growth rather than try to kill every single cancer cell in the body.

The Environment and Cancer

As we have seen above, most cancers result from the interaction of genes and the environment. In humans, genic factors by themselves are thought to explain only about five percent of all cancers. No doubt the situation is not much different with the canine. This is good news for cancer prevention in that environmental carcinogens—herbicides; insecticides; pollutants in the air, food, and water; drugs; radiation; and infectious agents—are theoretically preventable.

Carcinogens: Environmental Causes of Cancer
Carcinogens are identified by investigating unusually high cancer rates in groups of unrelated people that are exposed to a common substance. Epidemiological studies compare a group of people exposed to the substance with similar groups that have not been exposed. A higher rate of cancer in the exposed group is strong evidence that the substance is a carcinogen. That substance would also be studied in the

laboratory using animal studies. Carcinogens fall into three classifications: chemical, physical, and viral.

Chemical Carcinogens. Chemical carcinogens are strongly implicated in the development of many kinds of cancer. There are two groups of chemical carcinogens, the direct-acting and the indirect-acting.

Americans use some 2 billion pounds of pesticides each year. Some pesticide residues stay in the food chain for decades. DDT, for instance, was banned in the United States in 1972, but, since DDT has an environmental half-life of about 100 years, it is still with us. DDT and its main metabolic byproduct, DDE, can act as estrogenic compounds. These compounds have been linked to several problems in organisms, including cancer. Dioxin, another pesticide ingredient, has also been linked to cancer.[56] Some estrogenic compounds may be in the food we eat and in the wrapping that surrounds them because some of the chemicals used in the formation of plastics have been found to be estrogenic. Other such chemicals are PCBs.

Substances that are added or applied to foods are also suspected of causing cancer. These substances include some preservatives, insecticides, and chemicals used to control weeds. Many such substances that were once widely used are now prohibited. However, 2,4-D and other herbicides are still on the market and are commonly used weed killers at golf courses and on new lawns. It should not be surprising to learn therefore that there is a higher incidence of lymphoma among lawn-care workers. The herbicide 2,4-D acts to increase growth of broad-leafed plants to the point that the plant dies. One might suspect that such a mechanism might have a similar effect on animal cells and, therefore, be related to the origin of lymphomas.[57]

Some chemicals naturally present in food may become a cancer risk if they are consumed in large quantities. Diets high in fats for humans, for example, have been associated with cancer of the breast, colon, and prostate gland. Some studies have linked eating large amounts of smoked, salt cured and pickled food, and foods that sometimes contain molds, such as corn and peanuts, with cancers of the digestive system.

Cigarette smoke contains dozens of chemical carcinogens. It is estimated that smoking causes about one-third of all cases of cancer.[58] Cigarette smoke may also cause cancer in nonsmokers who live with smokers. As such, it should be a consideration when it comes to preventing cancer in dogs.

Many industrial chemicals are carcinogens. Such chemicals include dyes, arsenic, benzene, chromium, nickel vinyl chloride, and certain petroleum products. Industrial wastes containing such carcinogens have been released into the environment. Federal and State regulations are attempting to regulate such emissions into the air, water, and land, but many chemicals already in the environment will last for many years.

Physical Carcinogens. This category includes such things as ionizing radiation, ultraviolet radiation, and foreign material such as asbestos.

Certain kinds of radiation, for example, can disrupt the DNA, and such genetic defects lead to cancer. The sun is one of the most important sources of cancer-causing radiation, the most destructive of which is ultraviolet radiation. X-rays are also a cancer risk. Nuclear radiation from, for example, nuclear power plant accidents such as the explosion at Chernobyl, increased the rate of cancer (particularly thyroid cancer) and other genetic defects in those that were exposed to the radioactive fallout.[59]

Viral Carcinogens. It has been shown that certain kinds of viruses cause cancer by damaging normal genes (see p. 223).[60] I predict more will be learned about this cause of cancer in dogs.

Cancer in All Dogs

When one studies cancers in all dogs one finds that there are breed predilections to many cancers. Dr. Michael H. Goldschmidt, professor of pathology at the Veterinary Hospital of the University of Pennsylvania has studied the various breeds of dogs and the specific tumors for which they are at high risk. Dr. Goldshmidt concludes that by selecting for the specific external features of a dog, its phenotype, one is selecting specific genes that make that breed more or less susceptible to developing a specific cancer.[61]

Inheritance of Cancer in the Golden Retriever

Does a high frequency of cancer in the Golden Retriever mean that cancer is inherited? Certainly cancer has a genetic basis, meaning that the mechanisms involved in cancer involve the DNA of the cells. This does not mean, however, that cancer is necessarily inherited. In many instances cancer no doubt involves mutations, but these mutations only rarely involve the DNA of the egg or sperm (the germ cells) to be passed on to subsequent generations; rather, they are local mutations in a body cell (somatic cells), which leads to the cancer. Most people who develop cancer do not have inherited genetic abnormalities. Their genes have been damaged after birth by substances in the environment. As already noted, a substance that damages DNA in a way that can lead to cancer is called a carcinogen, and there are hundreds of these in the environment—both naturally occurring and man-made.

On the other hand, scientists have long known that the risk of some cancers increases for people with close relatives who also have the disease. The increased risk occurs because some types of genetic damage involved in cancer can be passed from parent to offspring. These forms of cancer in humans represent less than five percent of all cancers. Serious flaws in the DNA of an egg or a sperm would have a lethal effect on the embryo. However, defects carried on one chromosome while the other is normal might allow the growth of the embryo.[62] Because the product of the one gene is sufficient to allow normal development, this individual would be more susceptible to genetic damage later in life, as a result of having only one normal gene rather than two, in the event one is damaged. In addition to the nuclear DNA, there is DNA in the mitochondria of the egg. Because sperm have no cytoplasm containing mitochondria, only the mitochondrial DNA of the mother is passed on to the offspring. Therefore, defects in mitochondrial DNA would only be passed from mother to offspring.

It also seems to be true that there are families that have a tendency to escape cancer—at least until late in life. There is no doubt there can be a genetic basis for this longevity. For instance, there may be an inherited ability to resist the formation of tumors because of the presence of tumor-suppressor genes, e.g., p53 genes.

What the Breeder Can Do to Help Prevent Cancer

The breeder's responsibility in producing a puppy that can avoid cancer and live to a ripe old age is to choose breeding stock from a litter whose ancestors live long lives. Longevity is now being considered among serious breeders, along with other criteria such as hips, eyes, hearts, and elbows, and structure. It is not an easy criteria because dogs are used for breeding in their younger years so that one can only hope that they will reflect the longevity of their ancestors. A dog used for breeding will not necessarily live to be 13. In addition you cannot tell what impact carcinogens have had on the premature death of a particular ancestor. Only by reviewing many generations can you get a sense of what the genetic endowment of the puppy might be. Thus, the breeder has two approaches to the problem of how to produce a puppy that may grow up to live to a ripe old age. One is to select puppies from a litter in which the parents and other ancestors had long lives. The second approach is to reduce the amount of carcinogens in the environment that could cause a mutation from a normal to a cancer-producing gene, and to encourage new owners to continue to avoid carcinogens in the future.

Perspectives on Treatment

In recent years, there has been a tremendous growth in cancer research, knowledge about the subject, and methods of treatment. Traditionally, there have been three methods by which cancer has been treated: (1)

Surgery when the cancer can be easily and completely removed. (2) Radiation, which kills whatever cells it strikes and is used when the cancer is not easily accessible surgically. (3) Chemotherapy, whereby chemotherapeutic agents (toxic chemicals) are used to kill the cancer cells.

Discussion of Treatments

Veterinarians administer to dogs the same chemotherapy drugs used in human oncology. Drugs used in chemotherapy have been selected due to their specific action on dividing cells because cancer cells are dividing rapidly and are, therefore, more vulnerable than normal cells to these agents.

There are also multimodality therapies, which involve some combination of surgery, radiation, and drug therapy. In the most common multimodality therapy, drug therapy follows surgery or radiation or both. Such follow-up treatment is called "adjuvant drug therapy," meaning that the effectiveness of the second agent enhances result(s) from the first. Because the drugs reach all the cells of the body, they may destroy cancer cells that have metastasized throughout the body.

More recently, other modes of treatment such as immunotherapies have been developed as more information is gathered about the function of cells.

The Immune System

The Immune system is instrumental in fighting cancer. Disease-fighting proteins called antibodies are produced naturally in the body. Thousands of different kinds are made by a type of white blood cell called a B-cell lymphocyte. ("B" refers to Bone marrow, the site of production.) Antibodies circulate in blood and bind to foreign substances called antigens that appear on the surface of infected cells. An antibody attaches to an antigen attached to the cell surface and marks that cell for destruction by other cells (typically macrophages). Methods to increase the activity of the immune system and to mimic its cancer-fighting activities are now being used, such as monoclonal antibodies, interferons, Interleukin-2, and other proteins that stimulate the growth of certain blood cells.

Monoclonal antibodies are an important type of immunotherapy. Monoclonal antibodies are made in the laboratory by combining a cancer cell with a B cell. Cancer cells have antigens on their cell surface, and the combination of the cancer cell and B-cell produces an antibody that recognizes and attaches to the antigens on that cancer cell. By returning these monoclonal antibodies to the body the cancer cells will thus be marked to be destroyed by the other cells of the immune system.

Interferons are proteins that cells produce to resist infection by viruses. When given after cancer surgery, interferons have delayed or prevented the reappearance of the cancer.

Interleukin-2 is a protein released by certain white blood cells to support and sustain the growth of other white blood cells that have been active in the destruction of cancer cells.

Research in cell biology has shown that cells that become cancerous can be changed back into normal cells. Drugs called differentiating agents have caused certain cancer cells to appear normal again.[63]

Prognoses

Current cancer treatment protocols extend the survival time of an average lymphosarcoma patient from two months to a year, with some ten percent of these cases never relapsing. With osteosarcoma, the average survival time is two months without treatment and 8 to 12 months with treatment. Only 20 percent of patients are alive two years after diagnosis. While these statistics seem grim, only the dog's owner knows the importance of this added time.

The main goal in cancer treatment must be to maintain the highest quality of life for our beloved Golden. As his guardian we owe him that. Our goal must be to minimize his suffering. In light of that, sometimes the only option is euthanasia. Euthanasia is a humane and responsible decision (no matter how painful for the owner), and a responsibility one assumes when one takes home that delightful puppy.

Chapter 22:
Perspectives on Hip Dysplasia

I:
Understanding Hip Dysplasia

Introduction

Of all the problems that face dog breeders, dog owners, and veterinarians, none is so problematic and controversial as Hip Dysplasia. The purpose of this discussion is to set forth some of the current thinking on the subject and to share some of my own observations, experiences, and conclusions with regard to the nature of the condition in the developing Golden Retriever puppy.

Definition

Hip dysplasia (HD), or Canine Hip Dysplasia (CHD), is, in the simplest of terms, any deviation of the hip joint from what an orthopedist considers perfection. This state of perfection is termed normal. It has been the goal of the hip certifying boards such as the OFA (Orthopedic Foundation for Animals) to certify only those dogs whose radiographs show no imperfections. Because the OFA receives radiographic films for evaluation predominantly from people who wish to have their dog certified for breeding, they will be for the most part the radiograph of a dog that appears functionally normal and has a radiograph that shows no easily seen abnormalities. In general, the films of dogs that are

233

clearly dysplastic are never sent to the OFA. Therefore, the films the OFA receives (with few exceptions) are those of a very select group of dogs. Of these, the OFA is failing approximately 20.5 percent of the films. Clearly, the dogs that are certified are a very select, and more importantly, a relatively small group, when compared to the total number of Golden Retrievers. From this I would estimate that possibly 85 percent of all Golden Retrievers have hip dysplasia if one uses the OFA's determination of hip dysplasia. The predisposition to hip dysplasia among Golden Retrievers has been reported as anywhere between 85 percent and 95 percent.[64] Before one becomes too discouraged, however, it has also been estimated that more then seventy-five percent of Goldens have no clinical symptoms (ongoing discomfort) after maturity.[65]

Of the dogs that are rated as normal by the OFA, they are further classified as excellent, good, or fair. There are also a number of hip ratings for those that are not considered to be normal, i.e., dysplastic. It should not be surprising to learn, therefore, that along with the definition there are degrees of hip dysplasia, depending upon a number of factors such as the size and shape of the ball and socket, degree of abnormal remodeling, depth of the ball in the socket, and the formation of the femur.

Furthermore, there is a distinction between what is termed radiographic HD and clinical HD. Radiographic HD is any deviation from perfection of the normal configuration of the hip joint as seen by the radiograph. Clinical HD would be the manifestation of pain or unsatisfactory use or function of the hip joint. I have heard it stated many times by veterinarians that there is a poor correlation between the radiographic evidence of HD in dogs and the clinical presentation (how the dog functions). Many dogs are radiographically very dysplastic but function normally or with little discomfort and the owner never notices any problem. Less frequently, there are dogs with a great deal of hip pain that have little or no visible radiographic abnormalities.

A Description of the Condition and Clinical Manifestations

Puppies are not born with HD. In fact there is no hip joint as such in the newborn; therefore the condition may not be called, in any sense of the word, congenital (which, by definition, means "to be present from birth").[66] The newborn has merely flat cartilage where the acetabulum (hip socket) will form and a bar of cartilage for the femur without the presence of the femoral head or "ball." The hip joint develops over time, and it is said that the ball and socket grow in apposition to each other, meaning that they grow in response to one another, not just that they grow in close proximity. If the leg of a newborn puppy were to be removed, there would be no development of an acetabulum at all. Such factors as strong ligaments and muscles surrounding the joint, which help keep the femur in close proximity to the acetabulum, will lead to the formation of a deep acetabulum and a round femoral head. Conversely, factors that separate the acetabulum and femoral head will lead to a shallow acetabulum and an imperfectly shaped femoral head—in other words, hip dysplasia. In light of the above, you can begin to see that there are both genetic (pertaining to genes) and environmental factors leading to the outcome of the hip joint.

The first sign of hip dysplasia is often that of looseness in the hips. If you place your hands on that region, you can feel a clicking or popping (Ortolani's sign) in the hip joint as the puppy moves around. However, in many cases there is no progression to any additional symptoms, and by twelve months the clicking can no longer be felt. (There may be earlier signs of weakness in the rear but these observations are usually transitory and quite often they are the result of the uneven growth of the puppy and may not be a sign of dysplasia.) Looseness of the hip, termed subluxation (joint laxity), has also been defined as dysplasia or as causing dysplasia.[67]

In other cases, especially when the puppy is too active (which is traumatic to his developing hips), or is overweight (which in and of itself places stress on his joints), the situation may worsen. Such affected puppies, typically at six months or thereabouts, are seen to be limping or stiff and slow to get up. This would most commonly be noticed after too strenuous exercise. This situation can be reversed, or at least not worsen, if the owner changes the life style of the puppy. If conditions are not changed, however, the dysplasia may progress, and in this case, the puppy may become noticeably larger (more developed) in the front than in the rear. The puppy ceases to use his rear properly due to the discomfort in the hip. The hindquarters, therefore, exhibit less muscle mass and the muscles of the rear feel light and stringy.

In this worst-case scenario, the puppy typically develops a roached back (i.e., an arched back, typical of the Greyhound), and the hind legs lose their angulation; that is, there is a straight line of bone from the hip to the foot. Both the roached back and the lack of angulation are a function of both poor muscle development and hip structure and are a compensation for these deficits. The puppy prefers to sit but usually has what is called a "sloppy sit"—that is, off to one side. He also has difficulty getting up, and when running will use the rear as a single unit, i.e., "bunny hopping." The puppy, formerly active at three to four months, is now usually subdued or depressed. He may spend a lot of time sleeping, which is probably due in part to the ongoing inflammatory response. His appetite may be minimal. He is most likely in pain when he moves, and this probably contributes to his sedentary behavior.

A large-breed puppy such as a Golden Retriever is predisposed to developing hip dysplasia because the growing puppy's skeletal system grows faster or precedes the development of the muscle mass, making the puppy intrinsically weak and vulnerable to trauma until he is full grown. The skeletal system reaches its full size by ten to twelve months, but the muscle mass does not reach its full maturity until about eighteen months.

Any additional weight from excess fat on a puppy will compound the problem. The ball and socket of the hip joint are held together by connective tissue and ligaments that have little or no elasticity. When stretched too much by excessive weight or perhaps "trauma," ligaments do not recover; that is, they do not return to their original length, but remain stretched, thus leaving space or laxity within the joint.[68]

A loose joint is even more vulnerable to injury and is susceptible to microscopic breaks within the cartilage cushion at the articular surface between the femoral head and the acetabulum. Once this occurs, events are set in motion that will continue to exacerbate the situation.

When there is trauma or tissue damage to the cartilage or soft tissue of the joint, the body responds in several ways that lead to more tissue damage. (See Chart 1.) For example, lysosomal enzymes, prostaglandins, and histamines are substances that are released locally in response to injury. These often cause swelling, heat, redness, and pain—symptoms that occur when one is injured—and these symptoms also occur when the hip is injured. In addition, there is an increase in metabolic activity, such as in the breakdown of glucose or the synthesis of certain molecules. This increase in chemical reactions leads to the production of free radicals. Normally, there are enough enzymes present in cells to adequately remove these free radicals; however, in the case of injury to the hips, the free radicals are released faster than they can be removed. Free radicals are very reactive and will damage other molecules with which they combine, causing further damage to the tissue by interfering with the metabolic pathways handling nutrients and waste.

Chondrocytes, which are cells within the cartilage, normally break down damaged cartilage and then rebuild new cartilage. The degradative process is controlled by enzymes, which are released in response to the injury. The cartilage loses its thickness and elasticity. This degradation process further weakens the cartilage of the puppy at a time when the hip joint is already fragile because of the injury to the hip joint and the negative effects of the subsequent inflammatory response. Prostaglandin released at the time of injury suppresses the chondrocyte synthesis of cartilage so that the cartilage is not being rebuilt normally. Also, as a result of histamine release there is an increase in blood flow to the area and an increase in the permeability of the local capillaries. This causes swelling and a movement of fluid

Chart 1

VICIOUS CYCLE OF JOINT DISEASE

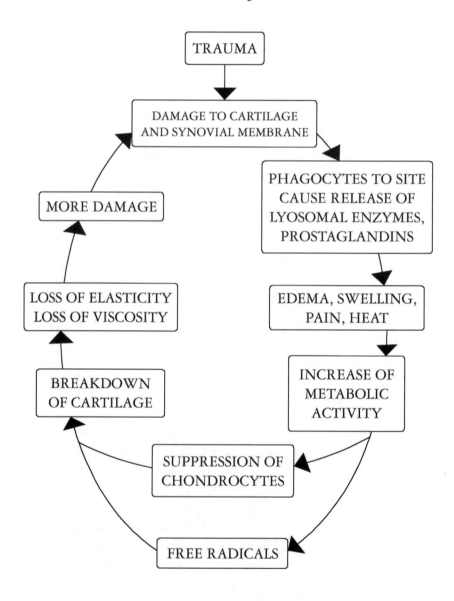

(edema) that also leaks into the synovial cavity in much the same way that "water on the knee" develops. The added fluid will cause additional separation of the ball from the socket. At the same time, the synovial fluid becomes less viscous not only because of this additional fluid, but because degradative enzymes enter the synovial space and break the long chains of hyaluronic acid into short segments, which adds to the loss of viscosity. In the acutely dysplastic dog, the synovial fluid is one tenth as viscous as normal synovial fluid. With the loss of viscosity, the synovial fluid provides less lubrication and cushioning to the joint. Also, with increased subluxation the joint becomes even more vulnerable to damage. The puppy in all his puppy exuberance continues to damage himself, and more wear and tear occurs.

If the femoral ball is not well-seated in the acetabulum, abnormal remodeling occurs. Remodeling in itself is a normal process by which mature bone is absorbed and gradually replaced by new bone. It is an ongoing process, but it can become abnormal, producing structures that are changed or malformed when acted upon by the abnormal forces present in the loose joint. What should be a round femoral head now becomes flattened and fits improperly into the acetabular space. With an improper fit there is a greater chance for damage to the joint, resulting in more inflammation and pain. And so the negative cyclical process continues: With the development of pain, there is less use of the muscles, which leads to the decline (atrophy) of the muscle mass. Without the muscles to protect the joint there is a greater risk of damage, and so, as this process continues, the puppy will become more and more lame (clinically dysplastic) and radiographically will show more space in the joints and more incorrect remodeling of the femoral head. This "worst-case scenerio" is estimated to occur in only five percent of Goldens. (HD exists in varying degrees: Some puppies have very mild symptoms that they outgrow, and some puppies have symptoms that are quite severe. But even the more serious cases will improve if the damaging cycle is stopped and if time is allowed for healing.)

There are basically two approaches to treat the symptoms of HD. One is called the "conservative approach." The other is surgical intervention. (See "Treatments and Prognoses," pp. 248–53.)

The Concept of Heritability

In the broadest of terms, heritability is an attempt to assign a proportion of the outcome of the hips (as with any trait for that matter) to a percent caused by genetic factors and percent caused by the environment. Heritability is the relative importance of these two factors (there are no others) as determined by statistical observations.

There are two points that I find interesting and that help explain the nature of the condition from a genetic perspective: (1) The heritability of HD has been shown over and over again in scientific studies to be between 12.5 percent and 40 percent for all dogs, and (2) Golden Retrievers, specifically, have been shown by scientific studies to be within the 20 percent to 25.9 percent range, meaning that approximately 20 percent to 26 percent of the outcome of the hips is determined by the genes and, therefore, 74 percent to 80 percent is due to environmental factors.[69]

Another way to understand heritability, and one that to my mind defines it more clearly is to put it in terms of a measure of how much of the variation, out of a given population's available variation, is inherited. If the heritability is low it means that most of the variation in the population is environmentally caused. Only if the heritability were 1.0 or 100 percent would the control of the development of the hip be due solely to the genes. "If heritability is high, selection has a large impact on future generations," and variation in the population is mainly due to the genetic endowment.[70]

Because Golden Retrievers have been shown to have a relatively low heritability, the formation of hip dysplasia is resistant to selection and is to a great degree under the influence of environmental factors. OFA statistics from 1972–1980, 1980–1988, and 1989–2000 show that there was no statistical improvement for Golden Retrievers during the first eighteen-year time period.[71]

To complicate the matter further, the recent study of genomics (the science of DNA analysis in order to determine the location of specific genes) is displacing classical techniques such as heritability analysis. Developmental factors are also being seen as more and more important in explaining the formation of hip dysplasia.[72]

To summarize: the outcome of the hips is a result of a genetic component in the Golden of 20 percent to 26 percent (in some breeds as high as 40 percent); and the genes are not disease-producing genes per se but are correlated to the type/conformation of the giant- and large-breed dogs. It is the interplay of both genetic and environmental factors that leads to the concept of heritability.

A Brief History

Let us examine briefly the history of the identification of hip dysplasia and then summarize three approaches in identifying and quantifying the condition that are each somewhat different but also complementary.

Identification of the Condition
In 1935 Dr. Gerry B. Schnelle (pronounced Schnell-e), later Chief of Staff of the Angell Memorial Animal Hospital in Boston, was the first to describe and name the condition called HD. Over a number of years he devised scores for measuring the severity of the disorder and the deviation of the hip from normal. In the 1950s and 1960s, others took up his work, sounded the alarm, and ran with it. Owners and breeders became increasingly worried, in fact even panic stricken. Dr. Schnelle soon became concerned about the damage his diagnosis-work was doing when he saw so many dogs being intentionally "put down," or subjected to the risk of surgery. Dr. Schnelle came to believe that the condition was not as threatening as he once believed, disavowed his "dire predictions," and recommended against surgery. He became an advocate for a more reasonable approach to understanding the condition. In a letter to a breeder of Golden Retrievers, he said:

In a very carefully controlled program the Swedes, in a ten year, ten thousand German shepherd dog program, did not succeed in reducing the incidence of HD. . . . I tell breeders to ignore the certification program and to breed the soundest, the best moving and the most suitable for the purpose for which the breed is intended and that is that. You have a somewhat acromegalic breed. . . . large size, loose skin, placid disposition and rapid growth and unless you choose to reduce these characteristics, you will have what is known as hip dysplasia in, I would guess, about a third of the pups. . . . The Swedes found that a wide pelvis and one that does not slope rearward too much (like the posed shepherd) provides a better "roof" over the hip joint and lessens the development of bad hips. They rightly call CHD a developmental disease and the "inherited" parts of it are those characteristics which allow it to develop or foster its development. I think that their work and their theories make the certification program a grand hoax on the breeder. Selecting dogs for breeding, in widely affected breeds, should not be based upon very slight differences in hip joint structure.[73]

Dr. Schnelle's observations were made in the 1970s and published in several journals. Unfortunately, his re-evaluation of the severity of the condition and its causes, and his more reasonable approach to understanding the condition, came too late to stem the tide of concern based on "dire predictions." Even today, Dr. Schnelle's retractions are not widely known and do not represent a majority opinion.

Current Approaches

Today, there are two approaches widely used in the United States with regard to measuring hip dysplasia and its severity: The oldest and most widely used is that of the OFA (Orthopedic Foundation of America), dating from the 1960s. More recent (1988) is that of PennHIP (University of Pennsylvania Hip Improvement Program).

The OFA: One of the first organizations to address the problem took place in the late 1960s and became known as the OFA (Orthopedic Foundation of Animals). Radiographs are taken by a local veterinarian and are then submitted to the OFA for evaluation and certification. The OFA was founded by Dr. Wayne Riser, who recognized an environmental component of the condition. He said that "all pups are born with normal hips. It is the physical stresses affecting this joint which can lead to laxity of the joint. And it is this laxity that promotes the degenerative changes characteristic of hip dysplasia."[74]

Under different management, the OFA's explanation of the condition called "hip dysplasia" is to refer to it as a "disease" that results in abnormal hip development, i.e., anything less than perfect ball and socket formation. At one time the OFA defined HD as joint laxity, but later defined it as any hip abnormality, whether of the ball or socket or femur or depth of fit. No credence is given to any environmental component, only that "some factors may affect the genetic expression of CHD." Nor is there any explanation other than that it is a hereditary or "genetic" problem"—an assumption not shared by others schooled in an understanding of heritability.

PennHIP: Originating around 1988, PennHIP uses a method whereby two radiographic views are taken: one with the femoral head compressed into the acetabulum (compression) and one with the head pulled out of the acetabulum (distraction). The two views are compared and the amount of femoral head displacement, called joint laxity, is measured and quantified. Dr. Gail Smith, chief of surgery at the University of Pennsylvania Veterinary School and the founder of the PennHIP program defines hip dysplasia as "a developmental hereditary (polygenic) condition characterized by progressive osteoarthritis of the hip joint beginning as early as 6 months of age." He states that he has made an in-depth study of hip dysplasia based on evidence and study that suggests that the cause of HD is hip joint laxity. Laxity, he says, "provides a conditional probability of the dog's susceptibility to hip dysplasia." Further, his approach measures degrees of passive laxity.[75] Furthermore, Dr. Smith's PennHIP data reveal that "Golden Retrievers were found to have a 42 percent to 60 percent incidence of CHD (based on the standard OFA method of hip evaluation). Moreover, data generated from the PennHIP diagnostic and scoring method . . . revealed that only 5 percent of Golden Retrievers in this study were truly unsusceptible to CHD"—i.e., 95 percent of Goldens are susceptible.

DLS: Not to be left out of the market of hip certification programs, researchers at the College of Veterinary Medicine at Cornell University have developed another imaging position called the dorso-lateral subluxation (DLS) position. A dog lying on his stomach is radiographed through his back (dorsally). Measuring femoral head coverage by the acetabulum in this position they hope to ascertain a more accurate measurement of the dysplastic or non-dysplastic status of the dog's hip—in other words, it is another way of determining the tightness of the fit of the femoral head into the acetabulum.[76]

The Importance of Selection

One cannot be an observer of the diversity of nature and the compelling and overwhelming evidence of evolution, without appreciating the great effect of both natural and artificial selection. In the past 400 years, dogs have evolved from a handful of breeds to 162 AKC recognized breeds and varieties.[77] When one considers the diversity that has resulted, from the tiny Chihuahua to the great giant breeds, it should not be surprising that selection has reduced the incidence of hip dysplasia. However, the tenets of population genetics tell us that you cannot select in every direction at once. You cannot select for perfect hips without changing other characteristics. For example, you cannot select for perfect hips and also select for large dogs with tremendous bone and huge heads. Certain traits are mutually exclusive.

A Closer Look at Environmental Factors

In summary, what can be said about the 74 percent to 80 percent of the outcome of the hips due to environmental factors? What are these environmental factors? From my experience, as well as from reading the literature, I would suggest the following possibilities:

1. Dietary Protein and Body Weight. The amount of protein fed the developing dog has been shown not to influence the development of hip dysplasia; however, nutrition is correlated with the appearance of HD. I believe that a high protein diet as well as moderate exercise has a protective effect on the developing Golden Retriever by fostering good bone and cartilage development and maximum muscle growth. This does not contradict the studies that have well documented the fact that excess food will lead to a greater incidence of HD because of the extra weight resulting from increased body fat having a negative impact on the developing hip.[78]

2. Trauma. Another suggestion has been that one should avoid having puppies romp, run, or walk on slippery floors, where minute slippage of the feet affects the hips and causes the femur to push against the capsule of the joint, and when done repeatedly will begin to strain or stretch the ligaments. Spurts of growth will also have this traumatic effect. It should be noted here that nowhere in the *Merck Veterinary Manual* (Seventh Edition, 1991) is it mentioned that HD is an "inherited disease." Rather it is stated that the "causes are unknown," but there is a strong implication throughout that "environmental stress," biomechanical stressors" or "biomechanical imbalance" may play a role in the development of the condition. Trauma is one such stress already mentioned.[79]

3. Exercise. Another factor is, of course, the kind and amount of exercise. People love to throw balls for adolescent puppies—perhaps something one shouldn't do; serious or severe exercise in a growing puppy could stretch the ligaments inappropriately, and as already noted, once stretched, ligaments never again recover their elasticity naturally. On the other hand, a Golden Retriever puppy doesn't need to go through long periods of inactivity, waiting for the owner(s) to return at the end of the day. In other words, an inactive puppy may be weaker than a puppy playing in the yard all day long, wrestling and romping with playmates (much as do dogs in the wild, where, incidentally, according to what I have read, puppies have not been observed exhibiting HD symptoms). It is the case that of the many

puppies that I have raised in my exercise areas, I have never raised a clinically symptomatic dysplastic dog. Perhaps this is due to my puppies wrestling and playing on the grass in an isometric fashion, which fosters muscle mass development, and maintaining an activity level of their own natural tolerance with playmates of the same size, age, weight, and energy level.

4. Muscle Mass. It is probable that all of the above factors may contribute to HD either acting alone or in combination. It is my further belief that insufficient muscle mass, whether depleted from crating or diminished from too little exercise, or even from an inherited genetic endowment for such, compounded by poor nutrition, can all contribute to poor musculature, and insufficient muscle mass may be the most proximate cause of HD. This agrees with my own observations of the dysplastic puppies that have been brought to me for examination and/or rehabilitation through the year.

Personal Insights and Experiences

As a result of my observations over a period of thirty years, I take serious exception to statements that suggest that HD is highly hereditary—as if the puppy was predetermined to have the condition. Such statements give a frightening impression to anyone not familiar with the scientific data and lead people to believe that they have been sold "defective goods" and that normal recuperative powers of the body will not be effective in overcoming the problems of the developing joint and musculature. On the other hand, I believe that HD may occur more frequently in certain types of individuals that have structures that predispose them to HD—for example, large Goldens with large heads and heavy bone and little musculature, or having weak ligaments and tendons that produce a greater tendency toward loose hips (joint laxity), which sets the stage for the trauma that leads to HD.

There are two points that I feel must be emphasized. One is this: Breeding for tighter hips, which is part and parcel of the certification programs, does reduce the frequency of HD, but it does inevitably change other characteristics of the dog, such as size, appearance, movement, and temperament. The second is: To label hip dysplasia as a purely genetic defect implies that surgery must intervene to correct the defective situation. If the dyplastic puppy is viewed as an injured puppy, going through a difficult period, rest and rehabilitation can be viewed as a normal recuperative process. Let's take a couple of real life examples:

A client comes to me in distress because in the course of a "routine examination" a radiograph was taken (suggested because "so many puppies have HD"), and the puppy was diagnosed as dysplastic even though he evidenced no signs or symptoms other than some joint laxity in the radiograph. Very often such a diagnosis is coupled with dire predictions that the "puppy will be crippled for life," with severe arthritis the inevitable result. It seems to me that the breeder and owner are not well served by such remarks. The owner is often sent to an orthopedic surgeon who warns the owner that there is a narrow window of opportunity for surgery to be performed to save the dog. The owner is understandably quite distressed but, after much counseling from me, the owner generally agrees to try the conservative approach of rest, weight loss if necessary, and gentle exercise until the puppy is fully grown. Inevitably such cases end happily with the puppy developing into a strong and fully functional adult.[80]

In another example, a young puppy named Winnie, who was particulary large and heavy boned and big headed, presented with symptoms of joint soreness and limping so severe that five orthopedic surgeons concluded that the puppy was too far gone even to undergo surgery. They recommended to the original client that the puppy should be "put down" after the client decided not to permit surgery and the puppy was returned for a full refund. Although my intuition about, and experience with, HD was not as strong as it is today, I decided that the puppy, after a few months of rest and recovery, could have a future after all, and gave him to a another client, with full disclosure, of course, about Winnie's history. Winnie turned out to be a magnificent dog; he came back to me over the years as a boarder. He could run like the wind and could even jump into the client's convertible in a single bound. He had no outward signs of arthritis. Later in life Winnie was hit by a car and had a pin placed in his femur; radiographs showed only minor malformation in one hip! Winnie made a full recovery from that car incident, too. He lived to be a few months more than 10 years of age, and he brought much joy to everyone.

Treatments and Prognoses

There are only two basic approaches to treating hip dysplasia that are presently in vogue in the veterinarian establishment: One is known as the "Conservative," or holistic approach; the other relies on surgical solutions. There are also a few alternative medical treatments as well as two approaches from authoritative sources.

The Conservative Approach
The conservative approach is that of doing everything possible, short of surgery, to stop the cyclical process of damage to the hip joint, and to allow the recuperative powers of the puppy's body to have time to heal and accommodate to those changes in the hip structure that cannot be reversed completely.[81] In summary, it involves the following: Rest or restricted exercise and nutritious diet; and nutraceuticals.

Rest and Diet. The puppy should have at least two weeks of enforced rest to allow microscopic breaks in the cartilage to heal. Exercise should be started only when no signs of pain are evident. Growth itself is an insult to the joints of a puppy. He should still be restricted to gentle exercise until at least ten months, when his bones have stopped growing. I prefer the puppy to exercise by himself in a small area so that he won't be stimulated to be overly active. The puppy should also be fed a nutritious diet to foster muscle development and healing, but the total calories should be limited to keep the puppy at a healthy lean weight. He should not have a heavy abdomen or fat on his ribs or have a great deal of subcutaneous fat.

Nutraceuticals: Dietary supplements such as Chondroitin Sulfate and Glucosamine, and antioxidants such as vitamins C and E that help in the healing process, can also be added to feedings. Chondroitin Sulfate and Glucosamine are natural substances found in animals. They are present in high concentrations in cartilage. As nutraceuticals they have been used for many years in Europe, but have just recently begun to be used widely in the United States. Some people report to me much success in feeding these joint-affecting nutraceuticals. Because they are the building blocks of cartilage, they have been found to be helpful in cartilage regeneration and are therefore useful in relieving the pain associated with the bone-to-bone contact that occurs when the cartilage is damaged or deficient. They are also believed to replenish and renew synovial fluid, which is important in the lubrication of the joint. In addition, Chondroitin Sulfate and Glucosamine also suppress the degradation process of tearing down damaged cartilage. Although the degradation is normally a beneficial process, it does cause additional problems in the already deficient cartilage.

Under normal circumstances the body is able to synthesize enough of these molecules for the chondrocytes to make all the cartilage needed. However, when there is damage to cartilage, the body does not synthesize enough, and supplements have been found to help the chondrocytes rebuild the damaged cartilage as well as to inhibit the degradation that occurs when cartilage is damaged.

In the synthesis of new cartilage, Glucosamine is involved in the production of glycosaminoglycans that combine with hyaluronic acid to form proteoglycans. The proteoglycans and collagen are the main molecules of cartilage. Chondroitin Sulfate is also necessary for the synthesis of glycosaminoglycans. However, it plays another very important role in the health of the joint. It is a necessary process that old cartilage be broken down so that it can be replaced with new cartilage. This is under the direction of enzymes from the chondrocytes.

As in many biological systems, there is a feedback mechanism whereby the degradative process is inhibited by the presence of a product of the degradation process itself. In this case it is the chondroitin. It is also important to remember that, as cartilage is broken down, glycosaminoglycans will release chondroitin. The chondroitin in turn will then inhibit the enzymes that break down the cartilage. It seems to be the case that in acute hip dysplasia the degradative process, in response to the damaged cartilage, overreacts and leads to a vicious cycle of more cartilage loss, which causes more bone-to-bone contact, pain, and soreness, which leads to muscle atrophy, thus making the puppy more vulnerable to joint damage, especially during bursts of play without the protection of the muscles. Also at this time the synovial fluid is less viscous probably due to the movement of inter-cellular fluid into the damaged and inflamed joint capsule. With more fluid in this space, the ball is being pushed farther out of the socket. With the addition of the chondroitin and Glucosamine to the diet, the process can begin to be reversed. Degradation of cartilage is slowed, the manufacture of new cartilage is enhanced, the damaged cartilage is repaired, the inflammation subsides, mobility returns, muscles re-spond, and although the puppy will never be a good as new, the crisis is over and the healing has occurred.

Antioxidants such as vitamins C and E as well as Dismutase are believed to help remove the free radicals that are present in increased amounts in the dysplastic joint.

Prognosis Using the Conservative Approach

In a mildly affected puppy, reducing the amount of severe and dam-aging exercise while increasing gentle, strengthening exercise such as trotting, can reverse the situation quickly. If the puppy is limping but has none of the other symptoms, two weeks of rest followed by gentle exercise is typically all that is necessary to put the puppy back on track. In the worst cases, however, I see little improvement in the symptoms of the severely dysplastic puppy until several months pass. With rest there will be little further damage, the breaks in the cartilage will be repaired, and the inflammatory response will end, but it seems to be necessary for some time to pass, probably for the puppy's growth to end, before compensations can be completed.

When the puppy reaches 11 or 12 months, the puppy will rapidly begin to improve. His demeanor changes, and he appears to be less depressed and more comfortable. The puppy begins to trot about and to regain better musculature and proper angulation in the rear. The roach in the back tends to disappear, and the puppy becomes much more playful and no longer sits or lies down excessively.

The puppy will continue to grow stronger until about 18 months, and then tends to remain the same until old age. It will always be to the dog's advantage for you to keep his weight down and keep him well exercised in order for the muscles to compensate for the weaker hip structure. Although much improved, dogs that have experienced the worst symptoms will usually evidence a front end that normally remains somewhat larger than the rear end. The dog may tire more rapidly with exercise than would a dog with "perfect" hips. Any illness that causes the loss of muscle mass through inactivity will have a negative but transitory effect of stiffness. The severely dysplastic dog seems less able to handle icy surfaces and could injure or re-injure the hip joint when on slippery surfaces.

I am not aware of any study that shows that a puppy exhibiting dysplasia will not substantially compensate for his hip deficit and greatly improve in function with rest and the passing of time (nor that degenerative arthritis is inevitable). Once the growth has stopped, the microscopic breaks in the cartilage have healed, and the inflammatory response to these breaks has ceased, the puppy can start an exercise program that will provide muscles to compensate for the lack of a normal hip joint. In most cases following this regime, the puppy will show a great deal of improvement and will be moving satisfactorily by eighteen months.

Surgical Solutions

There are several surgical procedures, depending on the age of the dog, that are used by the orthopedic surgeon. One is the triple pelvic osteotemy (TPO). This procedure is used in puppies younger than ten months of age. This is an expensive operation where the pelvis is broken in three places and moved closer to the femoral head. Generally, the less severe cases of dysplasia are considered to be better candidates for this surgery by the surgeon. The recuperative time is about six weeks—not too different from the time involved in seeing positive results from adopting "the conservative approach."

Another operation often performed on older dogs with problems that have not responded to the conservative approach is the femoral head excision. In cases where there is bone-to-bone contact within the hip, there will be a great deal of pain. Cartilage normally cushions the joint and does not have the pain receptors, so no pain is felt. The bone, however, has pain receptors, so that pain is generated when there is rubbing between two bones. In these cases, the head of the femur, if cut off, will regenerate a new surface within the hip joint that is cushioned with new cartilage and is therefore usually free of pain.

Total hip replacement can be performed on mature dogs. In this procedure, the hip joint is replaced by a prosthesis. This is expensive surgery and requires a three-month rest period, but can have good results, although a few people have reported to me that they were unhappy with the outcome.

Alternative Medical Treatments

In addition to those remedies mentioned in the "Conservative Approach" section above, pain killers such as buffered aspirin, corticosteroids, or non-steroidal anti-inflammatory drugs (NSAIDs, such as Rimadyl® [carprofen]) are usually prescribed. Although they make the dog more comfortable, they may have side effects and may also encourage the dog to be too active considering the state of his hips. Adequan® is another product that contains glycosaminoglycan, which is another compound that is used in the synthesis of cartilage. It is administered by a series of shots.

Massage and acupuncture have been used with some success. Both may improve circulation and diminish pain in the affected area, and may be helpful in strengthening muscles.

Two Authoritative Sources

Statements about the necessity of surgery and the poor prognosis if surgery is not performed are in conflict with advice set forth in *The*

Journal of Small Animal Practice, with statements by Dr. Gerry B. Schnelle, PennHIP, knowledgeable veterinarians, and with my own experience with caring for Goldens that have gone through the symptomatic phases of the condition. In addition, it is my considered opinion that the developmental instability that occurs in some growing puppies, which sometimes leads to dysplasia, is usually of no great consequence in the quality of life of the adult and what he can offer as a companion.

Finally, two authoritative sources in the foregoing paragraph commenting on the condition are instructive:

1. *The Journal of Small Animal Practice*, 28, 243–52, 1987: In this journal, it was concluded that conservative therapy, defined as controlling weight and restricting a dog's activity to short walks until the animal was 15 months old, resulted in a 76 percent recovery. By recovery is meant that the dogs had "either a normal gait or only slight abnormalities." In 63 percent of dogs, "lack of discomfort was noted," and "79% had a normal range of movement. Exercise tolerance was reported normal in 72% of the cases." Further, it has been observed that "spontaneous improvement" occurs in a high majority of cases as the animals mature.[82]

2. On the nature of surgical intervention: Dr. Gail Smith of PennHIP has concluded that it would be advisable for the surgeon to share with the pet owner the advice in 1., above; and further, that it is a major concern when TPO is offered as a preventive precaution when there is no clinical manifestation of HD.[83]

II:
From Old Ways of
Thinking (Reductionism)
to a New Science of Understanding

One serious misconception in present "scientific" thinking is still the old view that one gene is responsible for, or translates into, one trait. This has led to the gross oversimplification that problems in the development of the hip were due to the presence of "bad" genes that failed to code for the "right" proteins and therefore the hip was malformed. This kind of thinking grew out of what has been termed the reductionist method. From its beginning in the seventeenth century, modern science has largely worked within what is called a reductionist mode of thought, which maintained that breaking down complex situations into their basic parts could explain them. The reductionist method works very well for simple systems such as predicting the motion of planets, but fails when it comes to complex systems such as biology.

Although the "central dogma" of Biology, i.e., the view of life as a one-way directional flow from gene to protein, or from DNA (the molecule transmitting genetic information) to the total organism, remains generally intact, this explanation is now considered to be too simplistic. Moreover, as a consequence of recent discoveries, the explanation of the doctrine that one gene translates to one trait, and the old view of life as a simple one-way directional flow from the basic DNA to the formation of proteins that comprise the total organism, is now under attack. For reasons discussed below, it is now becoming clear that other genes and the environment play a role in the expression of genes and, in turn, how they function.[84]

Relevance of the Human Genome Project to Developmental Biology and Canine Development

Recently a great milestone has been reached in the history of science and genetic understanding when it was announced that the Human Genome Project had been completed. In light of this milestone it would behoove us to review our understanding of hip dysplasia and see where the scientific community stands in understanding the genetics and development of hip dysplasia and what new light this sheds on our understanding of the causes and even the outcomes of canine hip dysplasia.

The sequencing of the human genome is beginning to lead to new understandings of the function of genes. The key to the development of different and more complex organisms such as the mammalian body is not that of more genes per se, but rather more combinations and interactions of a few genes and their sequential timing. These interactions must be explained at the level of the turning on and off of genes that influence in turn not only the turning on (or off) of other genes of the organisms but also brings into play the effect of the environment on turning genes on and off. In other words, the organism cannot be explained simply as a summation of total genes.

Using the recent example of the completed sequencing of the human genome, it is estimated that there may be fewer than 40,000 human genes. The canine genome is estimated to between 60,000 and 100,000 genes. These genomes contain billions of bits of letter information: A,T,C,G, which direct the development of trillions of body cells. Another organism, the roundworm *C. elegans*, which has been well studied in the research laboratories, contains around 19,000 genes but only 959 cells. In other words, our bodies develop under the directing influence of only half again as many genes as the tiny roundworm needs to manufacture its simplistic form. Human complexity, it has been said, cannot be generated by 30,000 to 40,000 genes; it can only be explained if we envision several kinds of solutions for generating many times more messages (resulting in proteins) than genes. In the most widely accepted current mechanism, a single gene can make several messages because genes of multicellular organisms are not discrete strings, but composed of coding segments (exons) separated by noncoding regions (introns). The resulting signal that eventually assembles the protein consists only of exons spliced together after elimination of introns. If some exons are omitted, or if the order of splicing changes, then several distinct messages can be generated by each gene. Even more messages can result from a particular gene if one takes into account that the way proteins are "folded" also determines their function.[85]

The relevance of this to hip dysplasia is that one cannot rely on the removal of a "bad gene" for hip dysplasia as a method for removing hip dysplasia from the breed. This has been found to be a too simplistic and even harmful idea. The weight of evidence simply does not support the conclusion that hip dysplasia can be ascribed to the action of a particular gene or even a group of genes. It has long been known that the inheritance of hip dysplasia has been under the influence of both the environment and the genes. Furthermore, it is now becoming clear that the genes themselves are being turned on and off by the expression of other genes, which are in turn influenced by other genes as well as environmental factors. Is it any wonder that simple selection has not eliminated hip dysplasia?

III:
The Focus of Modern Research

Genetics vs. the Role of the Environment

For the past thirty years the main focus of bioscience has been on genetic research. So much has been written about the genome projects, genetic-marker research, and discovery of genes for certain diseases that one is left with the impression that very soon genes or DNA will hold the answer to eliminating every disease. Although there are some positive contributions made by the study of genetics, other scientists point out that there are risks in its over-commercialization.[86] Living organisms are complex and the effect of genetic tinkering is far more profound than replacing a "bad" gene with a "good" gene.

There are terms one often hears in discussions of hip dysplasia. By saying hip dysplasia is "polygenic," one means that many genes are involved in the predisposition to the condition. The situation, however, is far more complicated than simply identifying the responsible gene(s), or replacing genes that produce hip dysplasia with other genes. The genes involved have more than one effect on the development of the dog, and while some of these effects are involved in producing the condition, others are contributing to desirable traits.

It is also understood by many researchers that the genes that make dogs into large or giant breeds are also the genes that render a growing puppy susceptible to joint and other skeletal problems. It is for this reason that one does not change the susceptibility to hip dysplasia through selection without changing the breed—such as, for example, the size of the dog. There are undoubtedly other factors that are influenced by genes—such as muscle mass and the strength of collagen and muscle fibers. These factors, and probably many more, have an impact on the development of the hip joint.

Hip dysplasia is also said to be "multifactorial"; that is to say, a result of a genetic endowment and the influence of the environment. In other words, both genetic factors and environmental factors are involved in the production of the condition. Environmental factors include nutrition, weight, exercise, and trauma as well as many other external and internal factors that contribute to, and affect, the development of the hip structure and conformation as well as the progression of hip dysplasia.

Studies funded by the Purina Ralston Company during the past 14 years (see: www.purina.com) have shown that the amount of weight a puppy carries can be a predictor of the occurrence of hip dysplasia. This is just one of several environmental factors that influence the development of hip dysplasia. A greater knowledge of all the potential factors would contribute to a better understanding of the condition and thus help prevent the occurrence of hip dysplasia.[87]

One problem with thinking that all health conditions are linked to genes is that such thinking does not focus our attention and resources on what is happening in the environment that causes diseases. As I have already indicated, in large breeds of dogs such as the Golden Retriever, the genes that have been selected to make such a large dog are also genes that render a dog susceptible to joint problems such as hip dysplasia. These genes produce the rapid growth that is necessary if the dog is to attain its large size during its growth period. Because the growth of the skeletal system precedes the growth of the muscle mass, Goldens and other large-boned breeds are prone to problems during adolescence. In this intrinsically unstable adolescent period, the rapidly growing skeletal system does not yet have enough musculature to support it, and the joints can become loose due to the stretching of the ligaments and the less developed muscles of the hip joint.[88] It has also been suggested that a certain amount of laxity may even be "normal" to allow for growth.

After many generations of selection of parents without hip dysplasia, the condition in Golden Retrievers has not been eliminated. Yet millions of dollars have been spent on the X-rays and certification of breeding stock. Would it not be better to spend some of these funds on research to determine the environmental factors that lead to hip dysplasia? Furthermore, the dog owner will spend money on radiographs when it is already known that the dog has a problem. Yet little guidance and attention is paid to giving the puppy owner advice on how to raise the puppy to prevent hip dysplasia or, once started, how to limit its effect.

To look at a problem only in terms of a collection of genes leads us to conclude that there is nothing we can do to influence the prevalence of hip dysplasia. On the other hand, to view the puppy as a growing system that is largely under the control of the environment we provide him, gives us much more control by changing things such as food, diet, and exercise. The nature-nurture dialogue is complex.

Pleiotropy and the Complexity of Selection

As one begins to see that there is no such thing as a purely genic cause for HD, our attempt to explain the nature of the condition from a genetic perspective or to "blame" the condition on "bad genes" is not valid because of the relatively large role the environment plays. Furthermore, in our selection for certain characteristics that we love in the Golden Retriever, we are probably setting the stage for the development of HD. To repeat what Dr. Schnelle wrote: "The determining factors are: the heavier bones, the acromegalic type, the broader body, the placid temperament qualities, the fuller face, the more juvenile personality." These characteristics also go along with a more structurally unstable puppy.

In addition to the fact that the assortment of the genes is a "rolling of the dice," and one cannot know which genes will come together in a given puppy, we are dealing with a growth and development situation that has previously been characterized as polygenic and multifactorial, i.e., the factors impinging on the development of the hip are both environmental as well as due to the endowment of the genes and other developmental interactions. This definition needs clarification and more explanation in order to be understandable to today's dog owners or breeders.

Polygenic means not only that there are many genes involved in the predisposition of a condition, but that each gene is exerting a small quantitative effect. In other words, the phenotype is controlled by several genes, each having an additive effect.[89]

There is, in addition, another concept at work: "pleiotropy," defined as the effect a given gene has on more that one characteristic. These effects can be very important, especially when the gene acts in opposite directions.[90] This occurs if a gene increases one character and decreases another, or improves one feature while making another worse.

It is generally agreed that the concept of pleiotropy is the rule in Biology rather than the exception, and fits all we know from the study of the way in which development takes place. For example, as one selects for a tighter hip one may be simultaneously selecting for a stronger muscle mass, but one may also be selecting for a dog that is smaller. Or one may be selecting a more athletic dog, which could be considered a positive trait by some, but negative or "hyper" by others. Or it could be a dog that may move without great reach and extension due to the tighter conformation. (Some show people recognize that looser hips may result in greater reach and extension and beauty of movement.)

It is my further belief that the fact that hip dysplasia has not responded well to selection is because we are selecting for type and temperment of the Golden that we all love. In other words, to say it more succinctly, such breeds as the Greyhound, Borzoi, or Wolfhound have the most perfect joint conformation. These breeds are relatively free of hip dysplasia because they have a narrow pelvis: their hips are closer together than the hips found in the Golden or other breeds susceptible to hip dysplasia. The susceptibility is a result of the weight of the abdomen being partially suspended from the hips; the farther apart these points are from each other, the less stable the hip is. As we breed more perfect hips in the Golden Retriever, the conformation would be progressing more and more toward the conformation of the Greyhound or the Borzoi—the narrower hips, finer-boned, roached-back dog—not the type for which our breed is known, i.e., the heavy-boned, substantial, placid type that many prefer. In contemplating the difficulty of selecting in all directions at once, you will see not only the complexity of the problem but in some ways its insolubility.

Yet there is an answer. A Golden can be bred, and is being bred, that has most of the characteristics we want and at the same time, when raised under favorable conditions, will not develop hip dysplasia. Unfortunately, to quote Olsson & Schnelle, "anything that interferes with the normal growth and development of the hip joint can give rise to hip dysplasia."[91]

Heritability is not inevitability. I say this from my own experience of going from a situation in the 1970s, where most Goldens were dysplastic, to the situation today, where we rarely have a dog that we raise fail to pass the OFA. I attribute this to providing puppies in my care with the correct environment as well as exercising the power of selection, e.g., by breeding 10 generations of certified dogs and by using dogs in the breeding program that have demonstrated an unusual ability to produce offspring with sound hips and at the same time not changing the type and purpose. It is also my goal to advise owners how important environmental factors are in the development of normal hips and how important it is that they provide the puppy with the proper conditions for that purpose.

End Notes

Information about any of the citations below
may be obtained from the author.

1. Imprinting, which is distinguished from true learning, refers to "a critical (or sensitive) period when the phenomenon is most likely to occur.
After this period is over, there is little or no reversal—that is, once in
place, imprinting cannot be undone or even forgotten." (*The Animal
Mind*, by James L. Gould and Carol Grant Gould, Scientific American
Library, 1999, p. 36.) Although "imprinting studies have been done
mostly with antelopes, ducks, geese, and salmon, and some primates,"
my observations refer to Goldens specifically. I am not aware of any
studies on the breed, but the phenomenon would seem to be ubiquitous.

2. The discovery of this burial was mentioned in Kenneth J. McNamara,
Shapes of Time: The Evolution of Growth and Development (Johns Hopkins
University Press, 1997), p. 247. See also the article in *National Geographic*
(January 2002): "Wolf to Woof, The Evolution of Dogs," pp. 4–11.

3. Richard Dawkins, *River Out of Eden: A Darwinian View of Life* (Basic-
Books, 1995), pp. 1–29. This chapter is an excellent introduction to understanding life in a Darwinian way.

4. In the classic book *Man Meets Dog* (Penguin 1954) by Konrad Lorenz, the
world-renowned ethologist discusses his own deep bond with his beloved
canines. Lorenz was also the person whose studies of imprinting were
seminal and much admired. Another interesting reference to the historical bond between canines and their human companions is Angus Phil-
lips, "A Love Story, Our Bond with Dogs," *National Geographic* (January,
2002), pp. 14–31.

5. Charles Darwin, in *The Variation of Animals and Plants Under Domestication* (vol. 1: 1868; second edition, revised), pp. 15–45, offers an overview of the domestication of dogs from the Neolithic period through the
Bronze and Iron periods, and a perspective on the great antiquity of the
canine's relationship with *H. sapiens*. He makes a strong argument in
favor of several breeds of dogs being the descendants of distinct wild
stocks, pointing out that domestication was not a big issue, since the
Canidae are social animals "that inhabit nearly the whole world." "When
man first entered any country," he writes, "the animals living there
would have felt no instinctive or inherited fear of him," and he provides
several examples of a lack of fear of humans in different species of wild

263

animals, including canines. He also mentions the resemblance of half-domestic Asian and African dogs resembling jackals, which "agree closely in habit" [i.e., have similar traits] to tamed jackals, an observation also pointed out by Konrad Lorenz—traits that closely resemble those of our own Golden Retrievers today. Darwin also notes that selection by Man has resulted in a great variety of breeds being produced in a very short period of time, according to climate and purpose, a process akin to natural selection.

6. There are around 500,000 to 550,000 registered Goldens alive in the United States today, based on an average life expectancy of 10.5 years. Statistics are based on yearly litter registrations reported in the *AKC Gazette* (June 2003 through June 2004, during which time around 52,000 Goldens were registered).

7. Desmond Morris, *Dogwatching: Why dogs bark and everything else you ever wanted to know* (Crown 1986), pp. 17–27. Morris discusses barking, howling, and tail wagging in an informative way. The observations presented here, however, are my own.

8. Refer to Gould and Gould, *The Animal Mind*, note 1, above. The discussion of play behavior (pp. 163–69) covers mostly birds and mammals, the species that have been mostly studied. This book is one of the best studies on behavior and suggests that the gap between human and animal consciousness is not as great as many believe. More specifically, Patricia McConnell in *The Other End of the Leash* (Ballantine Books 2002) points out that humans and canids retain their play behavior into adulthood, and the games we love to play are those associated with our canids—especially, I might add, those of following and retrieving small or large objects, such as balls and birds.

9. For paedomorphosis in canines, see McNamara, *Shapes of Time: The Evolution of Growth and Development,* pp. 247–50. It should be added to this account, however, that, although it is generally believed that modern dogs are descended from wolves, especially those in Europe and North America, "other species of wild dogs, for example jackals, have probably contributed to their ancestry." In this regard see John Maynard Smith, *The Theory of Evolution,* (Cambridge University Press, Canto Edition, 1993), pp. 145–47, who also agrees with Darwin and Lorenz. See also note 5, above. It should be noted, however, that in a recent study comparing the DNA of 162 wolves worldwide with 140 domestic dogs representing 67 breeds as well as five coyotes and 12 jackals (of which two were Golden jackals and two black-backed jackals), the investigators

concluded that the wolves differed from domesticated dogs by 12 nucleotide substitutions and from the coyote and jackals by 20 substitutions (*Bioscience,* 1977, pp. 725–28). A more recent study using similar subjects and numbers for study indicates that Eurasian wolves may be the progenitors of New World dogs (*Science,* 22 Nov. 2002, pp. 161ff.). Not every dog researcher, however, is convinced. Some researchers believe that the origins of the dog are still controversial and insist that dogs probably stemmed from jackals or some hybrid canid or another extinct ancestor (*Science,* 22 Nov. 2202, pp. 1540–42).

10. Desmond Morris, *Dogwatching*, pp. 69–70.
11. Ibid., pp. 73–75. See also John Maynard Smith, *The Theory of Evolution*, p. 135.
12. This phenomenon was first brought to my attention by the molecular biologist, Bjørn Grinde. See his *Darwinian Happiness: Evolution as a Guide for Living and Understanding Human Behavior* (Darwin Press 2002), p. 30.
13. Morris, *Dogwatching*, pp. 71–72.
14. According to George C. Williams, "Deaths are not the data to be collected but merely the events that must end the data collection." The true data to be collected are "the vital functions of individuals through a succession of years." Williams correctly states that "there is no programmed *natural death*, nor any characteristic life span for [a] species. The age distribution of mortality rates results from an interaction between the evolved rates of senescence and the rigors of the environment in which the living takes place" (*Plan and Purpose in Nature*, Weidenfeld & Nicolson 1996, p. 126). Efforts to increase canine longevity by awarding ribbons to Golden Retriever owners after the death of their long-lived canines would therefore seem to be a waste of time and purpose.
15. One of the best introductions to the breed is *The Golden Retriever*, by Joan Tudor (Howell Book House: U.S. distributor, 1970). The opening chapter, "The Origin of the Breed," pp. 15–25, is an excellent overview of the beginnings of the breed. Chapters 2 and 3 bring the history up to 1939 and continues with the history of the breed in the United States and Canada to the end of the 1960s (pp. 168–81). See also, Jeffrey Pepper's book, *The Golden Retriever* (T.F.H. Publications, 1984), which is an excellent review of Canadian kennels (pp. 205–11) and United States kennels (pp. 223–77) through the early 1980s.
16. Quoted in *Golden Retriever News* (date unknown, probably 1948).
17. Personal communication. Warren Eckstein's book, *How to Get Your Dog to Do What You Want: A Loving Approach to Unleashing Your Dog's Aston-*

ishing Potential (Ballantine Books 1994) emphasizes an overall positive approach to raising a dog, beginning with puppy-hood. Reading this book will repay dividends to any dog owner.

18. Katherine Houpt, VMD, Ph.D., *DogWatch* (February 2003), p. 7. *Dog-Watch* is a publication of the Cornell University College of Veterinary Medicine.

19. Note 1, above.

20. Personal communication with a veterinarian reporting a conversation with a manufacturer of vaccines.

21. *The Merck Veterinary Manual*, Eighth edition (Merck & Co., 1998), pp. 949–50.

22. Marc Bekoff's research covers a variety of contexts in which animals and humans play. The complete title of his book is *Animal Play: Evolutionary, Comparative, and Ecological Perspective* (Cambridge University Press, 1998).

23. For overall balanced nutritional requirements, see "Puppy Diet Primer" and "Puppy Food Guide," by Amy D. Shojai in *Dogs USA, 2004 Annual*, pp. 78–95. Another good discussion may be found in *You & Your Puppy: Training and Health Care for Puppy's First Year*, by James DeBitetto and Sarah Hodgson (Howell, 1995), pp. 154–61. And an article entitled "Large-Breed Dogs: Feeding Proper Nutrient Amounts Can Help Prevent Developmental Bone Disease" (*DogWatch*, April 2002, p. 7) discusses in detail what the proper nutrients are and warns against supplementing a complete and balanced food diet with excess amounts of minerals and vitamins, which may be detrimental to a puppy's healthy development.

24. A super little booklet that may be quite useful in helping you understand how to prevent problems as well as how to raise a puppy in a positive way is Peter J. Vollmer's *SuperPuppy: How to Raise the Best Dog You'll Ever have!* (SuperPuppy® Press, 1992). Vollmer is also the author of *Super-Puppy Goes to Puppy Class: How to Train the Best Dog You'll Ever Have* (SuperPuppy® Press, 1992).

25. For a general overview of vaccinations, see *The Merck Veterinary Manual*, Eighth edition, pp. 1870–73. There is also a small pamphlet, "Roundtable on enteric Disease in Dogs," published by the Veterinary Forum (June 2001), in which different veterinarians discuss the reasons for various vaccination protocols.

26. Your veterinarian needs to be consulted about what protocol is best for your puppy.

27. In the laboratory, "challenge" testing means to give the animal a little

bit of the disease to see how it responds. Reference: AMVA Council on Biologic and Therapeutic Agents, *AMVA Journal*, 15 Nov. 2002.

28. Note 23, above.

29. In an article appearing in the *American Kennel Club Gazette* (n.d., 1977?), "Two Experts Address Developments in Canine Hip Dysplasia (CHD)," Dr. Wendell O. Belfield (Bel-Mar Orthomolecular Veterinary Hospital in San Jose, California) reported in *Veterinary Medicine, Small Animal Clinician* (October, 1976) as follows: "During the evolution of vertebrates, stress has been a constant companion of developing animals. . . . One of the main biochemical systems for neutralizing the adverse effects of stress, and one for whose importance is currently not fully recognized, is the enzyme system for converting blood glucose to ascorbate (incorrectly called vitamin C). This system is not situated in the mammalian liver. . . . The major biochemical functions of ascorbate are as an antistressor and detoxicant, and as a necessary metabolite for maintaining biochemical homeostasis in the animal's body." The complete article contains explanations by two medical experts, Dr. Schnelle and Dr. Belfield, on the subject of hip dysplasia—explanations that need to be taken more seriously. Belfield's comments about vitamin C (as ascorbate) have been questioned by those who insist on double-blind studies.

Further on the subject of vitamin C, John E. Craigie, VMD, wrote: "Vitamin C is non-toxic. If it is given in overdoses it does not cause any serious or permanent damage; it is merely secreted. Vitamin C is essential to practically every metabolic function of the body. Hip dysplasia is largely a disorder of the collagen of the ligaments and cartilage of the hip joints. Vitamin C is essential to collagen metabolism. Some of the first research that was reported on hip dysplasia showed that [the condition] was produced by a lack of vitamin C" (*Kennel Review*, 1978).

30. Free radicals are chemicals that can exist having one or more unpaired electron, so that there is a single unpaired electron in the outer orbit. The stable or non-reactive state is for the molecule to have two electrons in the outer orbit. A free radical is made by either the gain or loss of an electron. The remaining single electron strongly attracts a new electron from another molecule. When it bonds to this molecule, the reaction is very destructive to the molecule and to the cell that contains the molecule. See also the explanation in the Glossary.

31. Smith, G. K., Biery, D. N., Kealy, R. D. and D. F. Lawler, "Effects of Restricted Feeding on Onset, Incidence, and Severity of Hip Dysplasia and Osteoarthritis in Dogs: Diagnostic, Therapeutic, and Genetic Rami-

fications" (The Purina Pet Institute Symposium: Advancing Life Through Diet Restriction. St. Louis, Mo., September 20–21, 2002): "The mean protein content was measured at 27.5%. CD was more frequent, developed earlier, and became more severe in dogs with rapid weight gain caused by increased caloric intake, compared with dogs with low weight gain because of restricted feeding."

32. Chapter 19, "Your Puppy's First Visit to the Vet," by Jean H. Cunningham-Smith, VMD., p. 200.

33. In his first book, *Give Your Dog a Bone* (1993), Dr. Ian Billinghurst introduced this diet based on the canine's evolution. Another recent book, *The BARF Diet* (2001), is an updated version on the same topic. The acronym "BARF" is also used to refer to the diet in another way: Biologically Appropriate Raw Food.

34. Rutgers, H. C. et al. "Small intestinal bacterial overgrowth in dogs with chronic intestinal disease" (*J. Am. Vet. Med. Assoc.* 1995; 206: 187–93).

35. You cannot take gossip for granted, or even knowledge, that one litter shows evidence of megaesophagus. If subsequent litters were totally free of megaesophagus, then the entire premise that a major testing program is necessary would be entirely destroyed. Nor can a diagnosis always be considered accurate. In my experience, I have seen a vet diagnose a puppy as having megaesophagus, when in fact an autopsy revealed that the puppy had intussusception.

36. Stephen J. Birchard, DVM, and Robert G. Sherding, DVM, eds. *Saunders Manual of Small Animal Practice* (2nd edition, 2000, W. B. Saunders), pp. 1349–50.

37. Another hypothesis is that male puppies are affected (or feminized) by estrogen from female puppies in the litter. Only with the presence of a relatively higher level of testosterone will the gonad migrate to its position outside the body.

38. In an article, "Another Look at the Hip Dysplasia Question," appearing in *Pure-Bred Dogs, American Kennel Gazette* (n.d., pp. 31 and 38), two expert authorities presented their views on the impact of the environment on the condition of HD as follows: (1) "Hip dysplasia and its degree of severity as it is diagnosed on radiographs are influenced more by environmental factors not surely identified but which might include diet, exercise, etc. than by hereditary factors." (2) "Anything that interferes with the normal growth and development of the hip joint can give rise to hip dysplasia." (3) "If some laxity of the hip joints should be a criterion of abnormal hips, then there are no normal hips in the German Shepherd

breed. Nor are there any in Golden Retrievers, nor in beagles." The two authorities are Professor Sten-Erik Olsson (Head of the Department of Clinical Radiology, Royal Veterinary College, Stockholm, Sweden, and Special Consultant in Comparative Orthopedics at the Hospital for Special Surgery, Cornell University, New York City) and Dr. Gerry B. Schnelle (Emeritus Chief of Staff, Angell Memorial Animal Hospital, Boston, Mass.)

See also "Scientific Reports, Hip Dysplasia Symposium," *JAVMA*, Vol. 210, No. 10, May 15, 1997, p. 1466, a summary of a report entitled "Association between pelvic muscle mass and canine hip dysplasia" (George H. Cardinet, III, et al.): "Diminished pelvic muscle mass in dogs with CHD and altered muscle fiber size and composition in 8-week-old dogs that subsequently develop CHD strongly suggest that *abnormalities of pelvic musculature* [italics mine] are associated with development of CHD."

Reference is also made to a private communication (1993) from Dr. Gail K. Smith, VMD, Ph.D., Chief of Surgery, School of Veterinary Medicine, University of Pennsylvania: "Data generated from a new diagnostic and scoring method . . . revealed that only 5% of Golden Retrievers in this study were truly unsusceptible to CHD."

39. Statistical analysis of OFA evaluations between 1970 and 1988 notes that, out of 696,571 Goldens registered by the AKC during that time, only 42,822 were tested, or around 6%. During that 18-year time period, the incidence of HD in the number of Goldens evaluated as having been diagnosed with dysplasia actually *increased* by .03%. ("Role of the Orthopedic Foundation for Animals in the Control of Canine Hip Dysplasia," *Golden Retriever News*, November/December 1992, p. 99.)

40. In a personal letter dated July 29, 1974, Dr. Schnelle, the researcher who first identified the condition in 1935, actually wrote: "I am afraid that breeders and judges will have to alter their concept of what a Golden should look like before there will be much chance of reducing x-ray diagnosable HD." During World War II, Dr. Schnelle was in the U. S. Army assigned to securing German Shepherds for sentry duty. Before the war, not many breeders paid much attention to his findings, because affected dogs kept as pets and in kennels were not shown in the show ring and moved satisfactorily. In training, however, affected dogs broke down and could not be used. Fanciers, however, became alarmed at this finding, fearing that HD would eventually cripple the entire breed, and the "more conscientious" fanciers concerned with "saving the breed" began to destroy all their dogs diagnosed with HD. Over the years, Dr.

Schnelle became alarmed at what the breeders were doing, and in the 1970s he disavowed his dire warnings and stated that "selecting dogs for breeding, in widely affected breeds, should not be based upon very slite [sic] differences in hip joint structure. . . . Breeders are making too much of not quite perfect hips. . . ." (Private communication, 29 July 1974).

41. See note 38, above.

42. See notes 38, above, and 65, following.

43. Notes from the Symposium, University of Pennsylvania, School of Veterinary Medicine, Continuing Education program, 30 Jan. 2002.

44. In G. K. Smith, VMD, Ph.D., "Etiopathogenesis of Canine Hip Dysplasia" (Spring 2003): "In my 21 years of orthopaedic referral practice at the University of Pennsylvania, I have not found the need to euthanize a dog as a consequence of canine hip dysplasia."

45. Birchard and Sheriding, eds., *Saunders Manual of Small Animal Practice*, pp. 1201–7. Also refer to *The Merck Veterinary Manual* (Eighth edition, 1998), pp. 860–61, 876–78.

46. Gheorghe M. Constantinescu, *Clinical Anatomy for Small Animal Practitioners* (Iowa State Press, 2002), pp. 89–90.

47. Helena Cronin, *The Ant and the Peacock: Altruism and Sexual Selection from Darwin to Today* (Cambridge University Press, 1991), p. 329. The full quote is as follows: "There is, of course, nothing surprising about phenotypes venturing outside natural selection's expectations. There is no such thing as 'the' phenotypic effect of any gene. Phenotypes are always the result of an interaction between gene and environment. We have learnt, at tragic cost, that even genes for plantigrade feet and opposable thumbs will not express themselves as expected in the environment of the womb that has been exposed to some of the inventions of the drug industry." Helena Cronin's book is considered the definitive history and summary of altruism and sexual selection in modern evolutionary biology; she is a co-director of the London School of Economic's Centre for Philosophy of Natural and Social Sciences. See also note 90, below.

48. Note 6, above.

49. Such "inhibitory factors, for example, would be the tumor suppressor gene, p53, which has had an interesting and noteworthy history because of its role as a gene that protects and repairs cells damaged "by radiation and other insults." The cellular pathway involved in this gene is inactivated in most human cancers, and in approximately 50 percent of human cancers the gene malfunctions when "hit by a debilitating mutation." In the remaining 50 percent, different genes are involved, including a p53

inhibitor, MDM2, which blocks the p53 when it binds to it. Active research to find an agent that inhibits MDM2 effects on p53 are ongoing (see *Science*, vol. 393, 2 Jan. 2004, pp. 23–25). Familial cancers are rare and direct inheritance unusual, and when they do occur are incurred by DNA damage during postnatal life. Such occurrence is usually the result of damage to tumor suppressor genes. See also *How to Win the Nobel Prize: An Unexpected Life in Science*, by J. Michael Bishop (Harvard University Press, 2003), pp. 170–72.

50. An interesting discussion of osteosarcoma in dogs can be found in *Mutants: On Genetic Variety and the Human Body* (Viking 2003) by Armand Marie Leroi. He discusses the relationship between growth and osteosarcoma attributing it to the higher level of IGF (Insulin Growth Factor) circulating in the blood stream of large-size dogs, thus increasing the risk factor. He says, "Big dogs and tall children may be more susceptible to [these] cancers simply because that have more cells than smaller dogs and shorter children. More likely, however, it is probably not large size *per se* that is dangerous, but rather the high levels of growth hormone and IGF that big dogs and children tend to have. . . . why this should cause high levels of cancers is not exactly clear, but one idea is that IGF stops sick cells from dying. Cells that are stricken with a potentially carcinogenic mutation often [commit] suicide" (pp. 206–7).

51. *The Biology of Cancer*, by Armin C. Braun, Addison-Wesley Publishing Company, 1974, pp. 9–21.

52. Matt Ridley, *Genome* (HarperCollins, 1999), p. 234. An oncogene is a mutation of a normal gene that promotes growth, but unlike the normal gene, the oncogene fails to respond to signals from the environment to cease multiplying.

53. The germ-line theory, originally proposed by August Weismann, who is considered the father of modern genetics, is now deemed to be one of the most important paradigms in biology. As succinctly stated in *Exploding the Gene Myth* (Beacon Press, 1999), by Ruth Hubbard and Elijah Wald: "When we hear the terms, 'cancer genetics' or 'cancer genes,' we must understand that only rarely does a cancer mutation find its way into an egg or sperm and so get transmitted from a parent to his or her children. In fact, identical twins are not much more likely than other siblings to develop the same cancers, despite the fact that they were born with the same genetic material." And further: "There is general agreement that cancer-causing agents, or *carcinogens*, in the environment increase the likelihood that cancer-mutations will happen. Environmental carcino-

gens, such as chemicals, radiation, and probably viruses, are responsible for between 70 and 90 percent of cancers. . . . Presumably environmental factors play a part in the origin of cancers by increasing the probability of mutations. But no one believes that a single mutation is enough to produce a cancer" (p. 83).

54. *How to Win the Nobel Prize: An Unexpected Life in Science*, by J. Michael Bishop (Harvard University Press, 2003), pp. 160–66, offers an explanation about how the SRC gene, one of four genes present in the Rous sarcoma virus, can switch a cell from normal to a cancerous growth. J. Michael Bishop and Harold E. Varmus were awarded the Nobel Prize in 1989 for the discovery that normal genes under certain conditions can cause cancers, including cancers not caused by viruses.

55. Note 49, above.

56. See "Dioxin Dumps: Burning exposed trash pollutes soil" (*ScienceNews*, 29 March 2003, vol. 163), which notes that burning trash is creating hazardous environmental concentrations of dioxins and related contaminants in Asia and elsewhere. Air currents carry dioxin and furans across national borders, and the situation deserves international attention (p. 197). Another research study discounts industry claims that there is a safe "threshold dose, below which dioxin won't cause cancer." This new research claims that there is no evidence of a dioxin cancer threshold; that is to say, there apparently is *no safe dose* [italics mine] of dioxin. (D. Mackie and colleagues, Princeton University, Princeton Environmental Institute, October 2003. Refer *Cancer Res. Wkly* 40, 10/28/03.)

57. In an article, "Just Say No to Green Lawns," cited by *Animal Health Newsletter* (Cornell University College of Veterinary Medicine, October 1991), it was reported in *The Journal of the National Cancer Institute* that dogs allowed to romp on lawns treated with the herbicide containing the chemical 2,4-D (also called 2,4-D acid or 2,4-dichlorophenoxyacetic acid) were twice as likely to develop malignant lymphoma (lymphatic cancer) as dogs who did not have contact with the chemical or treated lawns.

58. *Scientific American* (September 1994), p. 112: "At present, the mounting toll of lung cancer provides incontrovertible evidence that smoking remains the single most important avoidable cause of cancer, responsible for about 30 percent of all cancer deaths in industrialized societies." The same article also identifies a number of significant environmental risk factors such as "past diagnostic and therapeutic radiation, . . . sunlight . . . long term low-level exposures to some environmental contaminants, such

as small particulates, chlorination by-products in domestic water. . . . Extensive animal studies indicate a clear risk. Some compounds may function by altering hormones, whereas others may directly affect gene expression."

59. It was reported in *Nature* (April 1996) that genetic studies after the Chernobyl reactor radiation accident showed an environment so contaminated that the animals themselves were radioactive, and mutations studied in voles who survived and thrived were "cumulative," that is to say, "increased with each succeeding generation." The body apparently is not only susceptible to high dosage but sensitive to low doses as well. In *Discover* magazine, January 2004, p. 47, it was reported that a German research team studying the effects of radiation concluded as follows: "All radiation can cause lesions in human DNA, known as double-strand breaks, which if unrepaired can lead to cellular mutations and cancer. The body moves quickly when it gets a high dose. . . . But with a low dose, the German team discovered, the body usually takes days to make repair—if it does at all."

60. Note 54, above.

61. Goldschmidt, M. H. and Shofer, F. S. (1992). *Skin Tumors of the Dog and Cat* (Pergamon Press, 1992).

62. Merrell, David, J. *Evolution and Genetics* (Holt, Rinehart and Winston 1962), p. 246: "Even recessive lethals may be present in a fairly high frequency, for when no recessive homozygotes survive or reproduce, affected individuals will continue to appear as the offspring of heterozygous normal parents."

63. See "Differentiation therapy" (www.medterms.com).

64. In a private communication (1993), the percentage is estimated as 95 percent. Elsewhere, it is listed as 85 percent.

65. "Clinical hip dysplasia in growing dogs: the long-term results of conservative management" (*J. Small Anim. Pract.* [1987] 28, 243-52), by A.R.S. Barr, H.R. Denny, and C. Gibbs. The Abstract reads: "The long-term results of conservative management in 68 immature dogs with clinical and radiographic evidence of hip dysplasia are described. Seventy-six percent of the dogs had minimal gait abnormalities despite radiological evidence of moderate or severe osteoarthrosis." See also *Dog World* (December 1987), p. 7.

66. "Animal Health Newsletter," Cornell University College of Veterinary Medicine, Vol. 3, No. 2 (April 1985), p. 4

67. In the 1970s the OFA defined CD as subluxation, but later changed the

definition to designate dogs with abnormal hip development, citing this as a "genetic disease." PennHIP, however, regards subluxation as the major component of HD, and this is true in the context that it can lead to increased vulnerability for trauma (and over-exercise when the musculature has not developed adequately) and other environmental influences, such as lack of exercise and overweight puppies, which are environmental components due to the canine's new tasks in the modern-day home.

68. Ligaments, the white fibrous tissue that connects bone to bone, "possess little or no elasticity, and when stretched do not recover" (quoted in *The Encyclopedia Americana,* Americana Corporation, 1957, p. 379). The observation has been confirmed in private conversation with a practicing orthopedist. See also, *Dog Owner's Home Veterinary Handbook,* by Delbert G. Carlson, DVM, and James M. Griffin, M.D. (Howell Book House, 1960), p. 225–26, where it is stated that "joint position is maintained by ligaments, tendons, and a tough fibrous capsule surrounding the joint. These combine to provide stability or tightness to the joint. Joint laxity is due to loose ligaments and/or a stretched capsule. . . . Growing puppies are especially susceptible to serious injuries to bones and joints caused by improper activity, improper diet, and trauma."

While it is generally agreed that there can be no hip dysplasia in the absence of joint laxity, I would not agree that joint laxity constitutes hip dysplasia—only that joint laxity contributes to the condition.

69. "Hip Scoring in the Golden Retriever: A Report to May 1988" (*Golden Retriever World* [July–August 1988]), pp. 14–20. This report was written by Dr. M. B. Willis, Senior Lecturer in Animal Breeding and Genetics at the University of Newcastle Upon Tyne, England. See, especially, p. 20: "Progeny tests are more reliable than a sire's own score. Few Golden Retriever sires show very low averages. In fact, the range in this breed is much lower than that seen in breeds like Labradors, German Shepherd Dogs, or Rottweilers, and this may indicate a breed with less genetic variation. This also explains a heritability around 20%, compared with figures around 40% for German Shepherd Dogs and Rottweilers, and around 30% for Labradors."

The OFA, however, maintains: "If it [the heritability estimate] is between 0.2 and 0.3, the heritability estimate is considered moderate," and selection based on the phenotype is slow but substantial. (See Greg Keller, DVM, *"The use of health data basis and selective breeding* [4th edition, 2003], p. 7.)

PennHIP, on the other hand, in "Summary of Research, 2000,"

states that heritability in a range of 0.2 and 0.3 is low: "If such low estimates for heritability of the OFA phenotype are found for the more popular breeds of dogs, it would account for the fact that the percentages of dysplastic progeny decreased only slightly over the study period (1971–93). On the other hand, heritability of passive hip laxity, using the PennHIP analysis yields higher values."

70. Richard Dawkins, *Climbing Mount Improbable* (W. W. Norton & Company, 1996), p. 165. The complete quote is as follows: "Heritability is a measure of how much of the variation, out of a given population's available variation, is inherited. If the heritability is low it means that most of the variation in the population is environmentally caused. . . . If heritability is high, selection has a large impact on future generations."

71. Golden Retriever statistics for the first 18 years of OFA records (1970–88), show that there was no improvement in the incidence of OFA negative certifications, despite the strong recommendations for selective breeding; in fact, the percentage increased 0.3 percent during this period, from 23.3 percent (1972–90) to 23.6 percent (1980–88). See "Role of the Orthopedic Foundation for Animals in the Control of Canine Hip Dysplasia," *Golden Retriever News* (November/December 1992), pp. 90–101. During the next 11 years (1989–2000), the incidence dropped to around 21 percent, as reported in *Golden Retriever News* (March/April, 2004), p. 22).

72. See "The Environmental Regulation of Animal Development," in *Developmental Biology* (Sinauer Associates, Fifth ed., 1997, pp. 805–41). "As we become aware of the complexity of development, we realize that development is critically keyed to the environment" (p. 841).

73. Private communication from Dr. Schnelle, dated 29 July 1974. In an oft-cited Swedish study—Hedhammer et al., "Canine Hip Dysplasia: Study of Heritability in 401 litters of German Shepherd Dogs" (*JAVMA* 174, May 1, 1979)—that lasted 10 years, sires and dams were apparently bred between 1965 and 1973 to determine the incidence and heritability of HD. After 1973 a program of selection was enforced to determine how to select breeding stock in order to lessen prevalence and severity of hip dysplasia, primarily by breeding sires and dams who both had "normal hips." The report emphasizes that such an approach did not take place until after 1973, and results were again analyzed in 1975, comparing the period 1965 to 1973 with the period ending in 1975 to test the new approach, and the results examined in 1976–77. The statistics are as follows:

Period	Total No. of offspring	No.(%) of offspring with hip dysplasia	
		Grade I-IV	Grade II-IV
1965–1967	791	404 (51)	176 (22)
1968–1970	943	468 (50)	298 (32)
1971–1973	670	220 (34)	127 (19)
1975	347	96 (28)	52 (15)

There is a serious lacuna in the report, which fails to explain why the incidence of HD dropped dramatically during the years 1971 through 1973, *after which* changes in the selection program were effected in order to reduce the incidence of CHD. The incidence had already been reduced (from grades I-IV by 16 percent and grades II-IV by 13 percent) before the new approach went into effect in 1973. Certain organizations for the genetic control of the "disease" of HD still cite the Hedhammer report as gospel, apparently unaware of the reported statistics.

There are other aspects to mention in the Hedhammer report. One is: "Weight at 60 days was estimated to have high heritability," whereas "there is nothing in the present investigation to point toward a correlation between weight at 60 days and later occurrence of hip dysplasia," although previous studies noted in the Hedhammer report suggest that "estimated heritabilities" indicate that environmental factors are also of considerable importance for development and severity of hip dysplasia.

Another observation is this: In 1975 it was found that "weaned pups on low caloric intake had a lower frequency of hip dysplasia than did normally delivered, bitch-fed pups." Later studies, however, indicate that a puppy's weight, although a result of "increased caloric intake," may be a more important criteria in the development of CHD (see note 31, above).

Still another point of interest: The Hedhammer report suggests that radiographs are the only way to identify "hip dysplasia"—a conclusion that may be challenged, as subsequent observations point out. The difficulty with the Hedhammer report is that the research unfortunately remains critically unexamined and has led to the unchallenged conclusion that HD is "a genetic disease." I would, however, agree with the overall conclusion of Hedhammer—namely, that progeny testing is an important part of the selection process. I would go further: Along with minimizing the environmental factors that contribute to the condition, it is the most important part of the selection process. Breeding dogs for tighter hips will in the long run result in dogs more free from dysplasia.

For years the OFA refused to acknowledge any environmental component: "No environmental component has been shown to cause CHD, but some factors may affect the genetic expression of CHD" ("Role of the Orthopedic Foundation for Animals in the Control of Canine Hip Dysplasia," op. cit., 1992, p. 97). Only recently has the OFA gradually awakened to environmental considerations: "Polygenic traits are influenced by environmental factors, which may minimize or maximize genetic potential." Some environmental factors include, but are not limited to "overweight, rapid growth early maturation, sex of the animal, etc. The most studied environmental influence on HD is caloric intake." (See Greg Keller, DVM, *The use of health databases and selective breeding* [4th edition, 2003], p. 8.)

The explanations of CHD may be various, but an understanding of the problem from a biological perspective seems to elude the establishment and most dog owners even today—perhaps because the concept of "phenotype" is still not well understood. It is the *environment* that plays the critical role in determining the organism's phenotype. It is the *environment* that yields different phenotypes from the same fundamental genotype. Once again, as stated by Theodosius Dobhzansky, nothing in biology makes sense except in the light of evolution. (See also note 89, below.)

74. Dr. Wayne Riser, founder of the OFA, has produced a number of studies that have shed light on the subject. Reference particularly: Riser, W. H., Cohen, D., and S. Lindqvist, et al. "Influence of early rapid growth and weight gain on hip dysplasia in the German Shepherd Dog" (*JAVMA* 145:661–68, 1964). There seems no doubt that "laxity" may be a proximate contributing cause of HD; however "laxity" is not a disease; it is a non-life-threatening condition. To say that HD is a "genetic disease" is a disservice that can only continue to contribute to a misunderstanding of the condition.

75. PennHIP basically agrees with Dr. Riser (see previous note 67). The PennHIP approach, however, does not address the question of functional integrity, although acknowledging its importance: "Clearly, the functional hip laxity is of greater diagnostic interest, but there are presently

no means to measure." (Smith, G. K., Biery, D. N., and Gregor, T. P. "New Concepts of coxofemoral joint stability and the development of a clinical stress-radiological method for quantitating hip joint laxity in the dog." *J. Am. Vet. Med. Association* 1990; 196[1]:59–70.) Indeed, functional tightness as a result of a strong muscle mass in the hip area is the most important area, especially, since the muscle function is completely removed under the required anesthesia. And, significantly, many breeders are seeking the services of radiologists who will radiograph the dog without anesthesia and are thereby receiving a greater number of passing OFA ratings than when their dogs are evaluated under anesthesia.

76. The DLS study is summarized in *Dog Watch* (Vol. 6, No. 5, May 2002, p. 4), published by the Cornell University College of Veterinary Medicine. See also "Canine Hip Dysplasia: The Dorsolateral Subluxation (DLS) Test," *Golden Retriever News* (July-August 2003), pp. 91–96.

77. The AKC website (2004) lists 150 recognized breeds classified in "seven groups or Miscellaneous Class." According to Eukanuba there are 162 breeds and varieties.

78. See note 31, above.

79. Olsson, Sten-Erik and Gerry B. Schnelle, "Another Look at the Hip Dysplasia Question" (*Pure-Bred Dogs, American Kennel Gazette*, n.d., p. 32): "Anything that interferes with the normal growth and development of the hip joint can give rise to hip dysplasia." Refer to note 38, above.

80. The Conservative Approach has worked in all the cases in which I have counseled clients. See also note 65.

81. See note 65, above.

82. Cited in the publication mentioned in note 65, on p. 251: "Spontaneous improvement will occur in a high proportion of cases as animals reach maturity and 76 percent of the dogs in this series were adjudged to have acceptable long-term function." Dr. Riser first mentioned that it had "been known for several years that spontaneous improvement may occur as dogs reach maturity" (W. H. Riser, "The dysplastic hip joint: its radiographic and histological development," *Journal of the American Veterinary Radiology Society* 14, 35–40). Dr. Riser was the founder of the OFA.

83. In a private communication (dated 1993), Dr. Gail Smith writes: "Because of the relatively poor scientific foundation of many of the treatments, the topic of CHD treatment is, at best, controversial. . . . To my knowledge, no study has been done to show the efficacy of TPO [triple pelvic osteotomy] versus any other treatment including surgical or no treatment at all." Another orthopedic surgeon, Dr. Charles W. Smith, of

the University of Illinois Veterinary Medicine Teaching Hospital, Urbana, Illinois, has stated that clinical signs do not correlate well with radiographs and that dogs diagnosed with hip dysplasia should be treated conservatively.

84. For scientists who consider genes to be the basis of our biology (rather than diet, nutrition, and exercise), genes are the fashionable explanation for health and illness. Some scientists prefer to study molecular transformations of genes and/or devise (expensive) diagnostic tests. But this approach must be placed in perspective: There are complex factors, variable and unpredictable, at issue here, and these involve a wide range of biological and environmental factors. See also Ruth Hubbard and Elijah Wald, in *Exploding the Gene Myth* ((Beacon Press, 1993): "Increased knowledge about DNA will improve our understanding of the structure and function of different proteins. [But] it is less likely to improve our understanding of the network of metabolic relationships underlying diseases and disabilities and the complex process of growth and development, because these depend on many factors that are not influenced by genes" (p. 158). Ruth Hubbard is a professor of Biology at Harvard University.

   According to another distinguished professor of Biology at Harvard, Ernst Mayr, "The gene is not the target of selection. A given gene can be highly favorable in one genotype and lethal in another context" (quoted in *Biology*, Third ed., Benjamin Cummings Publishing Company, 1994, p. 418). See also Mayr's *One Long Argument: Charles Darwin and the Genesis of Modern Evolutionary thought* (Harvard University Press, 1991) and *This is Biology: The Science of the Living World* (The Belknap Press of Harvard University Press, 1997).

85. Richard Lewontin, *The Triple Helix: Gene, Organism, and Environment* (Harvard University Press, Cambridge, Mass., 2000). Professor Lewontin informs us that the complete genome sequence, without additional biological knowledge, cannot describe the way a resulting organism will perform. The reason is this: No one can predict the way proteins fold since "not all information about protein structure is stored in the DNA sequence because the folding of polypeptides into proteins is not completely specified by their amino acid sequences" (p.73). Function, he says, "cannot be understood without information about shape and form" (p. 114).

86 Hubbard and Wald, *Exploding the Gene Myth*: "We need to have a realistic sense of the positive contributions genetics and biotechnology can

make, and of the risks inherent in the science, its applications, and its commercialization" (p. xiii). And on p. 6: "The myth of the all-powerful gene is based on flawed science that discounts the environmental context in which we and our genes exist." The social culture in which modern medicine is practiced in the United States has overtones in the practice of veterinary medicine as well. A belief that genes determine and can predict every health problem and that all of us have "genetic tendencies" to develop health problems, means that "we all become candidates for genetic diagnosis and therapy," no matter how healthy we are (p. 117).

Another useful book on the subject is: Richard Dawkins, *The Exended Phenotype: The Long Reach of the Gene* (Oxford University Press, 1999). Of particular interest is how Dawkins addresses the question of genic determinism: "The belief that genes are somehow super-deterministic, in comparison with environmental causes, is a myth of extraordinary tenacity, and it can give rise to real emotional distress" (p. 11).

87. Kealy, R. D., Lawler, D. F., Ballam, J.M. et al. "Evaluation of risk factors for degenerative joint disease associated with hip dysplasia in German Shepherd dogs, Golden Retrievers, Labrador Retrievers, and Rotweilers." *J. A. Vet. Med. Assoc.* 2001; 219:1719□24

88 Note 68, above.

89. A phenotype is the observable constitution of an organism. It is the appearance of an organism, the result of the interaction of the genotype and the environment. The genotype is the genetic constitution of the organism. It is the sum total of the genes that individual possesses, and these genes were transmitted to the individual from its parents. A gene does not really determine the trait of the organism but acts by way of the milieu of proteins and of other molecules that are in the organism. This determines the end result, the finished product, which is called the phenotype.

A mutation occurs not in the total organism but in a specific gene located in the DNA. A mutation is always in the genotype and may or may not be expressed in the phenotype. You really cannot say that a mutation acts directly on the phenotype; rather, it acts on the phenotype by way of the total organism. All mutations affect the genotype first, and then may or may not affect the phenotype depending upon the background of other proteins that are present within the organism. For example, suppose a mutation is in the heterozygous form. That gene has no impact on the phenotype because there is another gene in that organism that produces the needed protein and that will keep the phenotype from being affected.

How do you know what the genotype is? You can only know through breeding and the observation of the offspring or progeny. It is only by counting the progeny in the next generation that you can know if a mutation even exists. Over time, through counting the ratio of the expression of the gene in each generation, you can tell if the ratios are changing. Such changes in the ratio of the genes are the true meaning of evolution.

90. In order to understand pleiotropy, consider that a protein, which comes from a gene that has mutated, is now making a different protein. In pleiotropy, this changed protein will affect several parts of the body, with repercussions throughout the entire body of the organism. Genes affect the sum total of the organism. For example, heparin, which is determined by a single gene, is a protein that is important in that it has many different effects, including several different body reactions including those relating to coagulation as well as to the metabolism of fat.

For an interesting discussion of the relationship between pleiotropy and phenotype, and the pleiotropic effects that turn out to be adaptive, see Helena Cronin, *The Ant and the Peacock*, pp. 96–101. "What is pleiotropy, after all, but the various phenotypic effects of pleiotropy," she says (p. 99).

91. Note 38, above.

Glossary

How we define objects and concepts affects how we perceive and understand them. The following is a list of uncommon words I use in the text, along with brief explanations.

A

Acetabulum: The hip socket.

Adenovirus: A virus causing infectious canine hepatitis in dogs.

Adjuvant drug therapy: Treatment after a tumor has been removed surgically. Drug therapy may prevent recurrence of the cancer by destroying cells that may have previously spread from the original cancer.

Adrenal glands: Glands located above the kidney that release hormones, namely corticosteroids and adrenaline.

Ad Lib: Ad libitum ("at liberty"). Providing a puppy or dog with as much food as he wants to eat, whenever he wants to eat, and in whatever amounts.

Alpha dog: The head of the pack; the leader.

Amino acids: Organic molecules that serve as the building blocks of protein. The way in which amino acids are arranged in different proteins determines their various properties.

Amitraz: A potent pesticide used in treating Demodectic mange.

Anconeal process: Part of the ulna that contributed to the support of the humerus within the elbow joint. *See* Ununited anconeal process.

Angiogenesis: Development of the cells of the heart or blood vessels. This term encompasses the growth of blood vessels that cancers require. If the blood supply to a cancer can be inhibited, the growth of the cancer will be limited.

Antibodies: Proteins that are made by lymphocytes that bond to specific antigens (foreign material). The antibody-antigen combination will then be removed from the body by scavenger cells.

Antigens: The reactive part of a molecule that stimulates the formation of antibodies.

283

Antioxidants: Chemicals that will bond to, and remove, free radicals.

Apoptosis: Programmed cell death.

Articular cartilage: The cartilage that covers the articular surface, which is defined as the connecting surfaces between bones.

Autonomous growth: Ability to grow without external support or stimulation.

Autonomy: A property of cancerous cells by which cells have the ability to grow without responding to the chemical messages that normally regulate growth.

B

Bacteria: Unicellular microorganisms (also called prokaryotes) that have no true nucleus. Bacteria are classified into two groups based on a difference in cell walls, as determined by Gram staining (hence Gram positive and Gram negative bacteria.)

B.A.R.F.: Acronym for "bones and raw food"—a term coined by Dr. Ian Billinghurst of Australia that suggests following an evolutionary approach to feeding dogs. He points out that feeding raw, meaty bones and vegetable scraps is closer to the ancestral dog's diet than the large amount of processed grains present in today's commercial dog foods.

Base pairs: A pair of nitrogenous bases (one purine, which is either adenine or guanine; the other pyrimidine, which is either cytosine or thymine). The two double-helix strands (of deoxyribonucleic acid, which are complementary in terms of their bases) are held together with A bonding to T, and C bonding to G. Base pairing is also present in RNA (ribonucleic acid).

B-cell lymphocyte: Lymphocytes that are produced in the bone marrow.

Beta-carotene: A yellow-red pigment found in plants and animals. It is a precursor of vitamin A in that, when one molecule of beta-carotene is split, it yields two molecules of vitamin A.

Biological value: A term used in measuring the utilization of a food stuff.

Boosters: Subsequent inoculations that raise the level of antibodies (i.e., the titer) to the antigenic material in the vaccine.

Bordetella: A genus of aerobic, gram-negative, coccobacilli that are pathogens of the respiratory tract. Part of the "kennel cough" complex. *See* Kennel cough.

Bordetella bronchiseptica: A bacterial species that causes a highly contagious bronchopneumonia in dogs. Often called Kennel cough (q.v.).

C

Calcitonin: A hormone secreted by the parathyroid gland that lowers the level of calcium and phosphate in the blood.

Canine adenovirus. *See* Adenovirus.

Canine ehrlichiosis: *See* Ehrlichiosis.

Canine hip dysplasia: CHD. *See* Hip dysplasia.

Carcinogens: Agents that cause cancer.

Carcinoma: A cancer that arises from epithelial tissue.

Carpal bone joints: The bones of the wrist, located above the pastern in dogs. They are homologous to the wrist in humans.

Cartilage: A connective tissue characterized by its nonvascularity and firm consistency. It consists of cells (chondrocytes), an interstitial matrix of fibers (collagen), and a ground substance (proteoglycans). Cartilage is found in, among other places, joints and on the end of bones, where it is known as the articular surface.

Cell: The smallest unit of living structure capable of independent existence. Composed of an outer membrane enclosing the cytoplasm that contains the nucleus and various other intercellular structures. Cells are described as: (1) "well-differentiated," that is, having gone through changes to become specialized in certain ways, and (2) "undifferentiated," which is known as the classic cell and has no particular function. Cells that divide without stopping, thus forming a cancerous growth, are called malignant cells.

Central dogma: A hypothesis describing the one-directional flow of information used in the synthesis of protein from DNA to RNA to protein. Modern development theory suggests that this dogma is too simplistic an explanation or description.

Chemotherapy: Destroying cancer cells through the use of chemicals.

Chondral cartilage: A type of cartilage that gives rise to new bone growth (cartilage primordial) located at the end of the long bones (epiphysis), thus forming the growth plate.

Chondral fracture: A break in the cartilage.

Chondrocytes: Cells that produce cartilage.

Chondrogenesis: Formation of cartilage.

Chondroitin Sulfate: A building block of cartilage. Chondroitin Sulfate is available in pill form as a nutraceutical. It is normally extracted from bovine trachea.

Coccidia: A protozoan that lives in the epithelium (lining) of the intestine.

Collagen: The major protein of the white fibers of connective tissue, cartilage, and bone. It exists as a long molecule in a distinct triple-helix configuration.

Collar: There are different types of collars, but the most common are: (1) buckle collar—a collar that is closed by a buckle; and (2) choke collar—a collar that consists of either metal chain, nylon or leather strap with a ring at either end. The choke collar is passed through one ring to make a loop that goes over the dog's head; when the other ring is attached to the leash, the collar can be used to give corrections to the dog because the collar will tighten when the leash is jerked.

Colostrum: The first secretions of mammary glands. These secretions are rich in antibodies.

Cones: Specialized cells present in the retina of the eye that are sensitive to certain wavelengths of received light and are perceived as different colors. *See also* Rods.

Conjunctiva: The mucous membrane covering the anterior surface of the eye-ball and the posterior surface of the lids.

Conservative approach: An approach to healing through non-invasive remedies.

Coprophagy: Stool eating.

Corona virus: A canine corona virus (CCV). An acute contagious disease of dogs and puppies caused by a virus that invades the lining of the intestine and causes diarrhea and vomiting. It is one of the many causes of enteritis. Adult dogs are rarely seriously affected, and the virus is more dangerous in puppies. Vaccination for CCV is an optional part of the routine vaccination program for most dogs.

Crude protein: The total protein in a dog food, some of which may not be usable. For instance, hair, generally speaking, is not usable, although it is made of protein.

Cryptorchidism: The absence of descended testicles.

Cystitis: An infection of the bladder and/or urethra.

Cytoplasm: The material within the cell membrane not including the nucleus.

D

DDE (dichlorodiphenyldicholoroethylene): A chemical similar to DDT (q.v.) that has no commercial use, but is a contaminant of DDT preparations. It is also a breakdown product of DDT. Both DDT and DDE are stored in the body, and their concentration builds up in fatty tissue.

DDT (dichlorodiphenyltricholoroethane): A pesticide once widely used to control insects. DDT is a white, crystalline solid with no odor or taste. Its use in the U.S. was banned in 1972 because of damage to wildlife, but it is still used in some countries. One of the actions of DDT and DDE in low doses is to mimic the effect of estrogen. At high doses it affects the nervous system.

Dermatitis (atopy): Infection of the skin. Atopy means "of unknown origin."

Developmental biology: The study of the development of an organism.

Differentiating agents: Agents that cause cell differentiation.

Dioxin: Dioxin is the common name used to refer to the chemical 2,3,7,8-tetrachlodibenzo-p-dioxin or TCDD. Dioxin and related compounds, including PCBs, have a similar structure and activity and are commonly referred to as dioxin-like compounds or "dioxins." Dioxins are chemical contaminants that have no commercial usefulness by themselves. They are formed during such combustion processes as waste incineration, forest fires, burning trash, and manufacturing. Dioxin was a contaminant used in the manufacture of the herbicide Agent Orange—a defoliant sprayed on forest areas and crops—and used by U.S. forces in Vietnam. Dioxin accumulates in fatty tissue. It has been shown to be highly toxic, to cause cancer, and to alter reproductive, developmental, and immune functions.

Distemper: Also known as canine distemper virus (CDV). This is a severe, highly contagious, viral disease of dogs and other carnivores and is prevalent worldwide. Airborne exposure first leads to infection of the upper respiratory tract, followed by widespread systemic infection. By the 8th or 9th day the virus enters the central nervous system. The mortality rate can be high depending upon the virulence of the CDV strain and the strength of the host's immune system. Damage to the central nervous system is common, tends to be progressive, and can occur during, after, or in the absence of any systemic illness.

DLS: Dorsolateral subluxation. This is a new test for hip dysplasia, sponsored by researchers at the College of Veterinary Medicine, Cornell University.

DNA: Deoxyribonucleic acid. DNA consists of two complementary chains of polynucleotides wound into a double helix. Genetic information is stored in this compound. DNA is the macromolecule found in a chromosome that specifies protein production by way of RNA.

E

Ear leathers: The flap of the ear.

Ectoprasites: Parasites that reside on the outer surface of their host.

Ehrlichiosis: A disease whereby leukocytes are infected with rickettsiae bacteria (*Erlichia canis*, order Rickettsiales) carried by the tick, *Rhipicephalus sanguineus*. Also called canine ehrlichiosis.

Elbow dysplasia: Malformation of the elbow joint as seen in the radiograph of the canine elbow.

Electrolytes: A substance that dissociates into ions or charged particles in a solution. The atoms of salt molecules, for example, will separate into charged sodium and chloride ions when they are dissolved in water. These ions are called electrolytes because their charge allows the solution to carry a current. When fluids are lost from the body, they contain such ions. These electrolytes (sodium, potassium, chloride, bicarbonate, and others) must be restored to maintain the body's equilibrium.

Endochondral ossification: Certain bones formed by the laying down of calcium within the pre-existing cartilage by the action of osteoblasts within the cartilage.

Enteritis: An infection of the intestine.

Entropion: A rolling-in of the eyelid. Either eyelid can roll in, but the condition is more common in the lower eyelid of the Golden.

Enzymes: Proteins that act as catalysts to speed chemical reactions and are unchanged by the process. Enzymes control interactions between molecules, either by breaking them down or putting them together. "Life is a manifestation of catalysis by means of protein enzymes" (definition by A. I. Oparin, *Origin of Life*).

Epiphyseal growth plates: The region of growth at the end of long bone (e.g., femur).

Epiphysis: The end of the bone.

Epithelial cells: Cells that cover the outer surface of organisms as well as cells that line internal cavities. Their origin can be traced back to one of three original layers of cells in the embryo.

Epithelium: Cells that form a covering, as in the lining of the digestive tract.

Estrogen: A female hormone.

Ethoxyquin: A synthetic antioxidant originally developed as a rubber stabilizer. It was later refined and used as a preservative for many years because of its excellent anti-oxidant qualities. All dry commercial pet foods must contain preservatives. In the late 1980s companies began making high-performance foods containing more fat than regular dog food, and they began adding greater amounts of ethoxyquin to extend the shelf-life of their product. Public outcry against the use of ethoxyquin has led to the use of natural antioxidants in some cases.

F

Femoral head: Head of the femur (q.v.).

Femoral head excision: To cut off the femoral head. Synonym for femoral head resection.

Femur: The long bone of the hind leg.

Fibronectin: A large glycoprotein forming long fibers. It is important in growth and healing of wounds.

Fight-or-flight: A term coined by Hans Selye, meaning "to mobilize one's adrenaline to meet a challenge."

Flea: An ectoparasite (q.v.) that is common to the dog. An insect that sucks the blood of dogs; if no other host is available the flea will bite people.

Flora, bacterial: Mixture of the one-celled organisms that are present in the intestines.

Fragmented coronoid process (FCP): One of a collection of problems with the elbow joint. The coronoid process is a protrusion of the ulna, which contributes to the support of the humerus. Wear and tear can result in fragmentation of the coronoid process.

Free radicals: Chemicals that can exist having either gained or lost an electron, thus having a charge. They are produced by the metabolic reactions within cells. The free radicals strongly react with other molecules in order to share an electron. The reaction is very destructive to the molecule and to the cell that contains the molecule.

Frontal muscles: Muscles that are located on either side of the skull toward the front of the skull, and above the ear. They are above the temporal muscles.

G

Gene, Genes: A unit of substance of heredity that determines a particular characteristic of an organism. It was once thought to be a particular gene at a particular place (locus) on a chromosome that determined a characteristic, but now it has been found that one characteristic may be affected by a number of genes or one gene may affect a number of different characteristics. It has been shown that the environment also affects the expression of a gene. *See also* Pleiotropy.

Genetic: Common usage unfortunately interprets the meaning of the adjective "genetic" as referring solely to genes. The original meaning, however, was to describe the noun "genetics" (q.v.), meaning the concept or science of heredity that involves both the genes *and* the environment. The present use of this word has co-opted the original meaning and leaves a blank in our understanding of the true meaning of genetics, resulting in a misunderstanding of the term. For example, there is no foundation for referring to a condition such as hip dysplasia as a "genetic disease," implying that there is no environmental factor. This is confusing and misleading.

Genetics: Refers to the study or science of heredity, denoting the differences among organisms usually of the same species, owing to the interaction of the genes and the environment.

Genic: Pertaining solely to a gene or genes. Often used in combination, for example, as in "digenic" or "polygenic."

Genome: The entire genetic information, or full complement of the genetic blueprint, of an organism contained in the DNA (q.v.) This information is contained in the order of the arrangement of the four bases—A (Adenine), T (Thymine), G (Guanine), and C (Cytosine)—on a strand of DNA. The human genome, estimated to contain between 30,000 and 40,000 genes, is composed of more than three billion of these letters. The nucleus of every ordinary human cell contains two sets of chromosomes, each of which contains an entire genome.

Genome Project: The Genome Project is the scientific effort to establish the order of the genes in terms of the sequence of the four bases.

Genotype: The sum total of the genes of the organism.

Germ line: A process first identified by August Weismann ("the father of modern genetics"), in which the precursor cells of eggs and sperm separate off early in the embryo and travel to the gonads (testes, or ovary), where they eventually give rise to either eggs or sperm.

Giardia: A protozoan that infects the small intestine and interferes with food absorption. The infection is called giardiasis. Wild animals are potential reservoirs for the organism.

Glucosamine: An amino sugar found in organisms. It is a building block of cartilage.

Glycosaminoglycans: Glucosamines and glycans, which combine and contribute to the construction of cartilage.

H

HD: Hip dysplasia.

Head piece: Dog jargon term for the construction of the face and head. It includes such things as the squareness of the muzzle, the way the eyes are set apart and shaped, the shape of the dome of the skull, and the way the ears are set on the head.

Heartworm: A roundworm (q.v.) whose adult stage resides in the heart of the dog. The larval stage, known as microfilariae, is transported by the mosquito to infect another host.

Hemangiosarcoma: A cancer of the blood system resulting in tumors that lead to internal bleeding and death.

Hepatitis: Inflammation of the liver, usually due to viral infection but sometimes caused by toxic agents. In dogs the canine adenovirus type I (CAV-1) causes infectious canine hepatitis (ICH). It is related to, but distinct from, CAV-, which causes infectious tracheobronchitis (kennel cough). Vaccination has been highly effective for preventing CAV-1 infection.

Heritability: The degree to which the trait is controlled by the genes as opposed to the effect of the environment on the trait.

Hertz, Hz: A term used to define a unit of measure of sound.

Hip dysplasia: Any deviation from the ideal or perfect hip joint. Also known as CHD (q.v.) or HD (q.v.).

Hookworms: Internal parasites in dogs that embed their mouthparts in the mucosa of the intestine and suck out blood and tissue fluid. An important consequence of a severe hookworm infection is blood-loss anemia.

Homeobox, homeotic genes: Synonyms for hox genes, i.e., genes that control development. *See* Hox genes.

Hormones: Chemical messengers—such as growth hormone, estrogen, and testosterone—that travel by way of the blood stream and affect specific cells, causing them to modify their structure or function.

Hox genes: Genes that control development.

Human Genome Project: The massive identification program in humans to decode the genome (letters in the four-letter [base pairs] alphabet) sequentially.

Humerus: The bone of the upper arm.

Hyaluronic acid: One of the components of cartilage. A mucopoly saccharide that forms a gelatinous material in tissue spaces, it acts as a lubricant and shock absorbent throughout the body.

Hypertrophy: Increased growth in size and/or number of cells. The term is relevant to entropion of the eye because the rolled-in eyelid causes squinting, which results in hypertrophy of the musculature of the eye, further compounding the problem.

I

IGR: Abbreviation for Insect Growth Regulators (q.v.).

Imidacloprid: A pesticide that affects an insect's nervous system.

Imprinting: The changes that occur in the brain of the new born through sensory input, which causes those "imprinted on" to be perceived as family related.

Inguinal canal: The canal through which the testicle descends from the abdominal cavity into the scrotum.

Insect Growth Regulators: Chemicals that prevent the immature insect from proceeding through its normal larval stages to that of an adult that is sexually mature and can reproduce.

Integrins: Proteins found on the surface of cells that are involved in the control of growth.

Interferons: Glycoproteins found in the blood that are produced by cells infected with a virus and that have the ability to inhibit viral growth.

Interleukin-2: One of a family of proteins that stimulates the immune system. Specifically, Interleukin-2 stimulates the formation of T-lymphocytes.

Ivermectin: A pesticide used in dogs to control heartworm, roundworm, hookworm, and whipworm. It is also used to control some ectoparasites (q.v.).

J

Joint laxity: Looseness of a joint, also termed subluxation. The condition is of concern in discussions about hip dysplasia. *See also* Subluxation.

K

Kennel cough: A highly contagious infection of the upper respiratory tract in the dog. Because kennel cough is caused by several infectious agents, the collection of agents is called the kennel cough complex (KCC). The disease is characterized by a hacking cough lasting several days to a few weeks.

Kibble: Pieces of dog food extruded (formed) in various sizes.

L

Larva, larvae: A premature or pre-adult stage of some animals. Common in insects and nematodes, the egg hatches into a larva that is markedly different from the sexually mature adult. The plural form of larva is larvae.

LD$_{50}$: The amount of a substance that will be lethal to 50 percent of the animals tested.

Leptospira: A genus of bacteria characterized by a spirochete (q.v.).

Leptospirosis: A disease caused by a parasitic species of leptospira. Known as leptospirosis, the disease affects rodents, dogs, and other mammals and may be transmitted to people.

Lice: Plural for louse. A small, wingless, insect that is an ectoparasite (q.v.) of many mammals, including dogs.

Lumen: An anatomical term referring to an open space within an organ; for example, the center of the intestine is the lumen.

Lyme disease: A disease caused by a spirochete (q.v.) and transmitted by a tick (q.v.).

Lymphocytes: A variety of white blood cells (leukocytes). They are involved in establishing immunity.

Lymphoma: Cancer of the lymph tissue, characterized by enlarged lymph nodes. Synonym for lymphosarcoma.

Lysosomal enzymes: Enzymes stored within the lysosomes of a cell. When released, they catalyze the destruction of certain bacteria.

M

Macrophages: Large scavenger cells that remove bacteria and other foreign material from the body. They engulf the complex of the antibody and the antigen in order to break down the foreign material.

Mange: Several diseases of the skin caused by various kinds of mites living on or within the skin of the host.

Masseter muscles: The muscles that extend upward from the lower jaw and attach to the zygomatic arch (q.v.). Some of the muscle fibers go under the zygomatic arch from the lower jaw to the temporal region. The masseter is important in mastication and in closing the jaw.

Mast cell tumors: Cancer of the mast cells (cells that are circulating in the blood stream and in the tissues) that contain granuoles of chemicals that are released during inflammation.

Megaesophagus: A dilation of the esophagus caused by an obstruction that prevents food from passing through easily.

Mite: An arthropod belonging to the class Arachnida, which also includes the tick. The mite, however, is smaller than a tick.

Mitochondria: An organelle found in the cytoplasm of cells of higher organisms. Mitochondria are responsible for the energy reactions of respiratory metabolism production. They contain their own DNA (q.v.).

Monoclonal antibodies: Antibodies that are made in tissue culture by growing lymphocytes that produce immunoglobulins (antibodies) that are specific for a particular antigen (usually a cancer cell) because they are all alike. They are therefore considered to be clones.

Multifactorial: More than one factor. In the case of heredity, multifactorial refers to the influence of both genes and environmental factors.

N

Neoplastic growth: Another word for cancer.

Neotony: A tendency for the organism to stay in the larva or juvenile stage and yet become sexually mature.

NSAIDs: Non-steroidal anti-inflammatory drugs. A commonly prescribed drug for the treatment of dogs is Rimadyl®.

Nutraceuticals: Foodstuffs that are rich in certain molecules (e.g., glucosamine) that are utilized by the body.

O

OFA: The Orthopedic Foundation for Animals. The organization was founded in the 1960s for the purpose of evaluating hip radiographs of canines.

OFA evaluation: An evaluation of the radiographs presented to the OFA.

Oncogene: A mutated gene that encourages cell growth and does not respond to the chemical signals that normally turn it off. It is a mutated normal gene that produces cancer.

Oncoviruses: Viruses that cause cancer.

Osteochondrosis: The abnormally rapid growth of the cartilage precursor to bone formation in the growing puppy.

Ortolani's sign: Palpation of the hip joint to test for subluxation, which is felt as "clicking" in the hip.

Osteoblasts: Cells that lay down calcium for bone formation.

Osteochondritis dissecans: A growth problem involving the separation of small fragments of cartilage or bone from the surface of the joint.

Osteogenesis: Formation of bones.

Osteosarcoma: Bone cancer.

P

Paedomorphosis: Retention by an organism of structures that are normally only present in juvenile stages.

Panosteitis: An inflammation of bone due to growth. The center or medulla of the bone grows and exerts pressure on the outer layer of the bone called the cortex. The pressures that cause the reabsorption of bone can produce pain.

Parinfluenza: A canine virus that is another cause of kennel cough. It causes a mild respiratory infection in otherwise healthy dogs, but can be severe in puppies or debilitated dogs.

Parvo, Parvovirus: A deadly intestinal virus that may cause severe dehydrating diarrhea in dogs. Parvovirus infection is especially dangerous for puppies.

Pathogen: An organism, such as a virus or bacteria, that causes disease.

PCBs: A class of man-made chemicals known as polychlorinated biphenyls that have had many industrial uses. They were first manufactured commercially in 1929 by Monsanto, the sole U.S. manufacturer. Since the 1970s many health problems have been associated with PCBs. Among these are skin ailments (called chloracne), reproductive disorders, and liver disease. PCBs are a known carcinogen in animals and are resistant to degradation. They may persist for many years in the environment and accumulate in the food chain. They are stored in the body fat of animals and humans. The manufacture of PCBs is now banned in the U.S.A., and the disposal of PCBs is regulated.

PennHip: A certifying organization that tests for subluxation, which can lead to CHD. The technique involves compression and distraction of the bones of the hip, with the dog under anesthesia. The two radiographs are taken and then compared. *See* Subluxation.

Permethrins: Another insecticide, close in structure to pyrethrins.

Persistent Ductus Arteriosus (PDA): Persistence of an opening in the heart that allows blood to go from one side to the other. The opening is normal in the unborn but closes off when the blood begins to circulate through the lungs rather than only through the placenta.

Phenotype: The appearance or structure of an organism.

Play-biting: A natural instinct to bite; a play term, not an aggressive term.

Play-bow: A position where a dog wishes to invite play by lowering his front legs.

Play-face: A grimace made by a dog when the dog wishes to play.

Pleiotropy: The many effects of a gene, not just one.

Polygenic: Involving many genes.

Precursor cells: Cells that formed before specific cells, and give rise to those cells.

Promoter carcinogen (or co-carcinogen): A chemical or condition that needs to be present in order for an agent to become a carcinogen.

Prostaglandin: A group of hormone-like chemicals that are present in many tissues and body fluids. They have many actions such as the contraction of smooth muscles and dilation of blood vessels; they are, therefore, important in producing inflammation.

Proteins: A class of molecules found in the body. Protein is comprised of amino acids, which are universally present and involved in everything that happens in a living organism. Some proteins are structural, such as those found in connective tissue; others are involved in chemical reactions as enzymes. Proteins fold themselves into various shapes, which designate their functions.

Proteoglycans: Another of the building blocks of cartilage.

Proto-oncogene: A gene that promotes cell growth and division. If damaged by a mutation, it becomes an oncogene (q.v.).

Puppy acne: Another colloquial term for a bacterial infection of the skin. Also known as puppy dermatitis.

Purebred dogs: Dogs that are recognized by a registry. The oldest and largest registry in the United States is the AKC (American Kennel Club).

Pyrantel pamoate: A commonly used de-wormer (antihelmintic drug), which removes intestinal worms, especially roundworms. Trade name: Nemex®.

Pyrethrins: Insecticidal chemicals found naturally in pyrethrum flowers and used to treat various conditions caused by parasitic insects.

R

Rabies (hydrophobia): An acute, fatal, viral disease of the central nervous system that affects all warm-blooded animals. It is usually transmitted by a bite from an infected animal.

Radius: The bone located in the forearm that carries about 80 percent of the weight on the forearm.

Remodeling bone: The construction of the bone changing in response to pressures on the bone. It is a normal developmental and growth process.

RNA: Ribonucleic acid. Similar in composition to DNA, except the base uracil is present instead of cytosine. RNA is formed on the DNA template and produces ribosomes, transfer RNA (tRNA), and messenger RNA (mRNA)—all of which are used in protein synthesis.

Rods: Receptors in the eyeball and retina that are exquisitely sensitive only to the presence of light.

Roundworms: The most prevalent internal parasites of the dog. In dogs they are classified as Ascarid nematodes. Nearly all puppies are born infected with Ascarids because of the migration of the mother's encysted larvae into the fetus during pregnancy.

S

Sarcoma: A type of cancer arising from connective tissue. It can be found in any part of the body since connective tissue is found in all structures.

Scolex: The anterior part, or head, of the tapeworm that attaches to the intestine by means of suckers and hooks. New segments are generated from behind the scolex.

Spirochete: Corkscrew-shaped bacteria that form a taxonomic group. Other bacteria are: spherical (coccus), rod-shaped (bacillus), comma-shaped (vibrio), or spiral-shaped (spirillum).

Staph: Refers to Staphylococcus bacteria, a genus of gram-positive spherical bacteria.

Stop: In a dog, the angle between the bridge of the nose or muzzle and the forehead. In a bitch, the angle is shallower than in the male dog.

Subaortic stenosis (SAS): An anomaly of the heart characterized by constriction of the left ventricular opening leading into the aorta. With Doppler echocardiographic examination, the condition is characterized by a high-velocity flow (>2.0m/sec) across the aortic valve.

Subluxation: Looseness, or partial dislocation, of the joint. It is of particular interest with regard to the hip in the dog.

Synovial fluid: Viscous fluid within the joint capsule (synovial cavity) that cushions and lubricates the joint.

Synovitis: Inflammation of the synovial cavity.

T

Tapetum lucida: In nocturnal animals, a membrane that covers the retina and reflects light back through the retina. The *tapetum lucida* is thus responsible for the illumination one sees at night when a light is directed on an animal's eyes.

Tapeworm: A parasite of the small intestine. Adults are comprised of a head (scolex) and a long chain of segmented structures called proglottids. The scolex attaches to the intestinal wall and begins forming proglottids. The proglottids absorb nutrients from the digested food in the intestine. The oldest proglottids are sexually mature and contain eggs. They are highly motile when released from the end of the tapeworm and can be seen crawling on the dog's stool or around the anus. Tapeworms require an intermediate host to complete their life cycle. Outside of the body the proglottid dries and releases the eggs. The eggs are consumed by either a flea or a mouse, which is the intermediate host. When ingested by the intermediate host, the egg hatches into a larval stage, which remains in the tissues of the flea or mouse until it is eaten by a dog. The consumed larval stage is transformed into a scolex in the dog's intestine, which completes the life cycle.

Temporal muscles: The temporal muscles on the sides of the skull that cover the temporal bone.

Throwback: An individual who resembles a more distant ancestor than the parents and represents a recombination of the genes that were present in that ancestor.

Tick: A blood-sucking, external, parasitic Arthropod that belongs to the same group as mites. Ticks transmit diseases, such as Lyme disease and Rocky Mountain fever.

Triple pelvic osteotomy (TPO): Common, but expensive, surgery done to reposition the acetabulum in the hip joint around the femoral head in order to provide more coverage.

Transcription: The process by which the base sequence of DNA is used to produce an RNA molecule of complementary base sequence.

Translation: The process of information carried in the DNA sequence being used in the production of protein.

Transplantability: A characteristic of tumor cells in that tumor cells can be transplanted to another site and will continue to grow as tumors.

Tumor progression: The change of tumor over time to more aggressive forms.

Tumors, conditional: A type of tumor that needs certain chemicals to be provided in order to grow, such as tumors that are hormone dependent.

Tumor-suppressor genes: Genes that code for substances that inhibit the growth of tumors. A common tumor-suppressor gene is "p53." If p53 is not operating, a cancer may grow—especially when there are no back-up genes to intervene.

Type: A word used in the dog fancy to describe a particular overall look and behavior of a dog.

U

Ulna: A smaller bone in the forearm that carries approximately 20 percent of the load on the forearm.

Ununited anconeal process (UAP): In the puppy, the anconeal process develops from a separate center of ossification and is united with the rest of the ulna at 20–24 weeks of age.

UTI: An abbreviation for Urinary Tract Infection. *See* Cystitis.

Z

Zoonosis: A disease organism that affects more than one species, including humans, and therefore can be transmitted to humans from other animals, specifically dogs.

Zygomatic arch: The bone forming the upper boundary of the cheek.

Index

Page references in boldface indicate where an entry has been defined.
References to trademark products are not included.